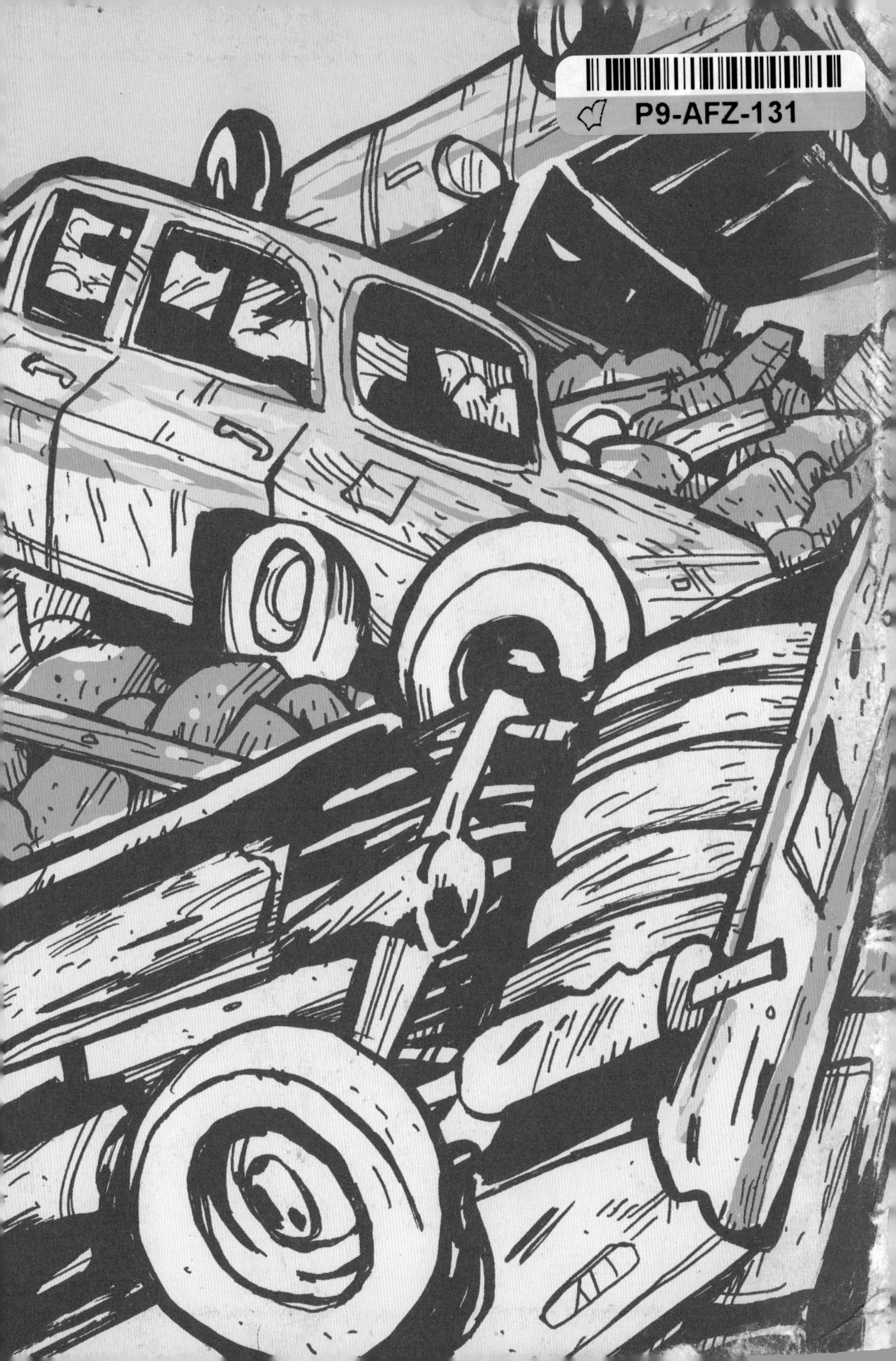

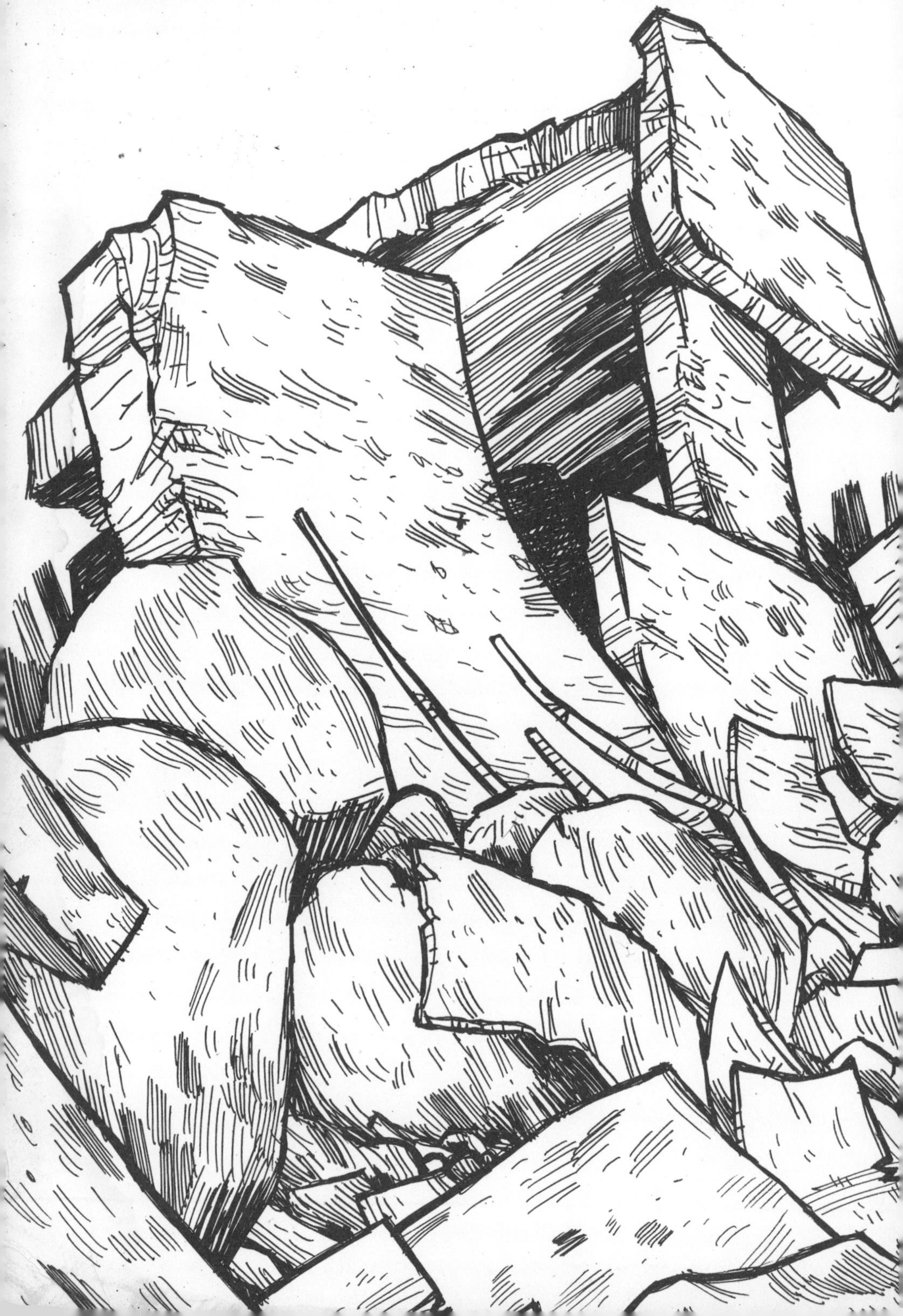

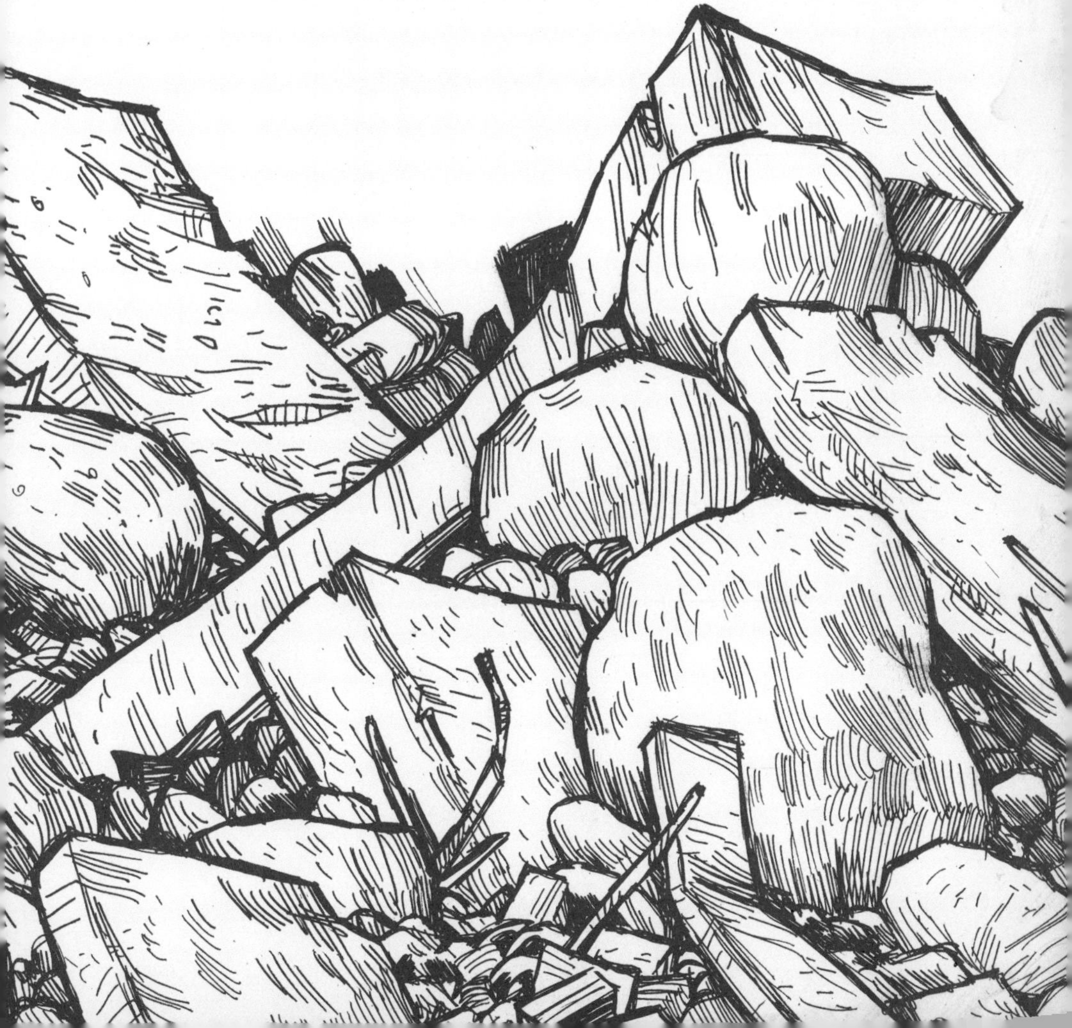

DAYBREAK

BRIAN RALPH

DRAWN & QUARTERLY

MOST OF THIS BOOK WAS PRINTED IN PAMPHLET FORM
(DAYBREAK 1, 2, AND 3) BY BODEGA
PRODUCTION BY RANDY CHANG WITH ASSISTANCE
BY RAY SOHN, ANDREW ARNOLD, AND SHANNON TIEN.

DRAWNANDQUARTERLY.COM

978-1-77046-383-7

FIRST HARDCOVER EDITION: AUGUST 2011
FIRST PAPERBACK EDITION: FEBRUARY 2013
SECOND HARDCOVER EDITION: OCTOBER 2019

PRINTED IN CHINA

10 9 8 7 6 5 4 3 2 1

CATALOGUING DATA AVAILABLE FROM
LIBRARY AND ARCHIVES CANADA

PUBLISHED IN THE USA BY DRAWN AND QUARTERLY, A CLIENT
PUBLISHER OF FARRAR, STRAUS AND GIROUX

PUBLISHED IN CANADA BY DRAWN AND QUARTERLY, A CLIENT
PUBLISHER OF RAINCOAST BOOKS

PUBLISHED IN THE UK BY DRAWN AND QUARTERLY, A CLIENT
PUBLISHER OF PUBLISHERS GROUP UK

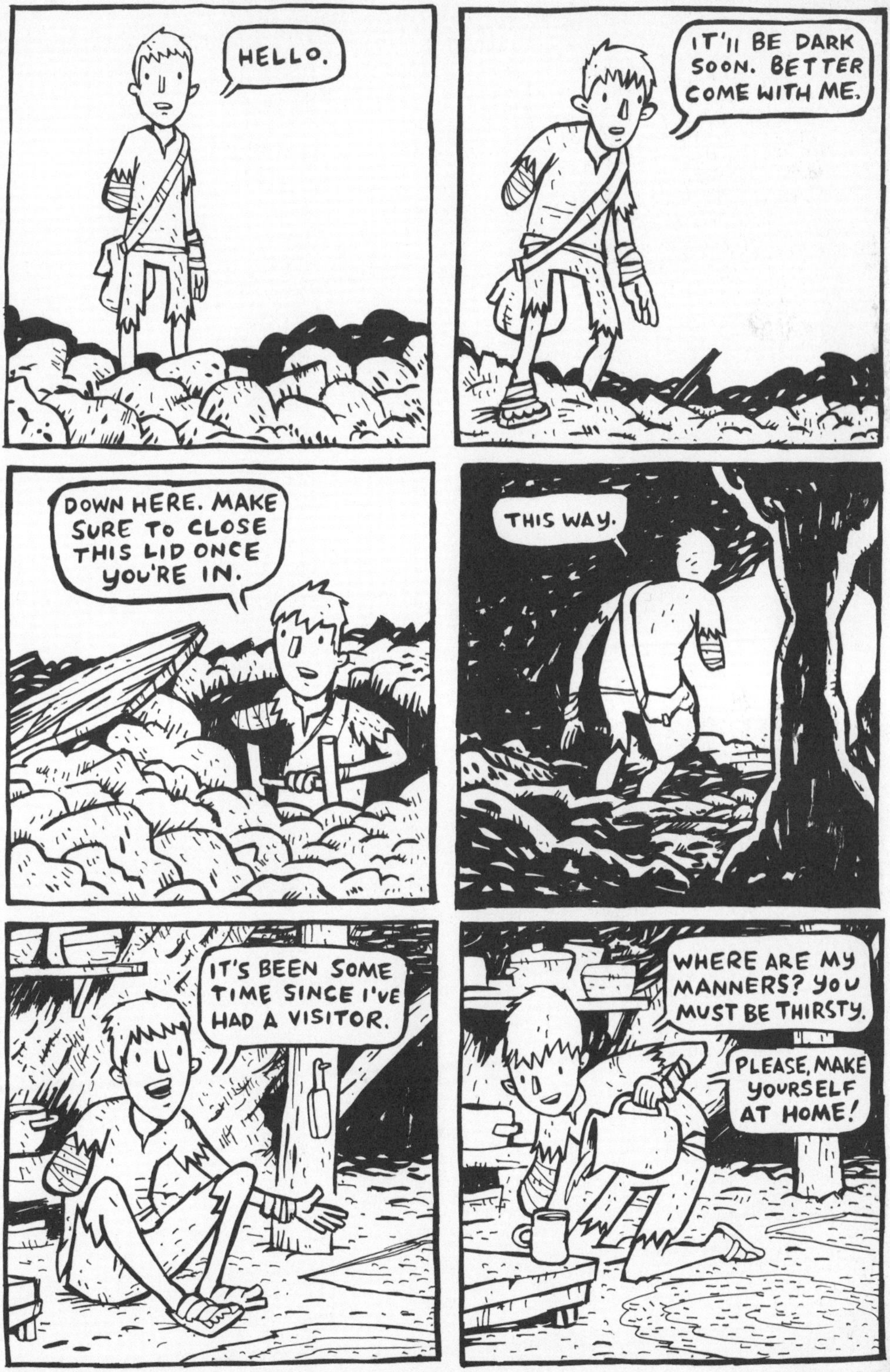
HELLO.
IT'll BE DARK SOON. BETTER COME WITH ME.
DOWN HERE. MAKE SURE TO CLOSE THIS LID ONCE YOU'RE IN.
THIS WAY.
IT'S BEEN SOME TIME SINCE I'VE HAD A VISITOR.
WHERE ARE MY MANNERS? YOU MUST BE THIRSTY.
PLEASE, MAKE YOURSELF AT HOME!

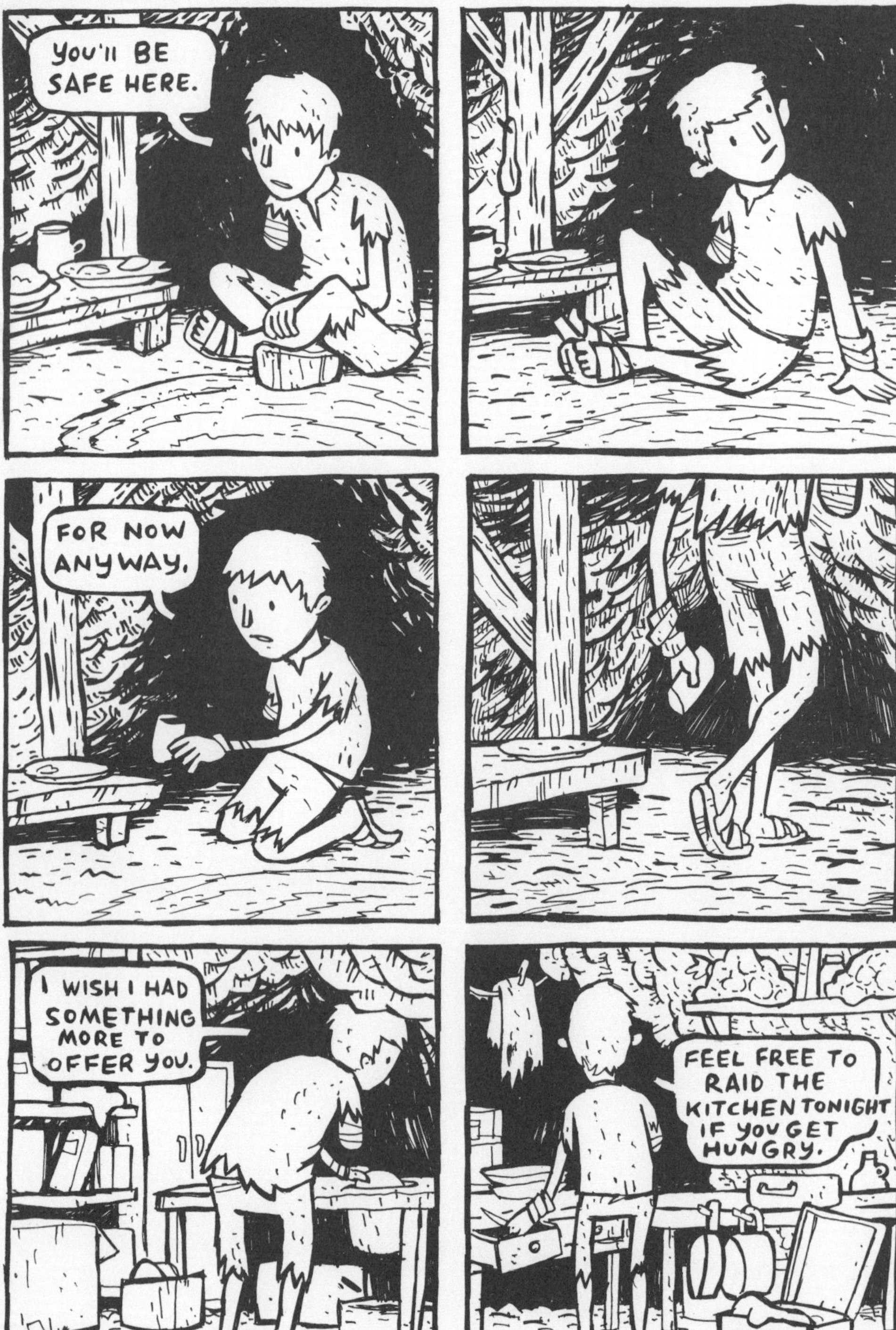
YOU'll BE SAFE HERE.
FOR NOW ANYWAY.
I WISH I HAD SOMETHING MORE TO OFFER YOU.
FEEL FREE TO RAID THE KITCHEN TONIGHT IF YOU GET HUNGRY.

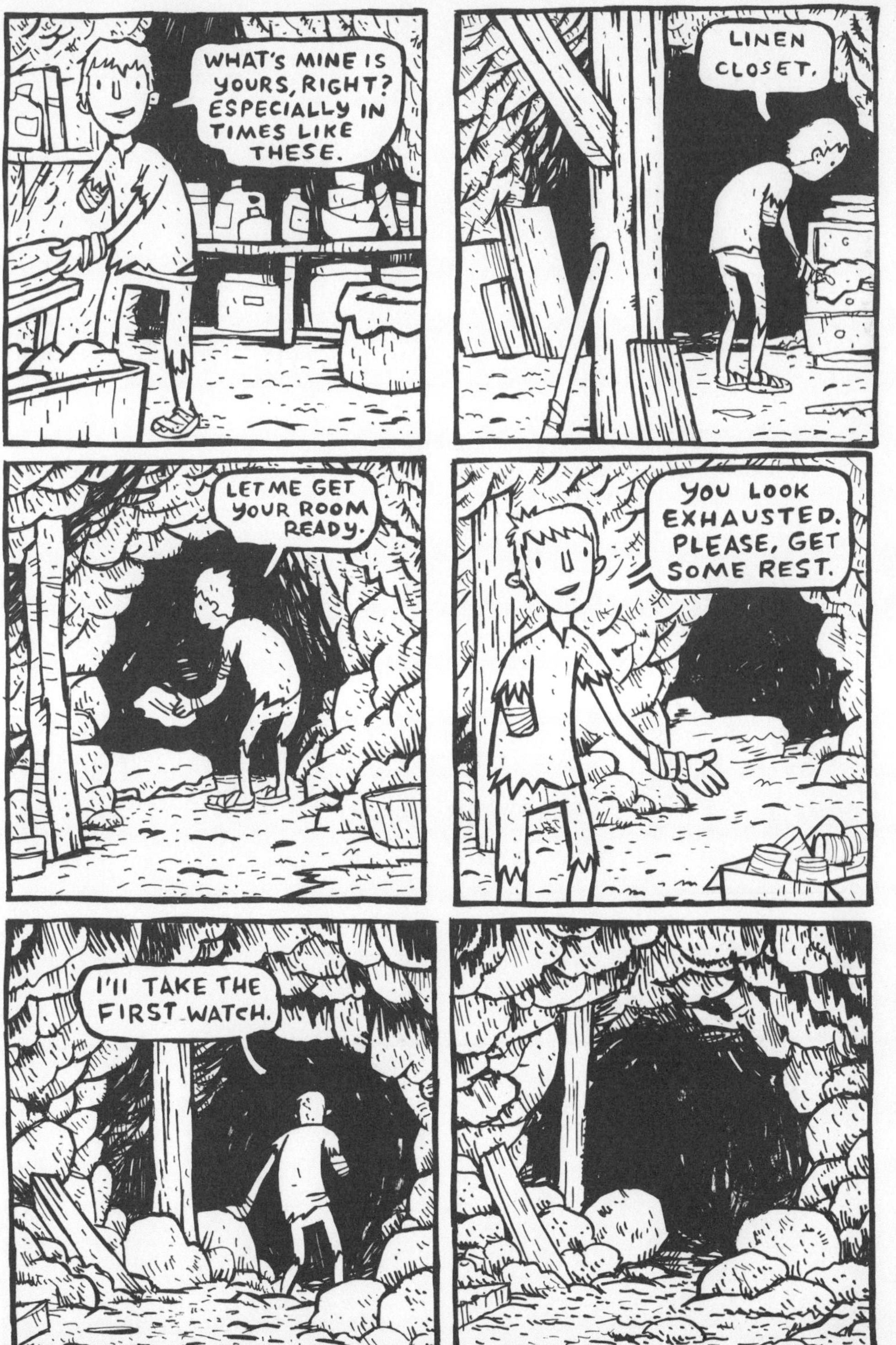
WHAT'S MINE IS YOURS, RIGHT? ESPECIALLY IN TIMES LIKE THESE.
LINEN CLOSET.
LET ME GET YOUR ROOM READY.
YOU LOOK EXHAUSTED. PLEASE, GET SOME REST.
I'll TAKE THE FIRST WATCH.

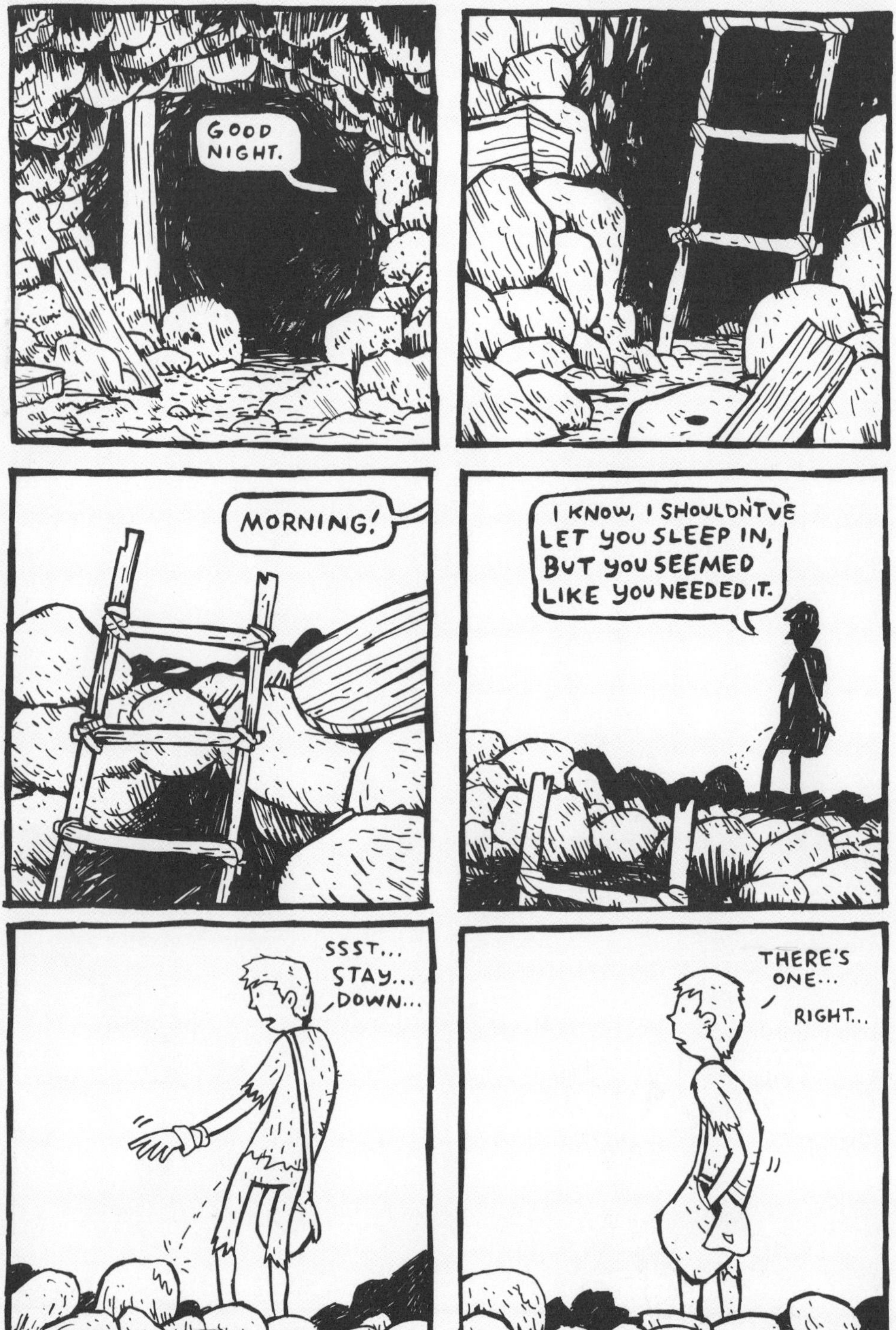
GOOD NIGHT.
MORNING!
I KNOW, I SHOULDN'TVE LET YOU SLEEP IN, BUT YOU SEEMED LIKE YOU NEEDED IT.
SSST... STAY... DOWN...
THERE'S ONE...
RIGHT...

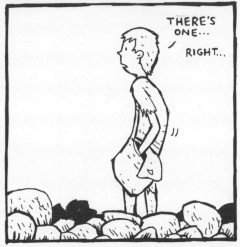

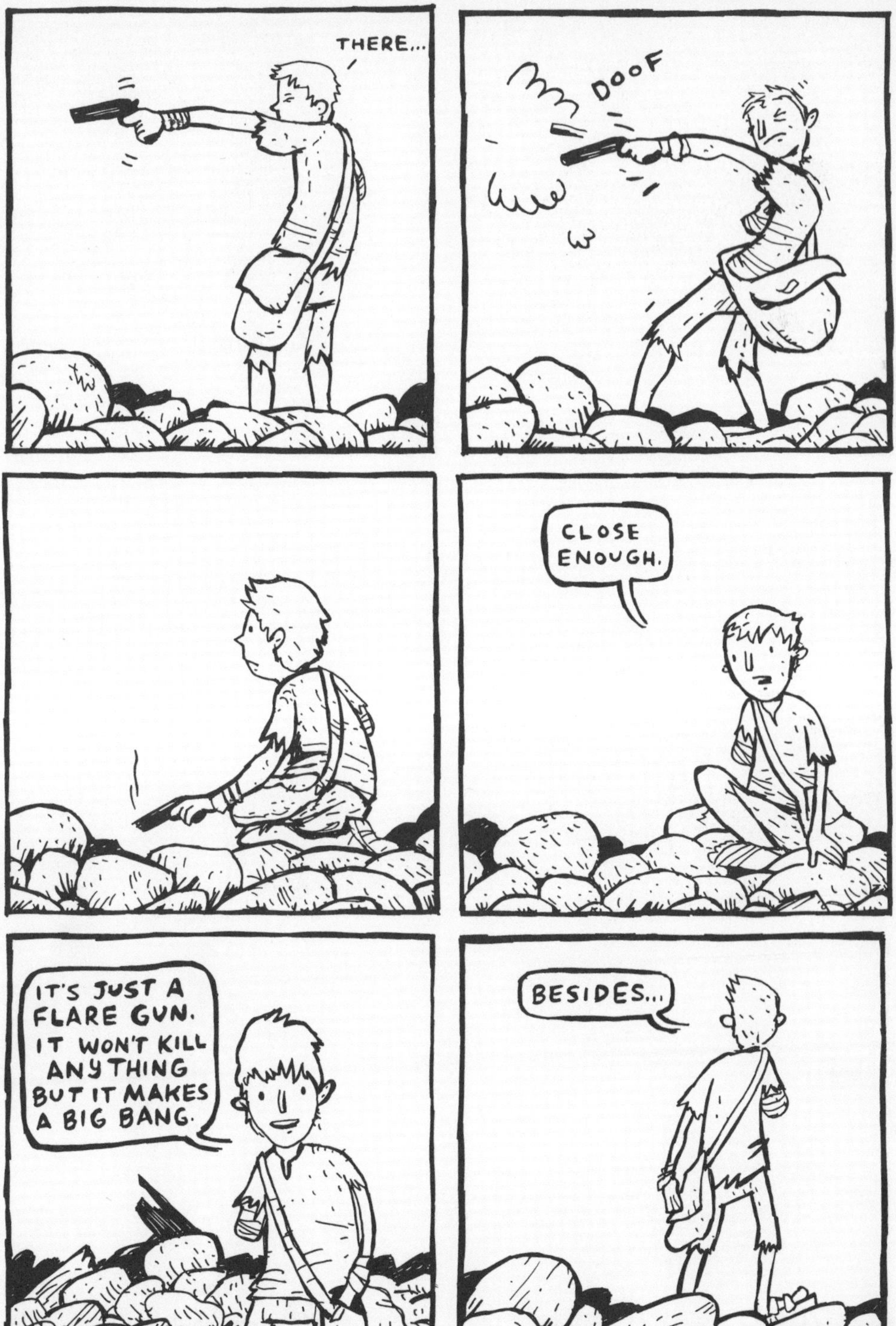
THERE...
DOOF
CLOSE ENOUGH.
IT'S JUST A FLARE GUN. IT WON'T KILL ANYTHING BUT IT MAKES A BIG BANG.
BESIDES...

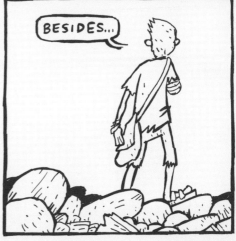

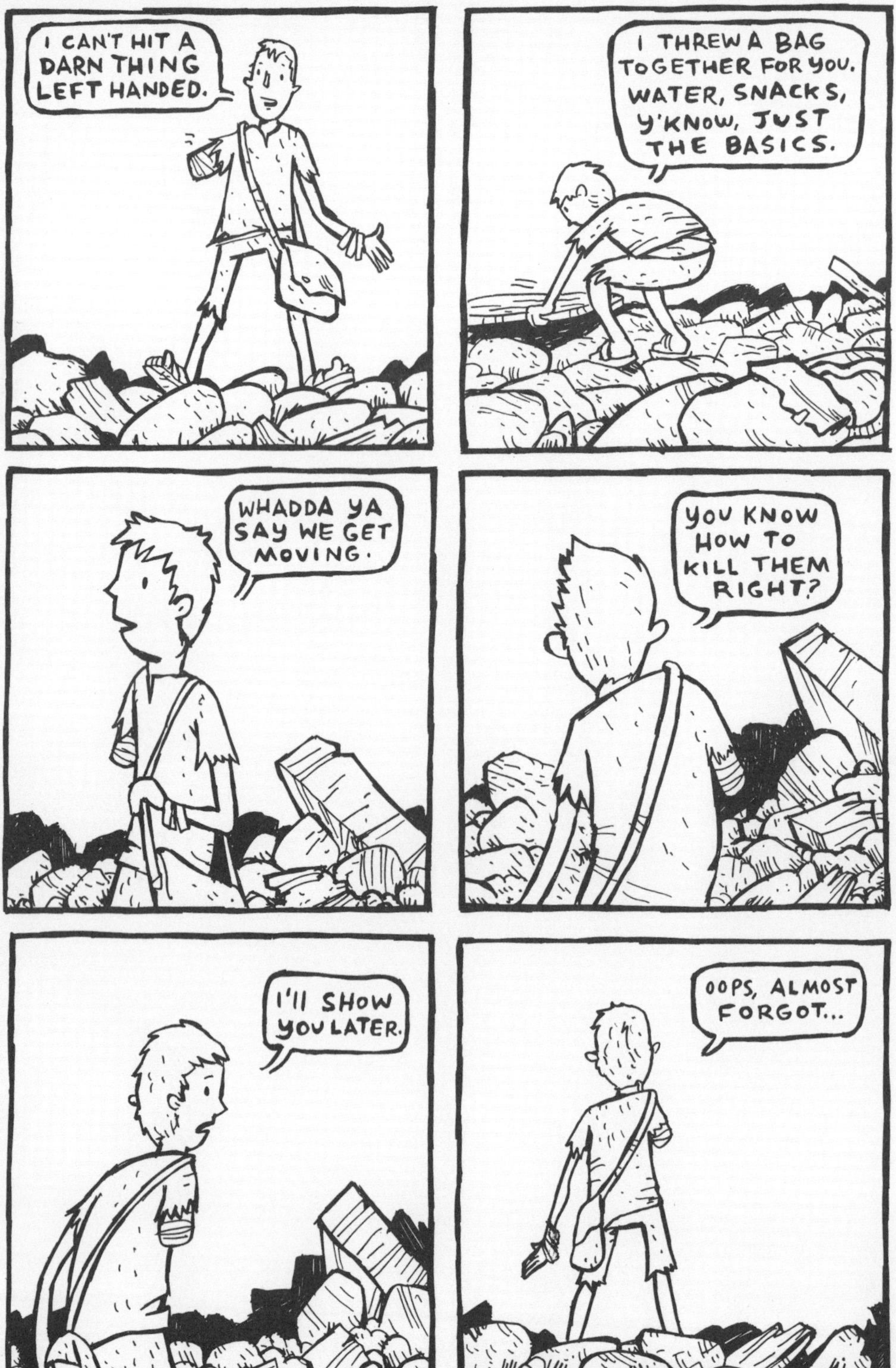
I CAN'T HIT A DARN THING LEFT HANDED.
I THREW A BAG TOGETHER FOR YOU. WATER, SNACKS, Y'KNOW, JUST THE BASICS.
WHADDA YA SAY WE GET MOVING.
YOU KNOW HOW TO KILL THEM RIGHT?
I'LL SHOW YOU LATER.
OOPS, ALMOST FORGOT...

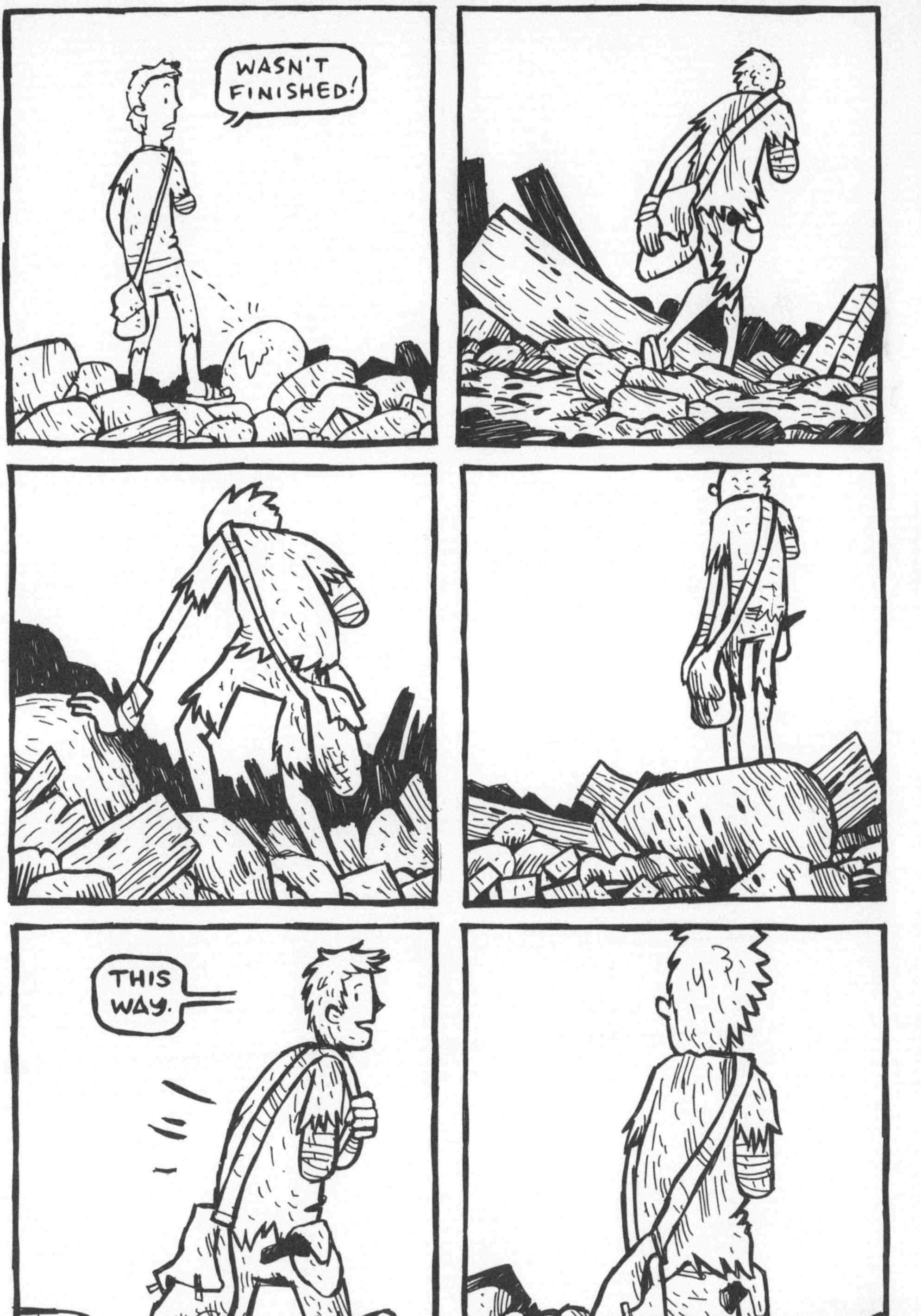
WASN'T FINISHED!
THIS WAY.

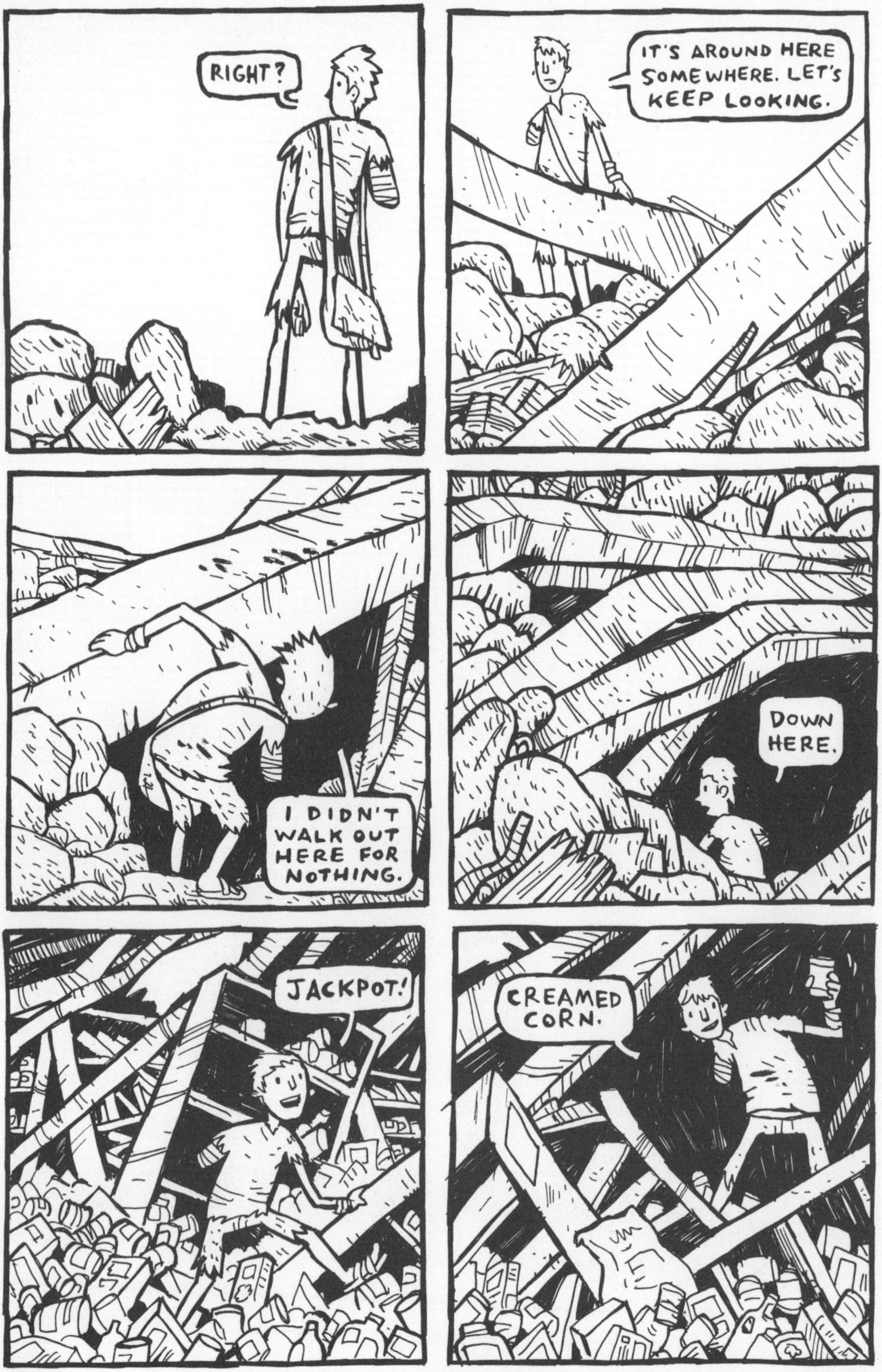
RIGHT?
IT'S AROUND HERE SOMEWHERE. LET'S KEEP LOOKING.
I DIDN'T WALK OUT HERE FOR NOTHING.
DOWN HERE.
JACKPOT!
CREAMED CORN.

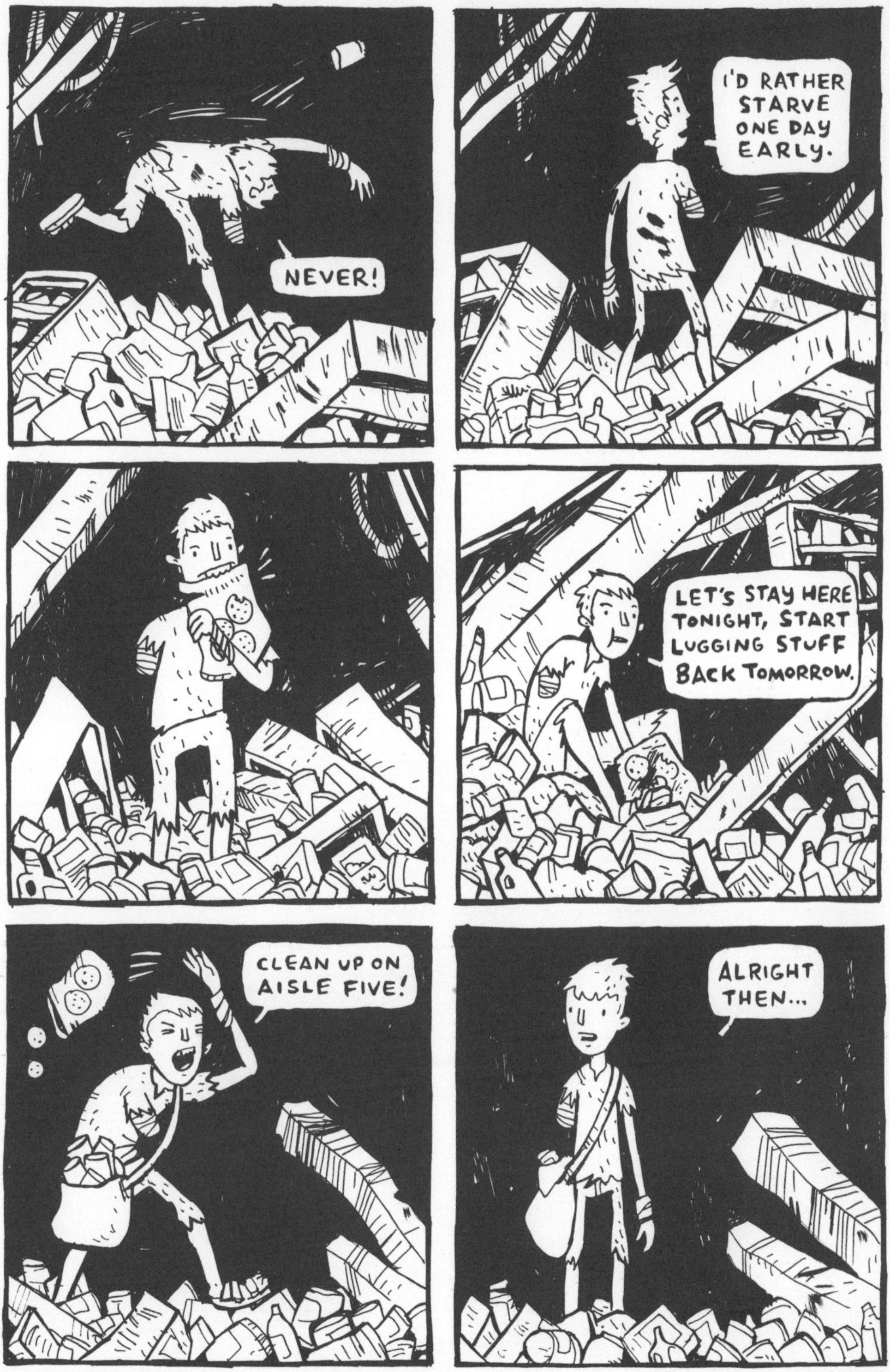
NEVER!
I'D RATHER STARVE ONE DAY EARLY.
LET'S STAY HERE TONIGHT, START LUGGING STUFF BACK TOMORROW.
CLEAN UP ON AISLE FIVE!
ALRIGHT THEN...

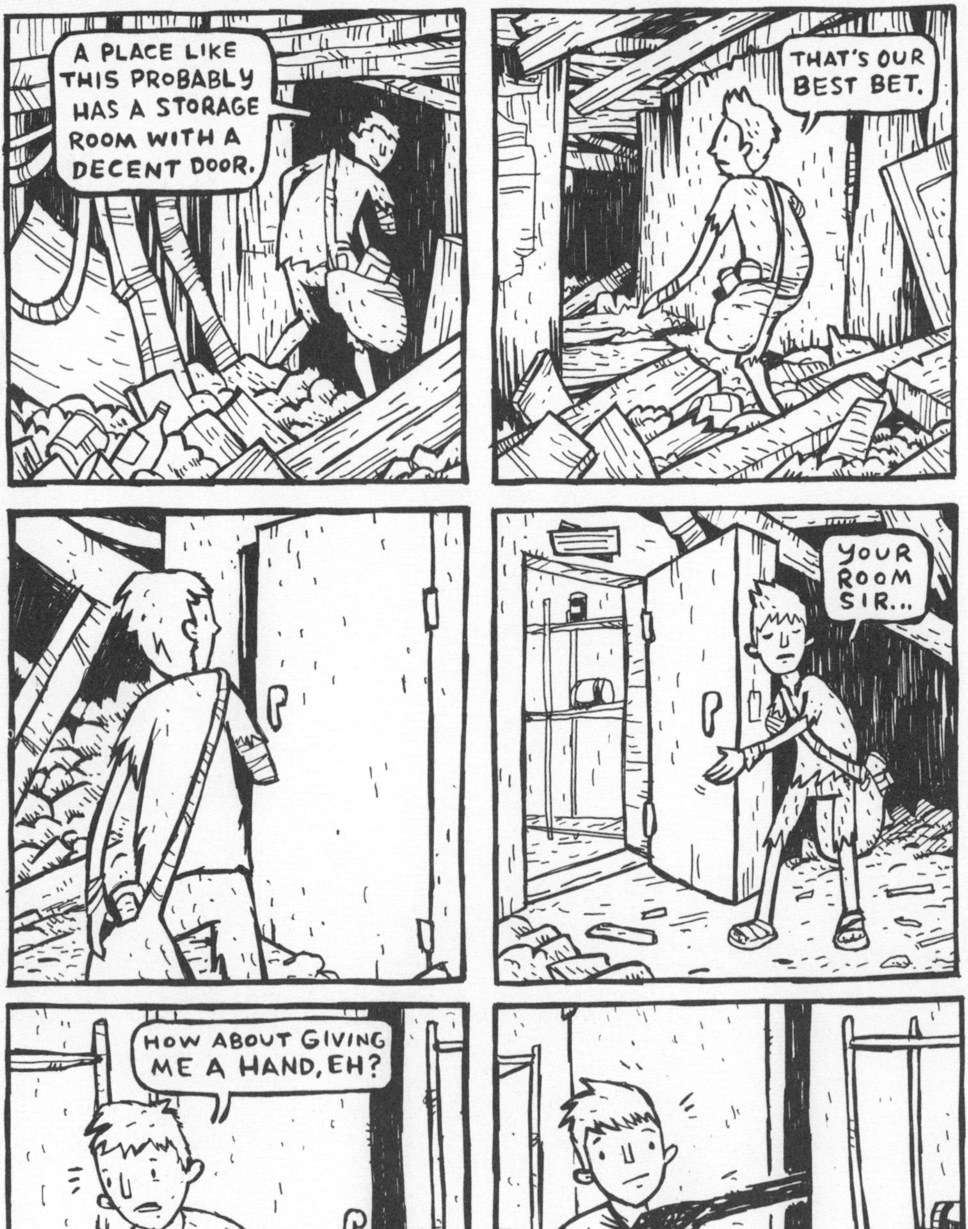
A PLACE LIKE THIS PROBABLY HAS A STORAGE ROOM WITH A DECENT DOOR.
THAT'S OUR BEST BET.
YOUR ROOM SIR...
HOW ABOUT GIVING ME A HAND, EH?

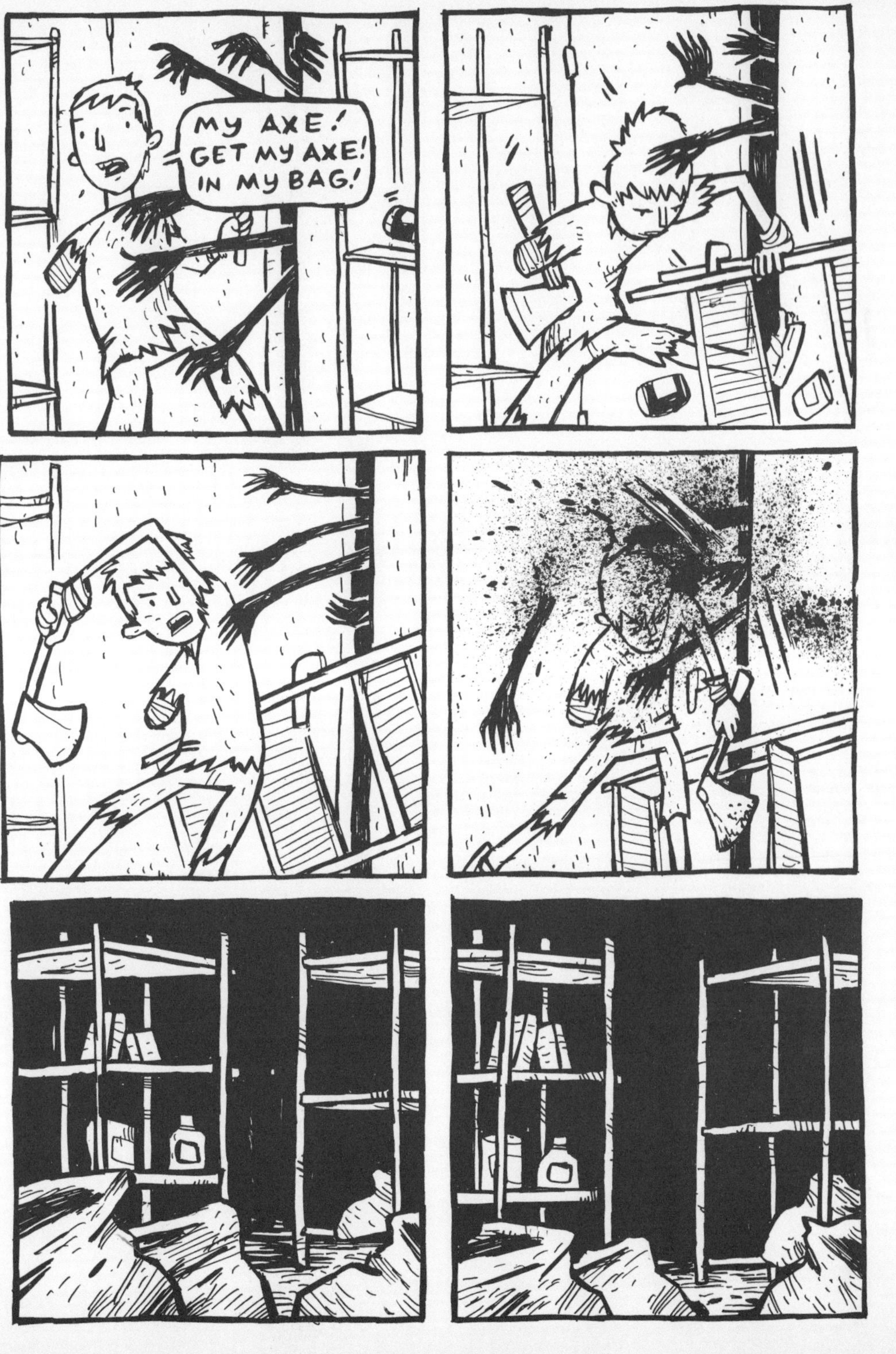
MY AXE! GET MY AXE! IN MY BAG!

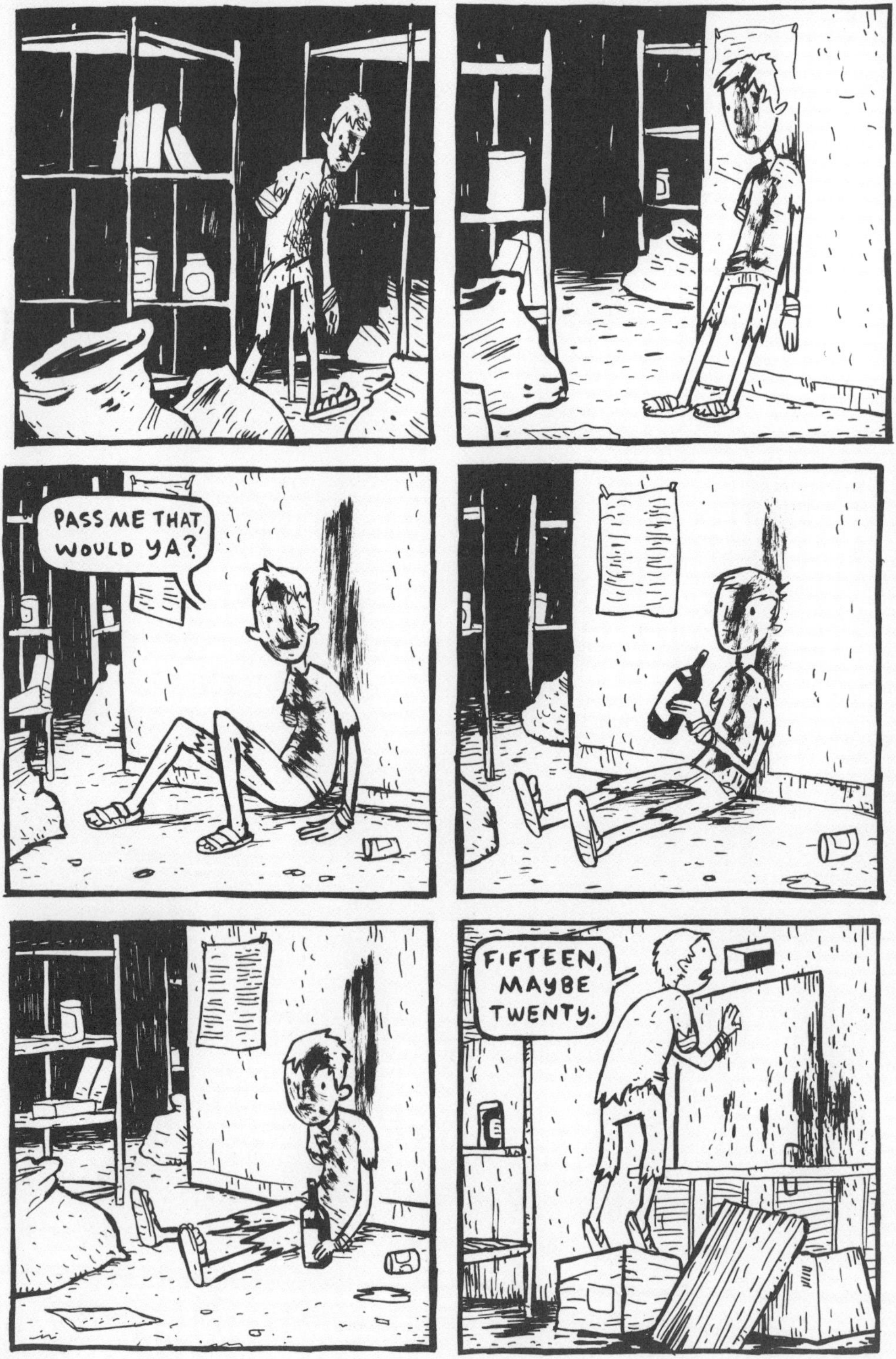
PASS ME THAT, WOULD YA?
FIFTEEN, MAYBE TWENTY.

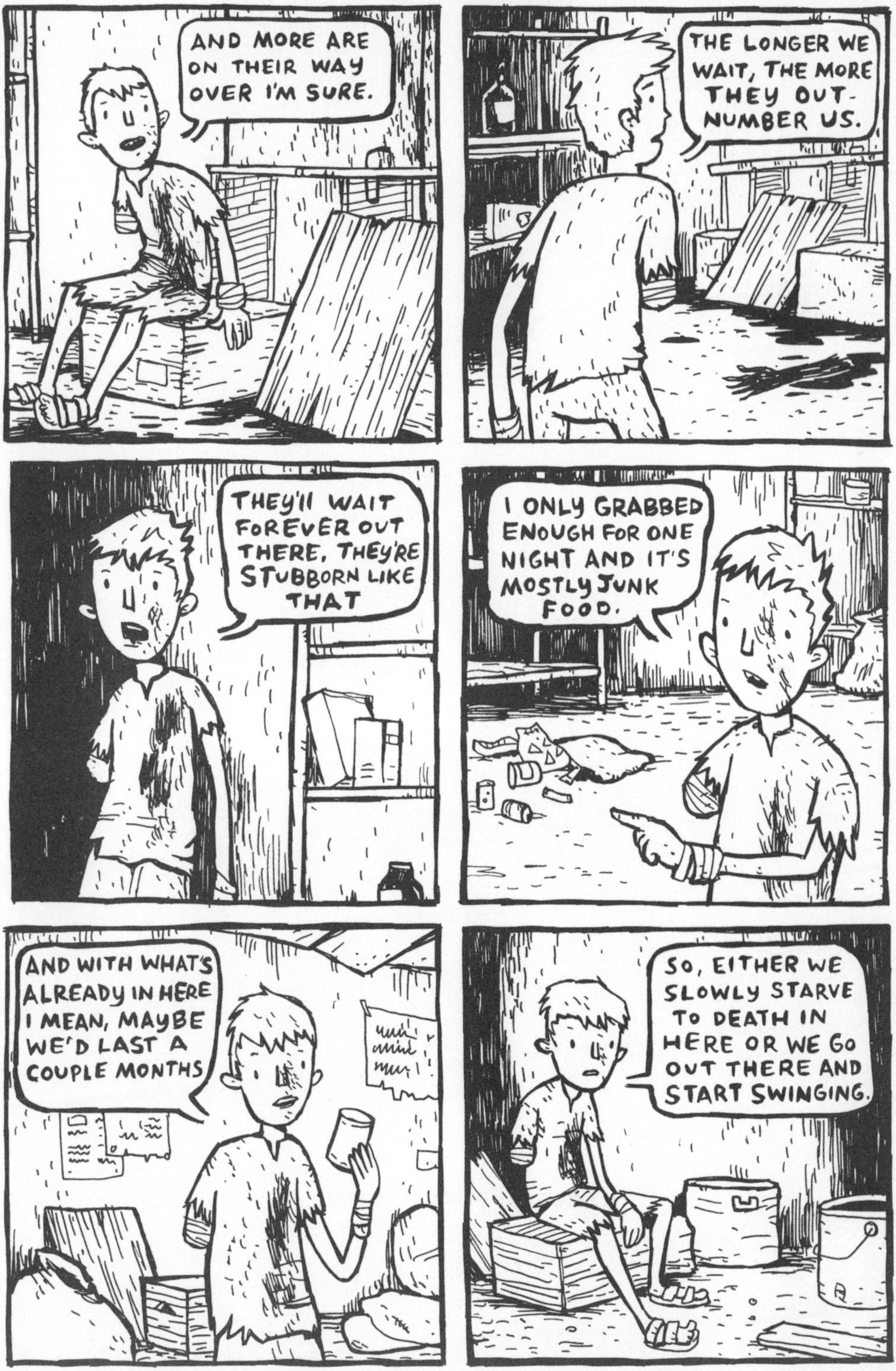
AND MORE ARE ON THEIR WAY OVER I'M SURE.
THE LONGER WE WAIT, THE MORE THEY OUT-NUMBER US.
THEY'll WAIT FOREVER OUT THERE, THEY'RE STUBBORN LIKE THAT
I ONLY GRABBED ENOUGH FOR ONE NIGHT AND IT'S MOSTLY JUNK FOOD.
AND WITH WHAT'S ALREADY IN HERE I MEAN, MAYBE WE'D LAST A COUPLE MONTHS
SO, EITHER WE SLOWLY STARVE TO DEATH IN HERE OR WE GO OUT THERE AND START SWINGING.

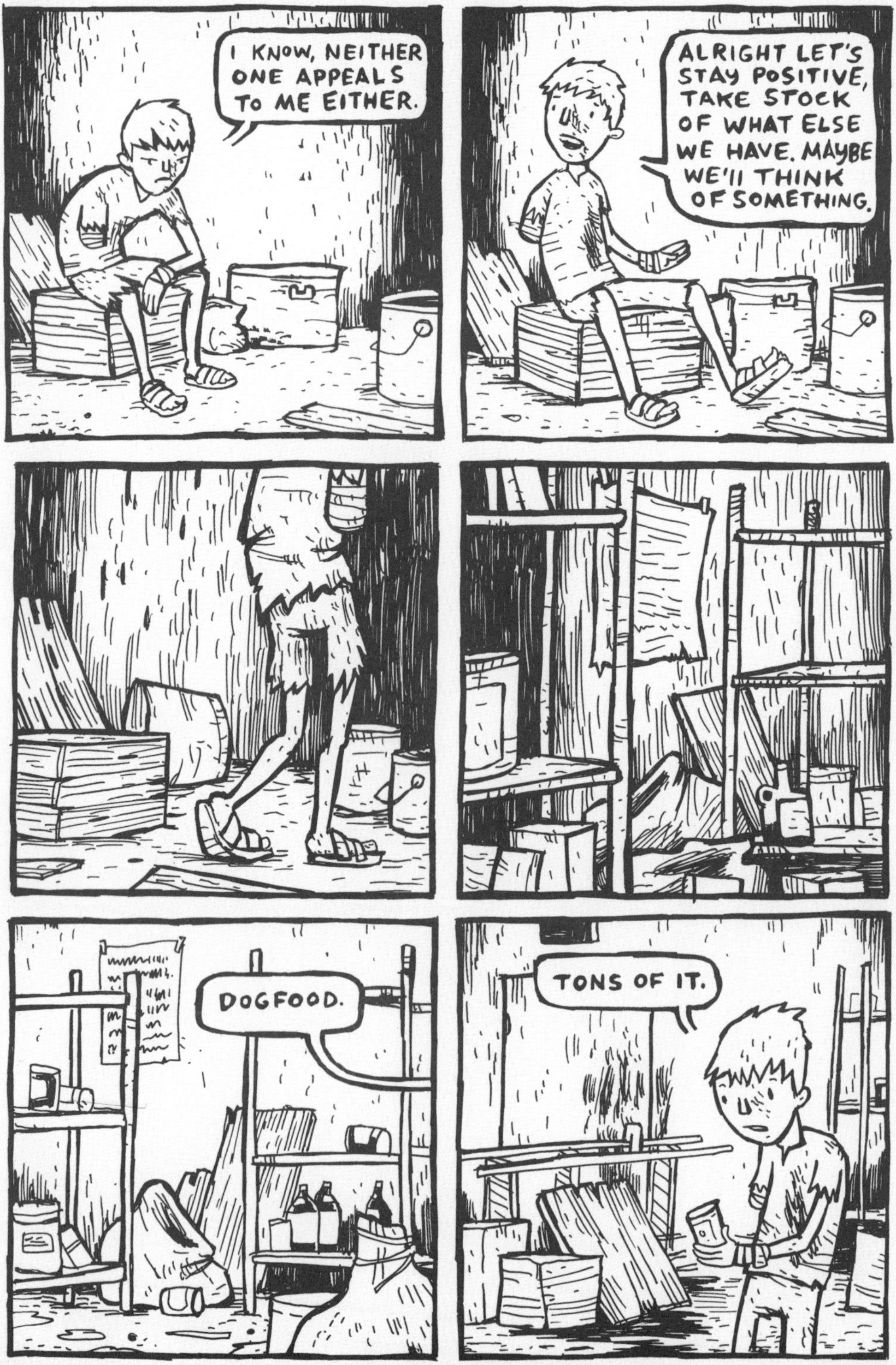
I KNOW, NEITHER ONE APPEALS TO ME EITHER.
ALRIGHT LET'S STAY POSITIVE, TAKE STOCK OF WHAT ELSE WE HAVE. MAYBE WE'll THINK OF SOMETHING.
DOGFOOD.
TONS OF IT.

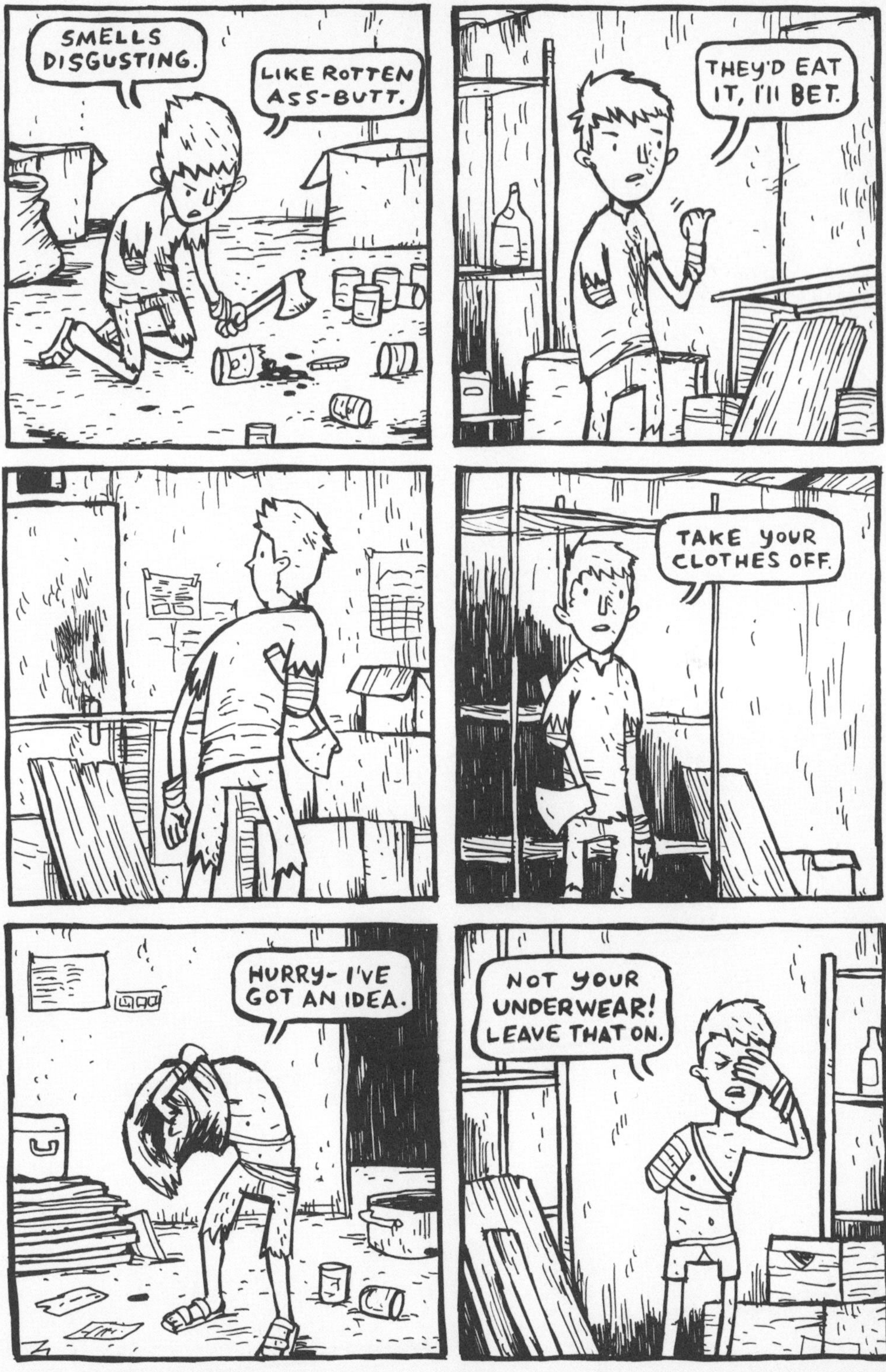
SMELLS DISGUSTING.
LIKE ROTTEN ASS-BUTT.
THEY'D EAT IT, I'll BET.
TAKE YOUR CLOTHES OFF.
HURRY- I'VE GOT AN IDEA.
NOT YOUR UNDERWEAR! LEAVE THAT ON.

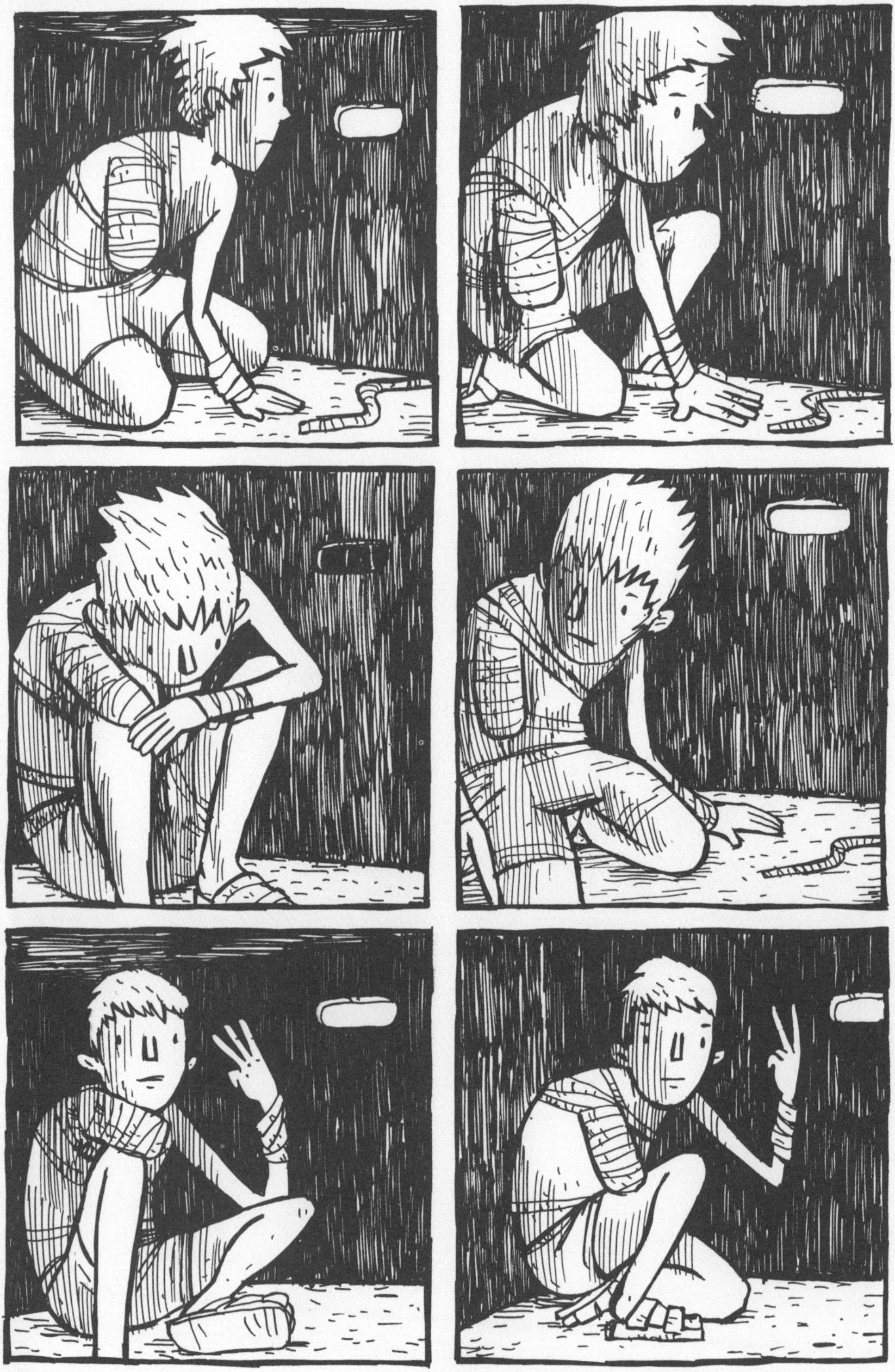

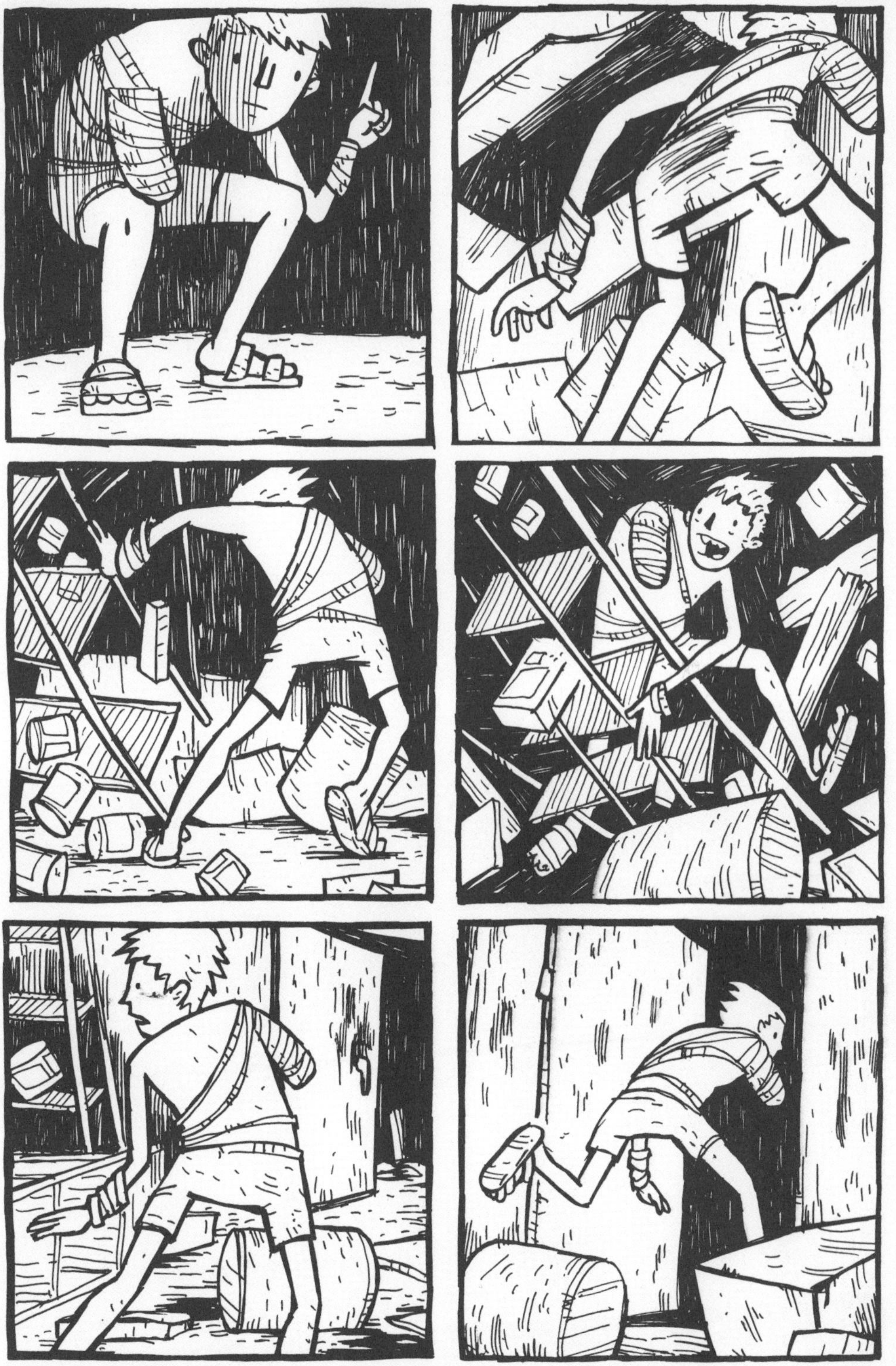

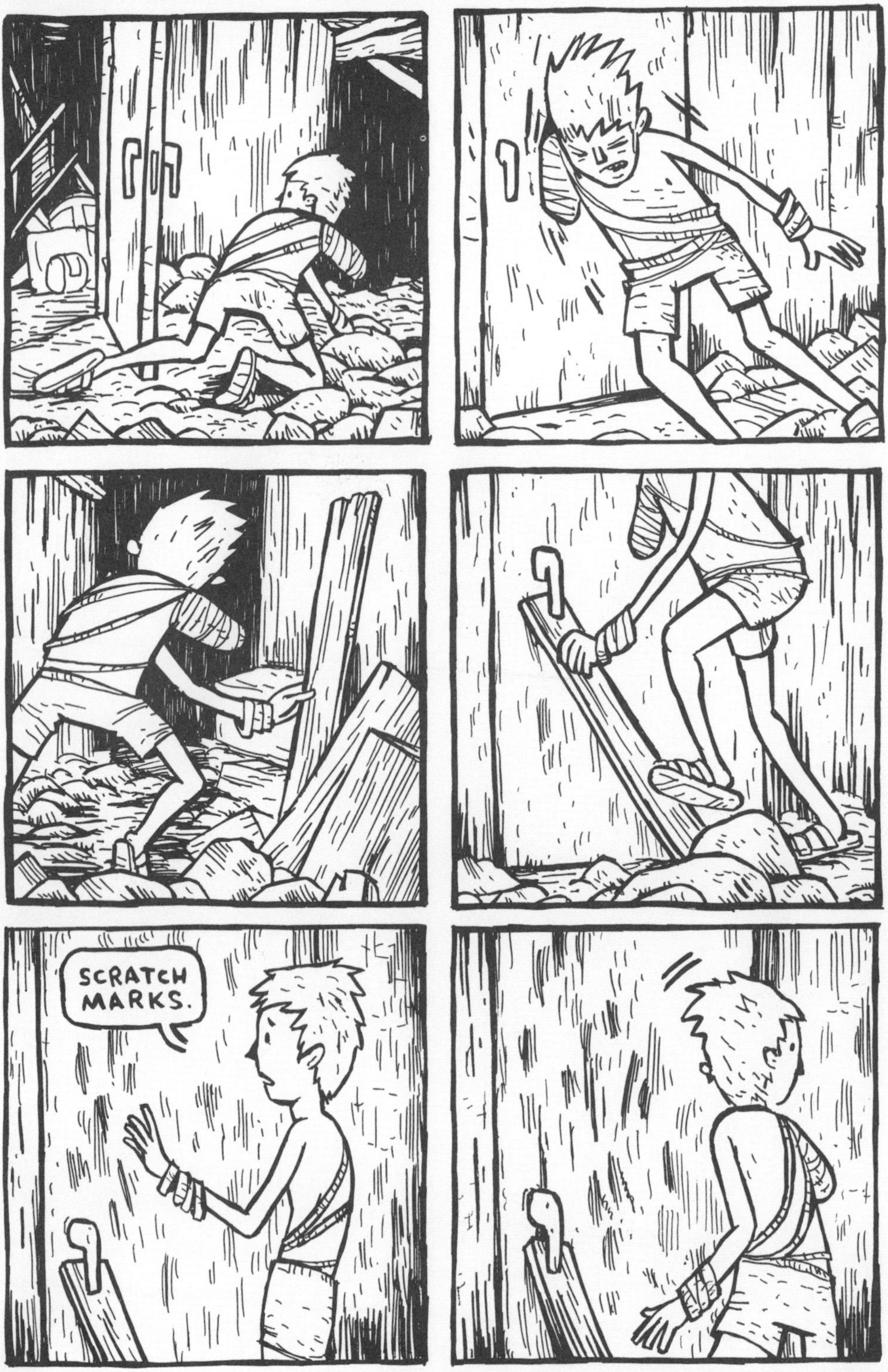
SCRATCH MARKS.

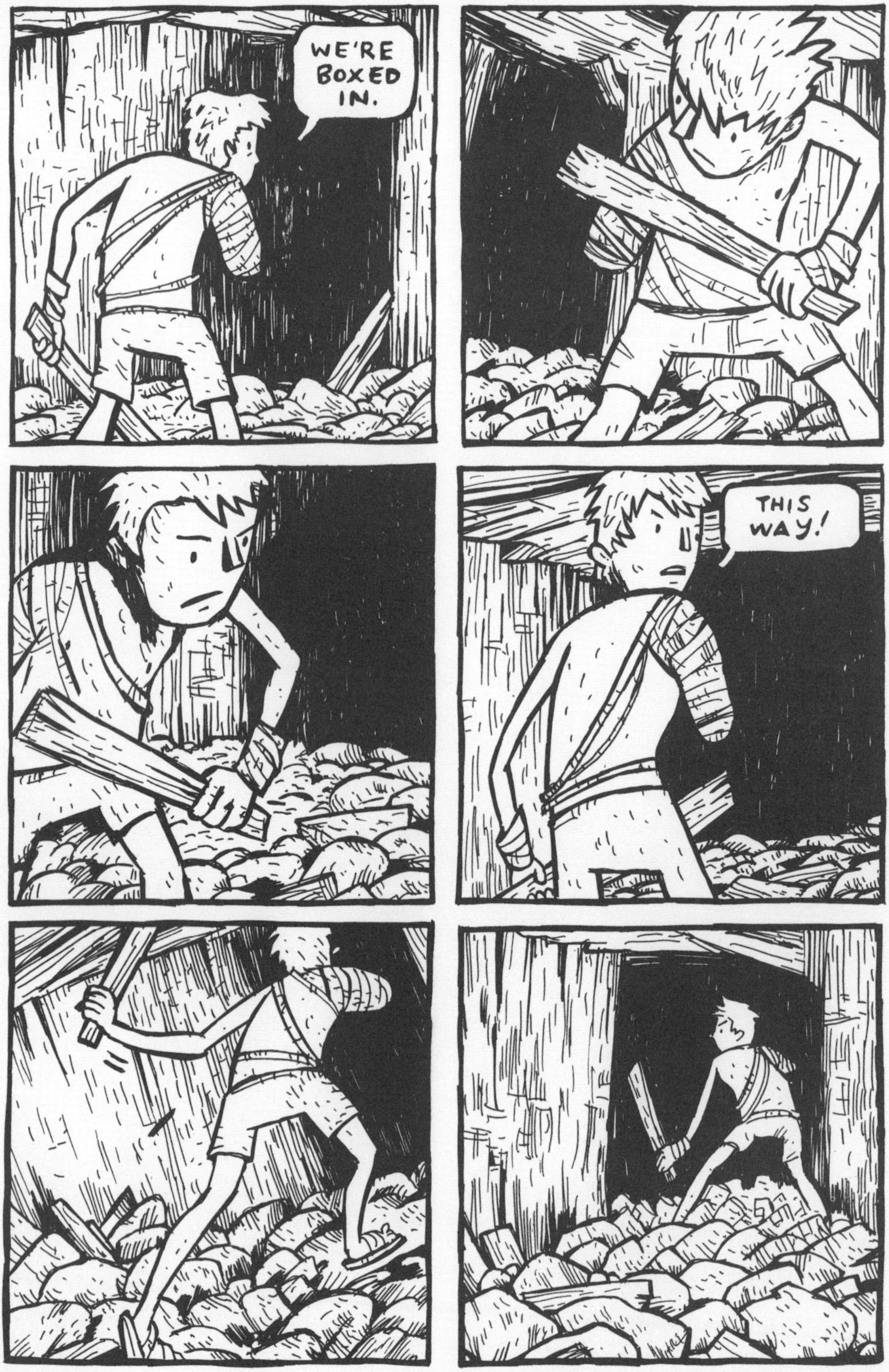
WE'RE BOXED IN.
THIS WAY!

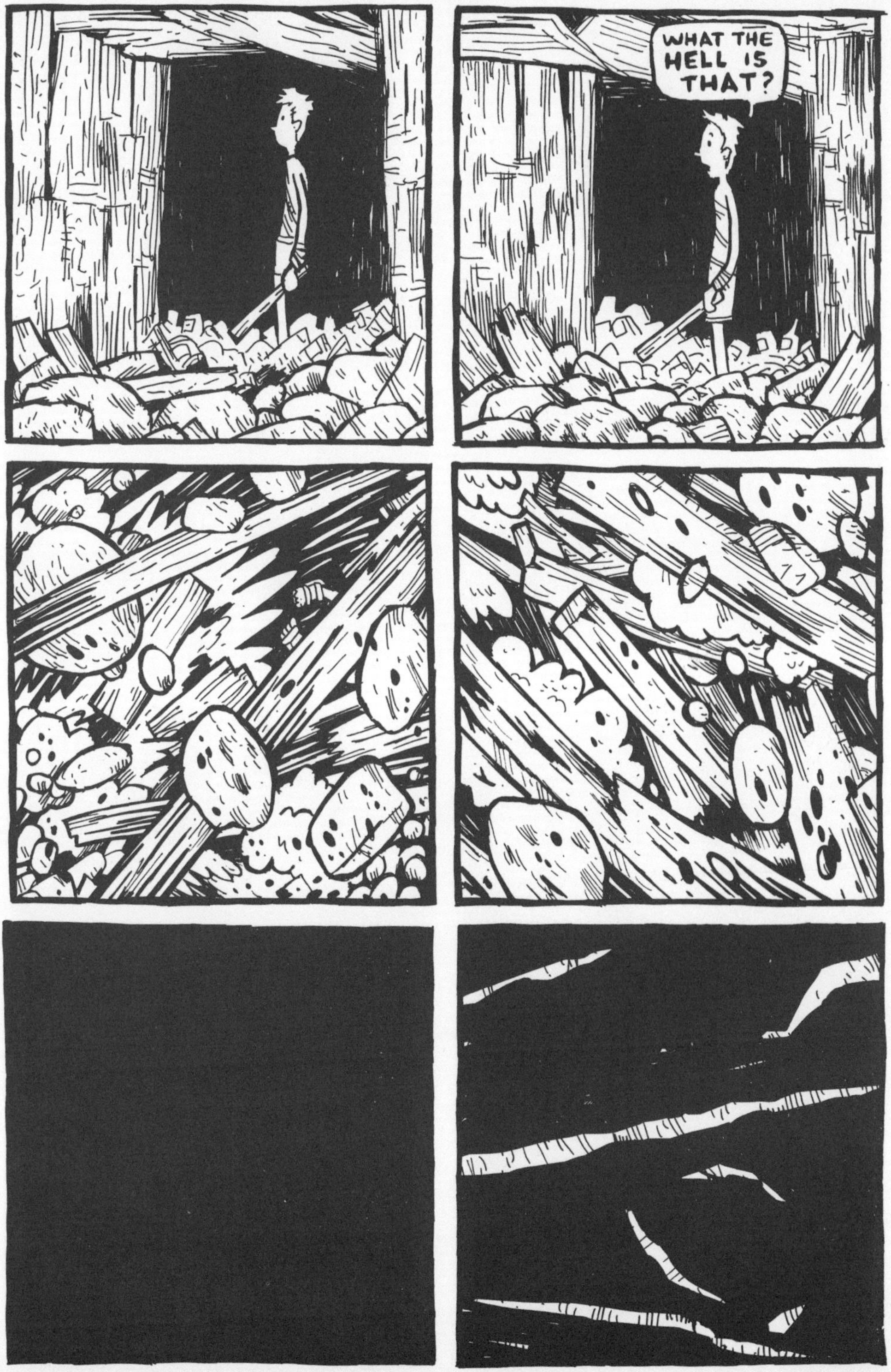
WHAT THE HELL IS THAT?

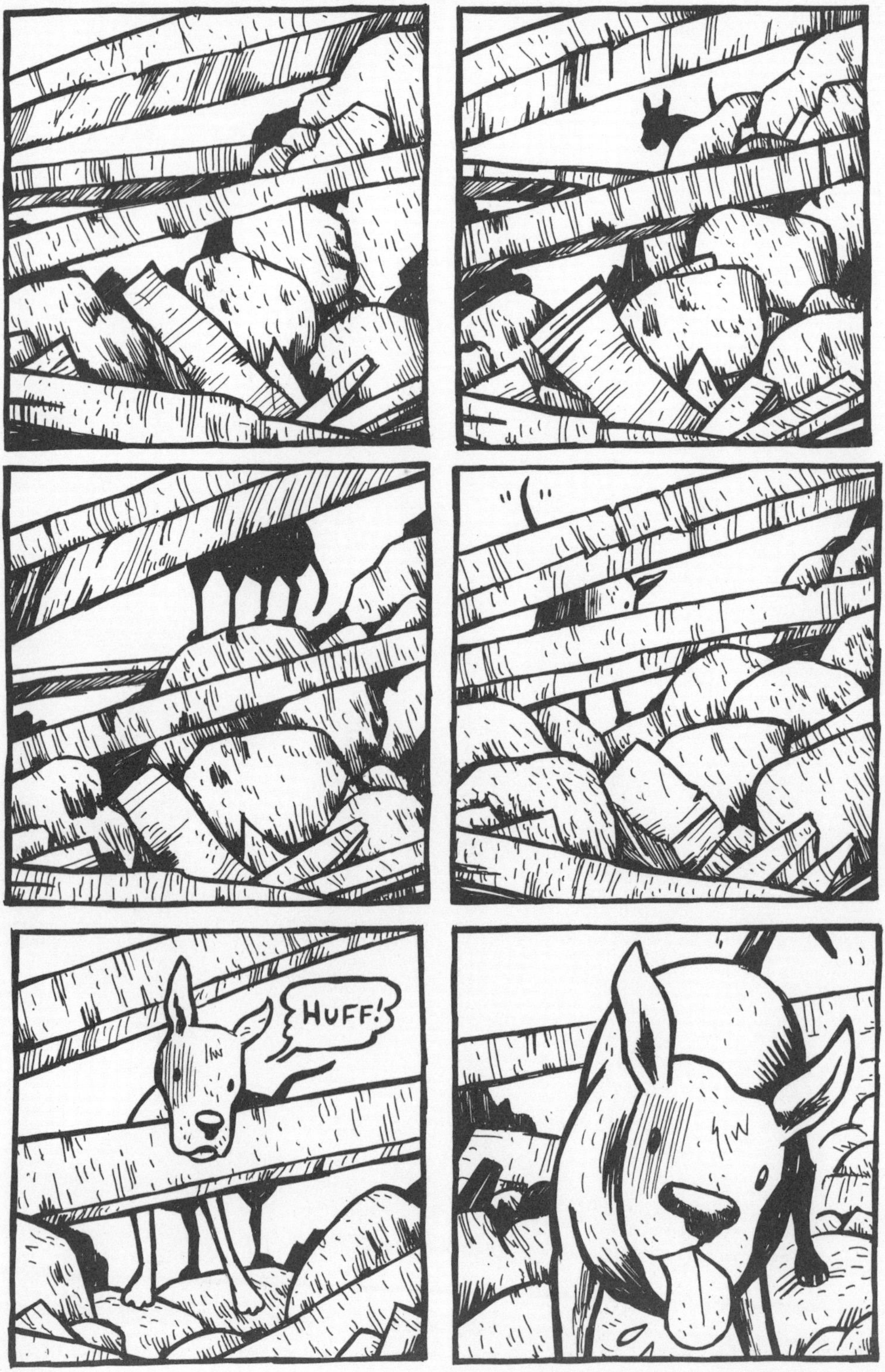
HUFF!

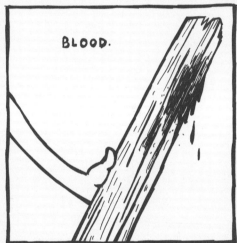

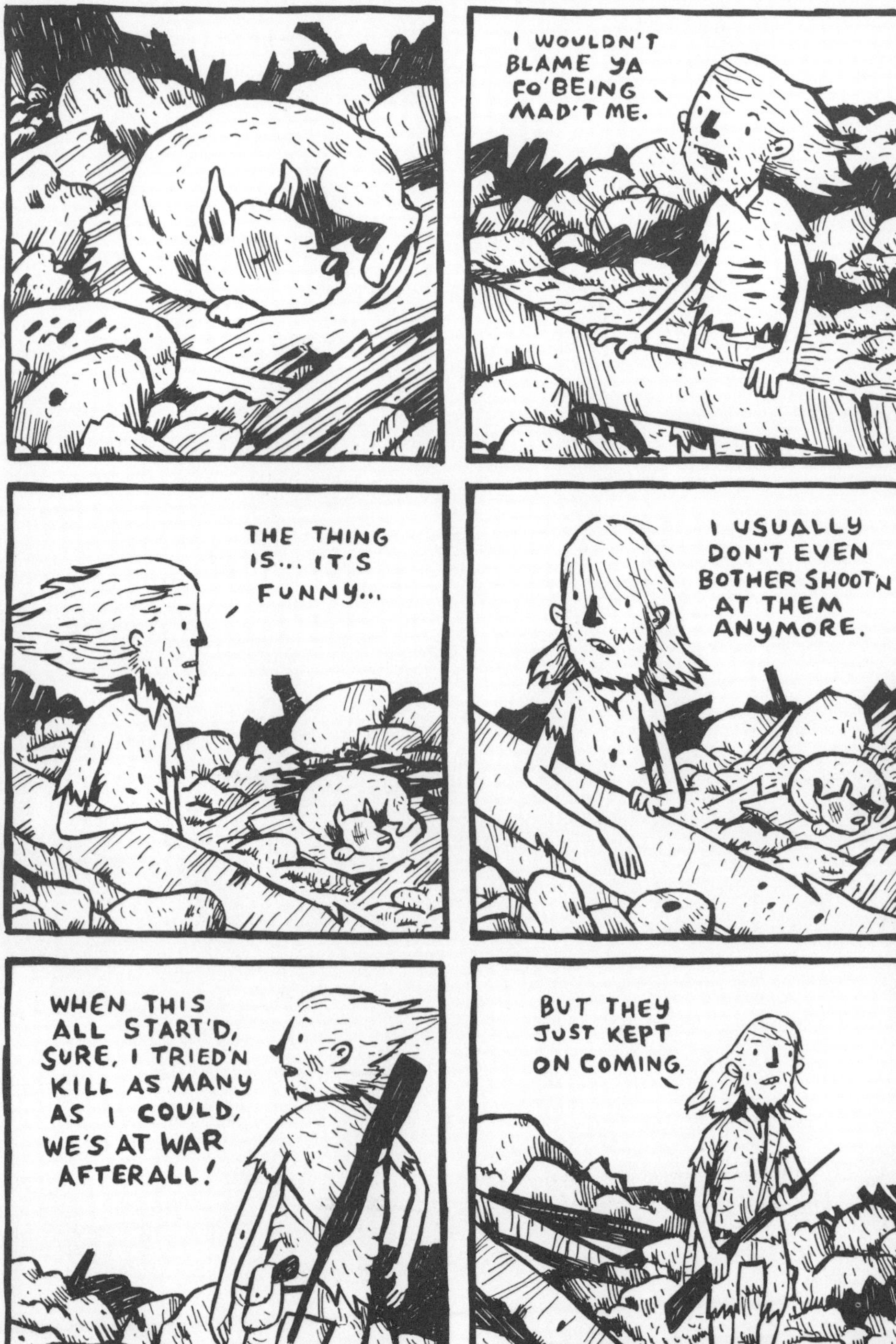
I WOULDN'T BLAME YA FO'BEING MAD'T ME.
THE THING IS... IT'S FUNNY...
I USUALLY DON'T EVEN BOTHER SHOOT'N AT THEM ANYMORE.
WHEN THIS ALL START'D, SURE, I TRIED'N KILL AS MANY AS I COULD, WE'S AT WAR AFTERALL!
BUT THEY JUST KEPT ON COMING.

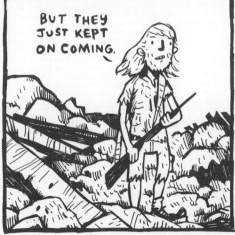

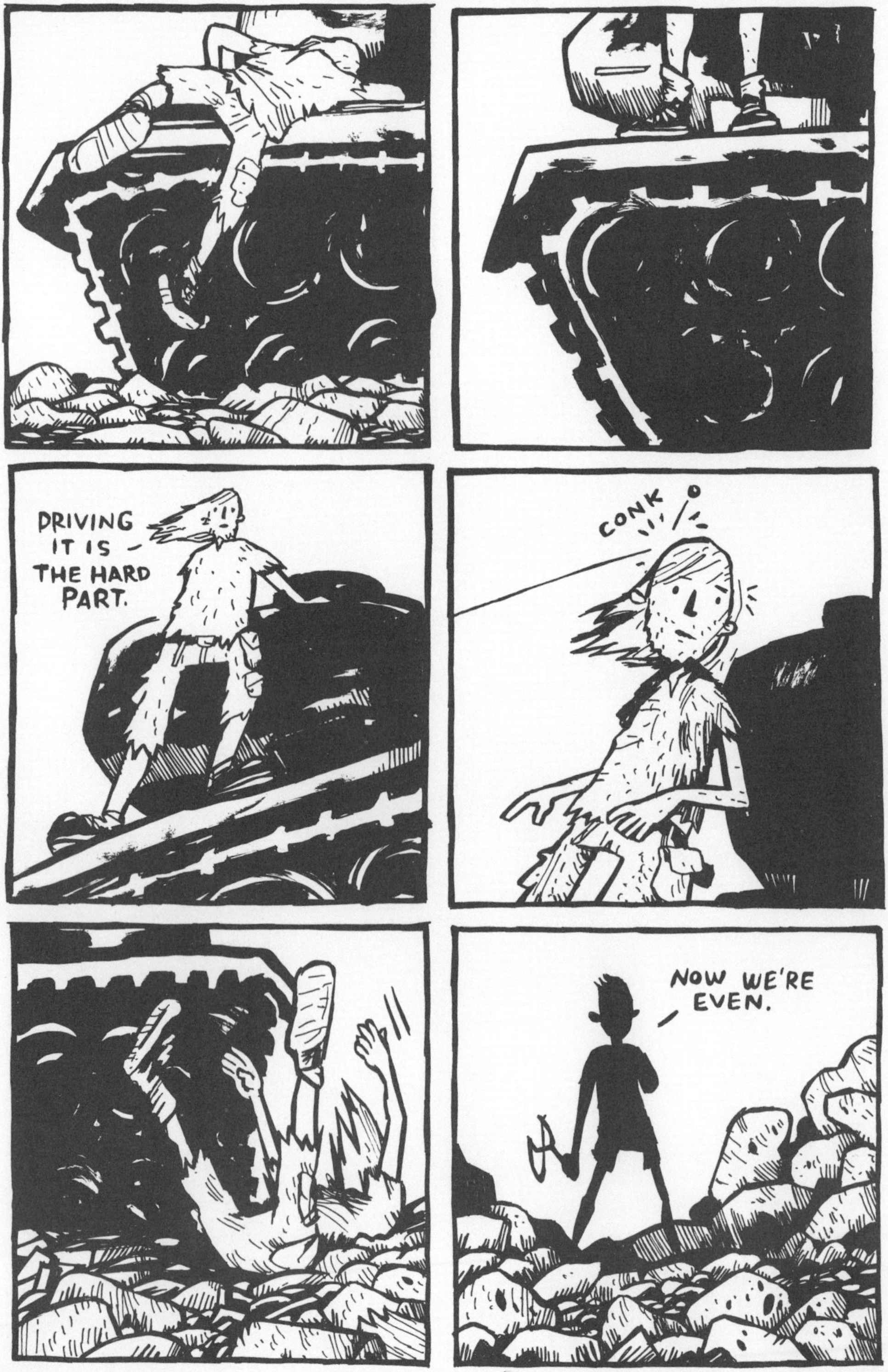
DRIVING IT IS THE HARD PART.
CONK
NOW WE'RE EVEN.

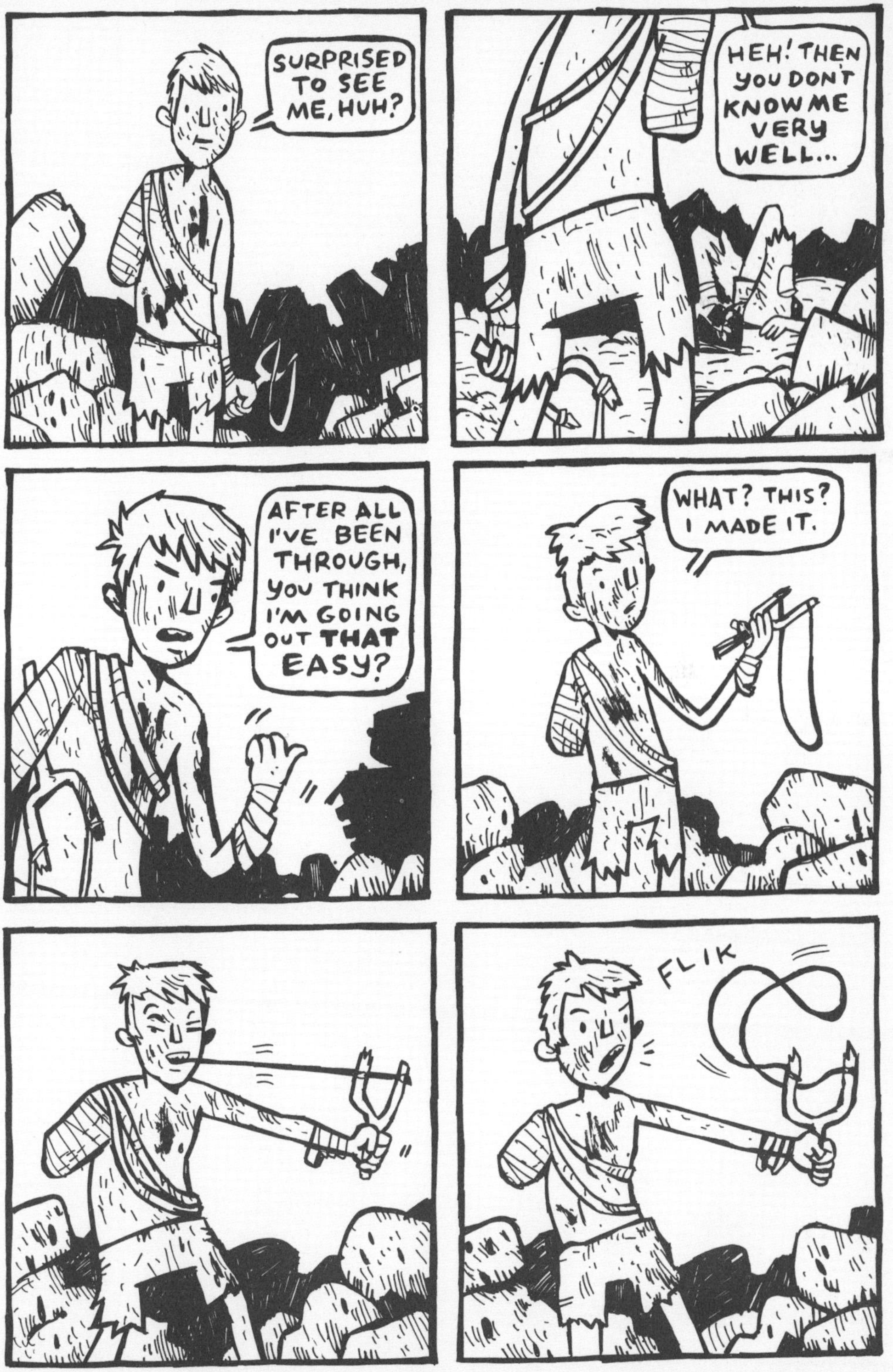
SURPRISED TO SEE ME, HUH?
HEH! THEN YOU DON'T KNOW ME VERY WELL...
AFTER ALL I'VE BEEN THROUGH, YOU THINK I'M GOING OUT THAT EASY?
WHAT? THIS? I MADE IT.
FLIK

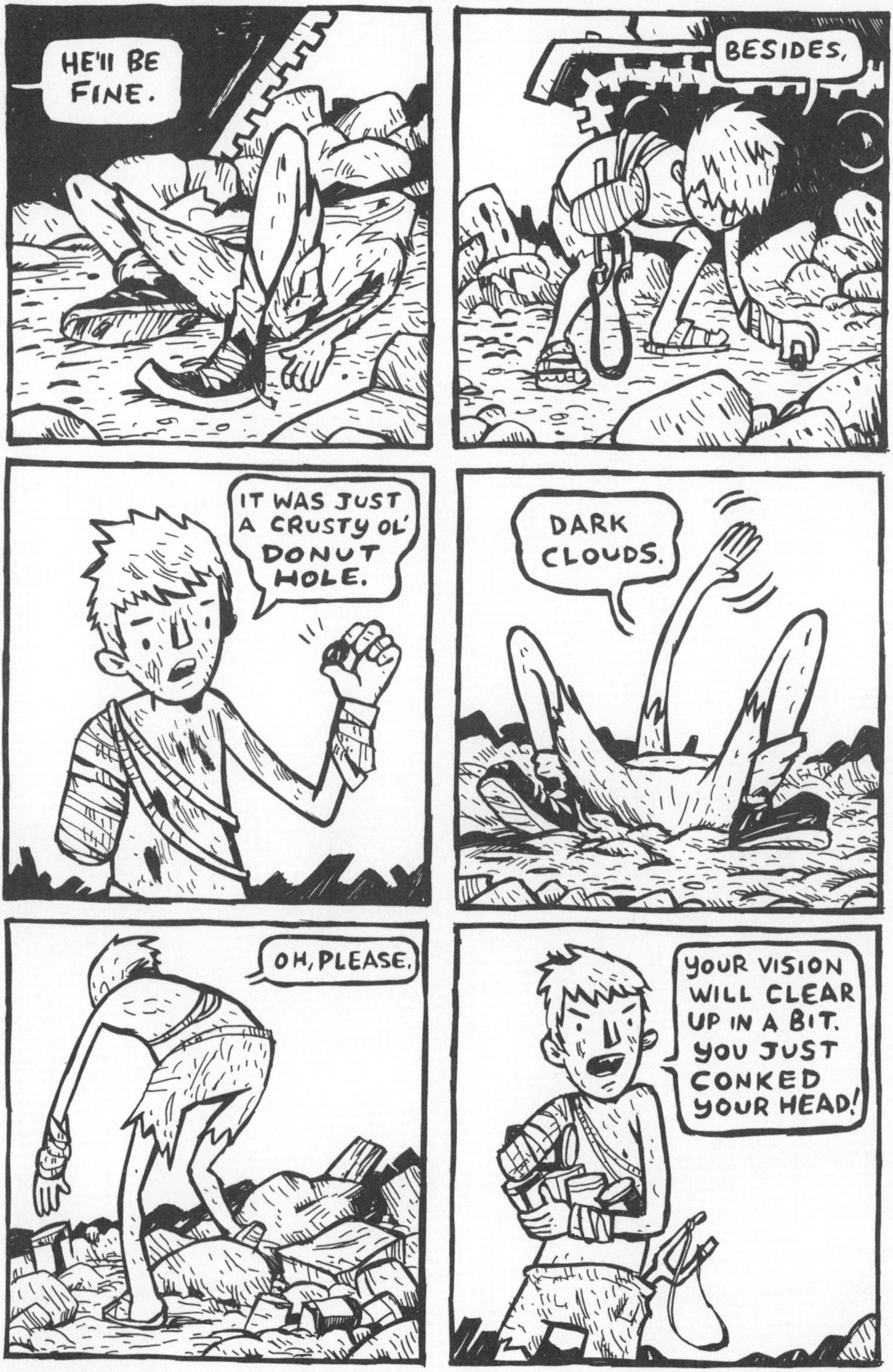
HE'll BE FINE.
BESIDES,
IT WAS JUST A CRUSTY OL' DONUT HOLE.
DARK CLOUDS.
OH, PLEASE.
YOUR VISION WILL CLEAR UP IN A BIT. YOU JUST CONKED YOUR HEAD!

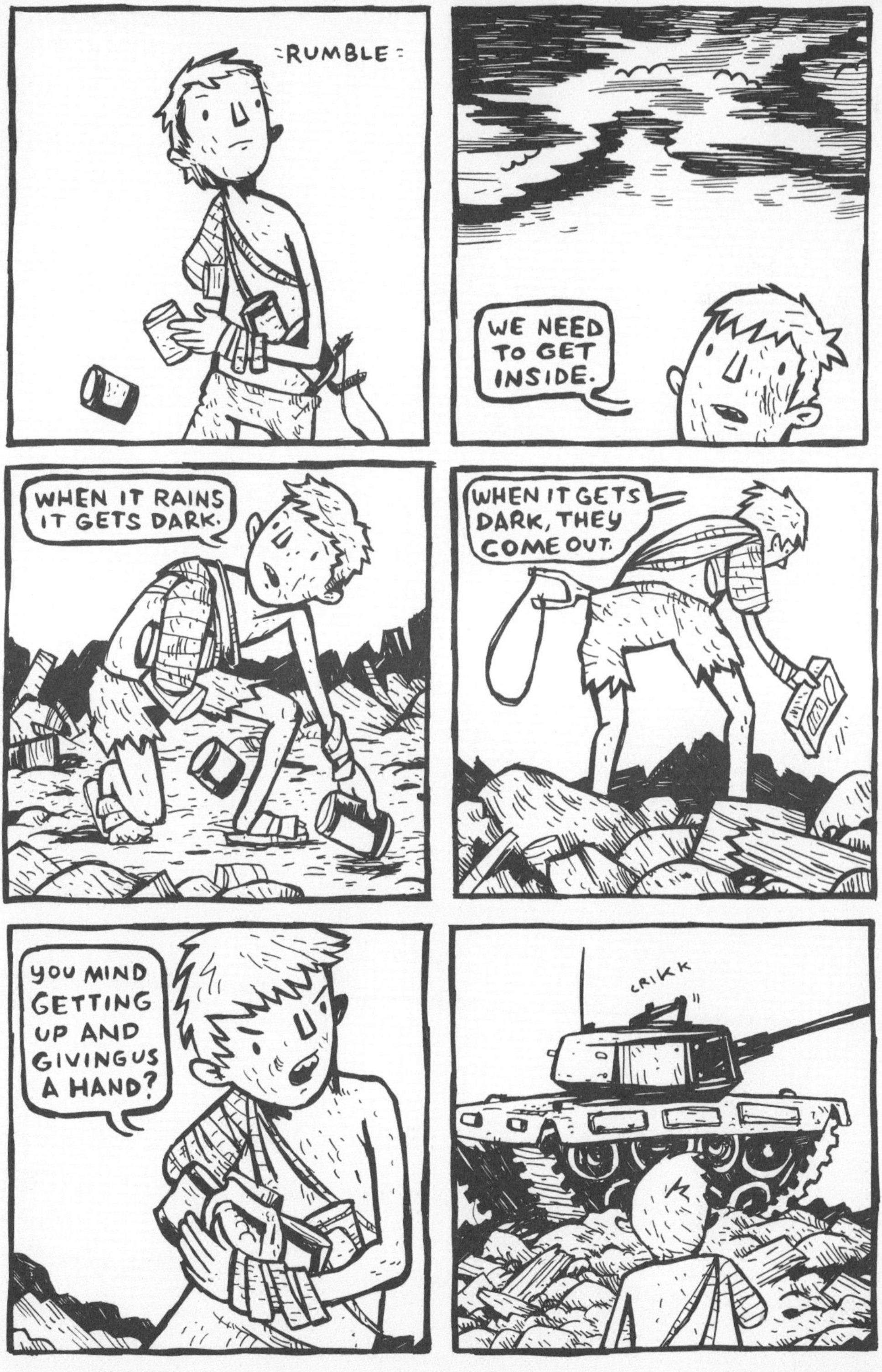
RUMBLE
WE NEED TO GET INSIDE.
WHEN IT RAINS IT GETS DARK.
WHEN IT GETS DARK, THEY COME OUT.
YOU MIND GETTING UP AND GIVINGUS A HAND?
CRIKK

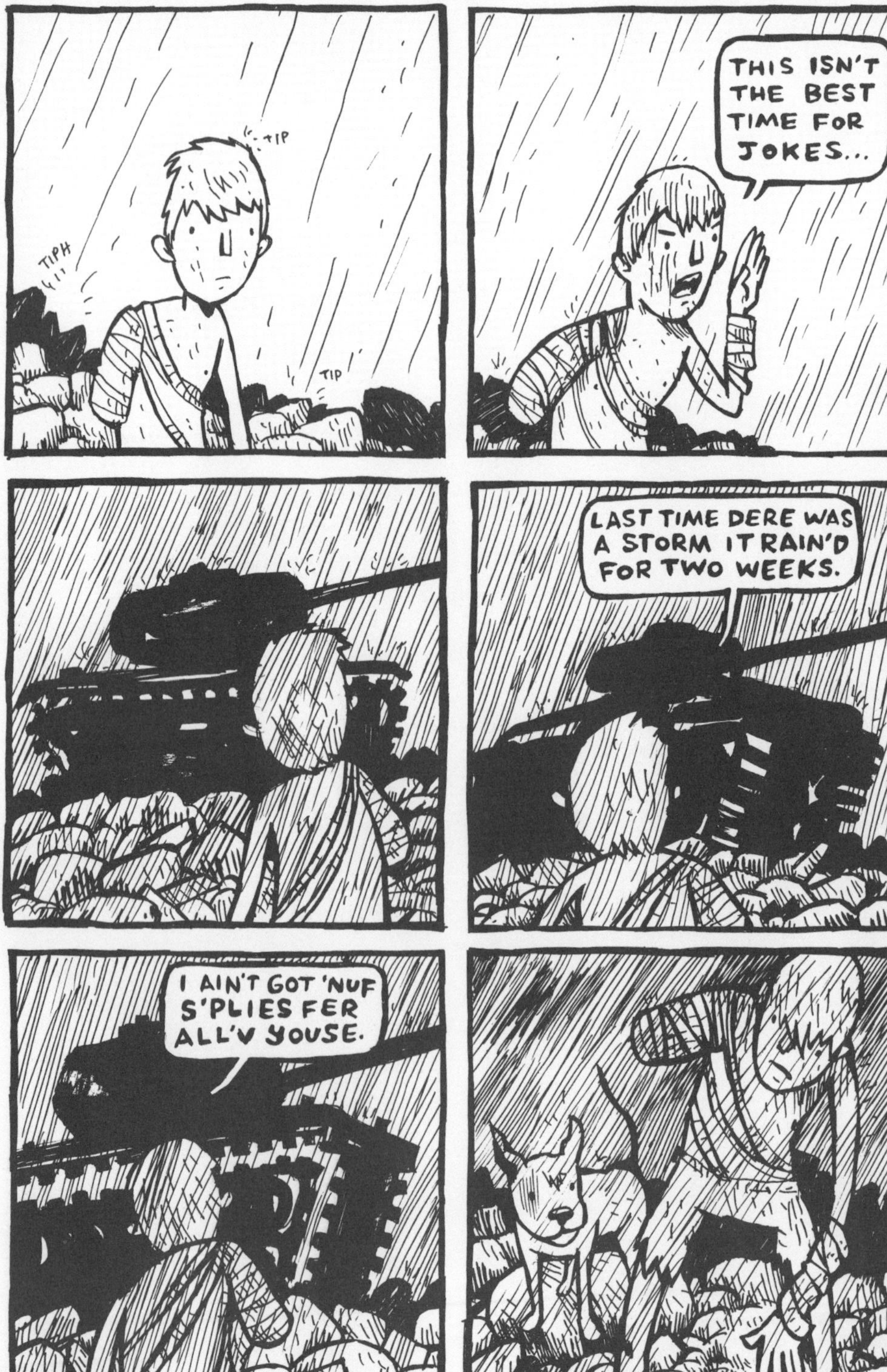
TIP
TIPH
TIP
THIS ISN'T THE BEST TIME FOR JOKES...
LAST TIME DERE WAS A STORM IT RAIN'D FOR TWO WEEKS.
I AIN'T GOT 'NUF S'PLIES FER ALL'V YOUSE.

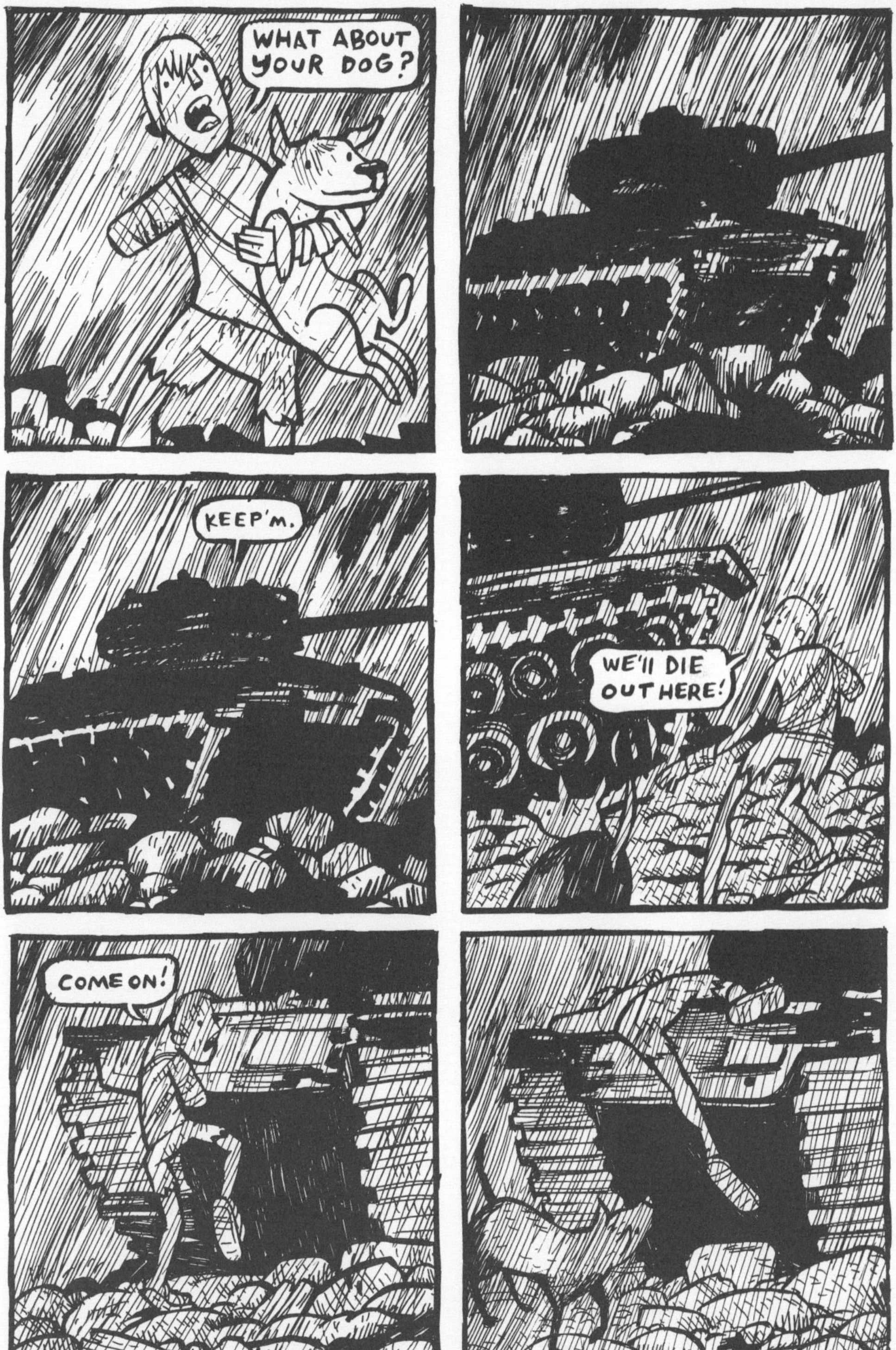
WHAT ABOUT YOUR DOG?
KEEP'M.
WE'll DIE OUT HERE!
COME ON!

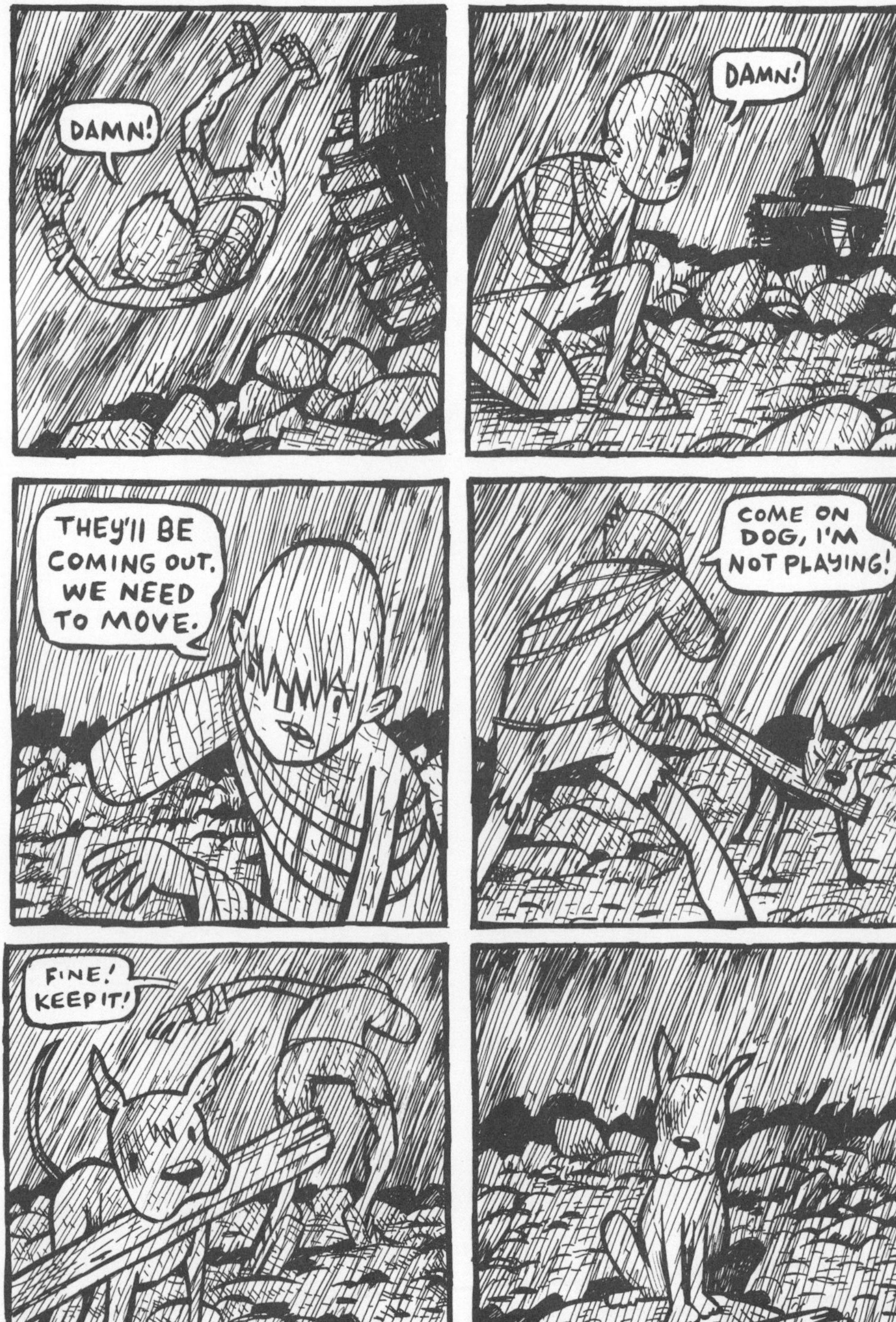
DAMN!
DAMN!
THEY'LL BE COMING OUT. WE NEED TO MOVE.
COME ON DOG, I'M NOT PLAYING!
FINE! KEEP IT!

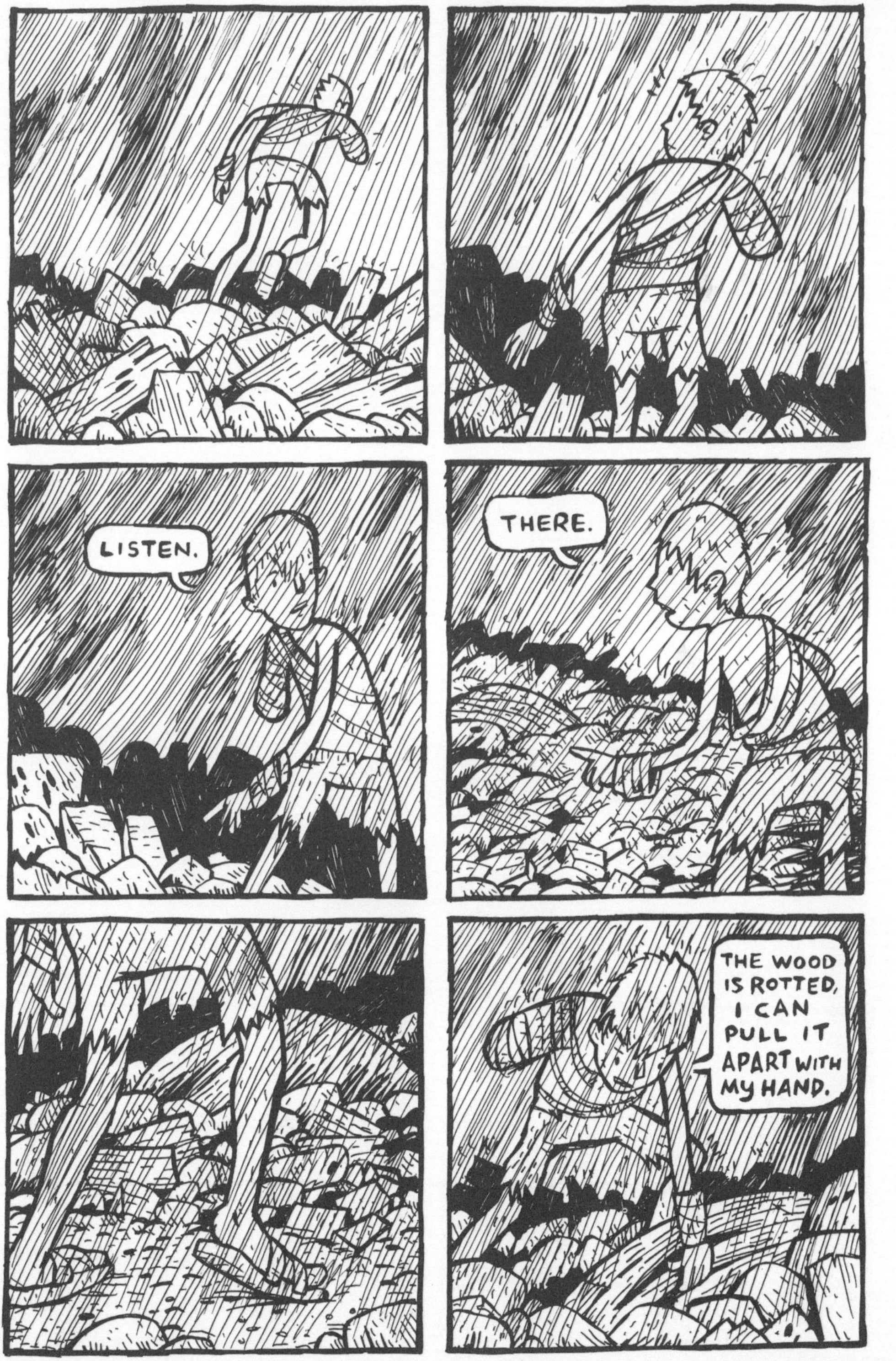
LISTEN.
THERE.
THE WOOD IS ROTTED, I CAN PULL IT APART WITH MY HAND.

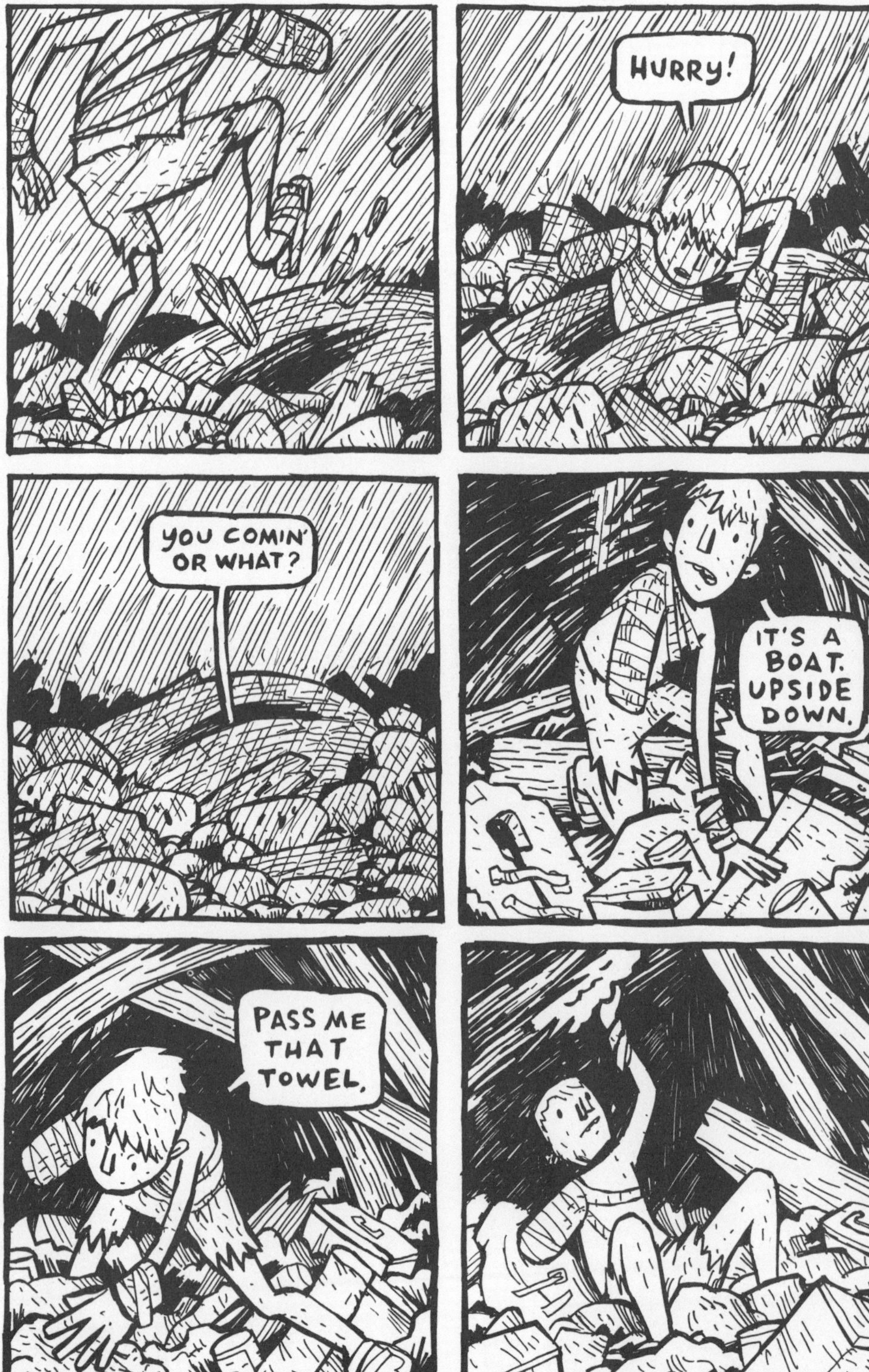
HURRY!
YOU COMIN' OR WHAT?
IT'S A BOAT. UPSIDE DOWN.
PASS ME THAT TOWEL.

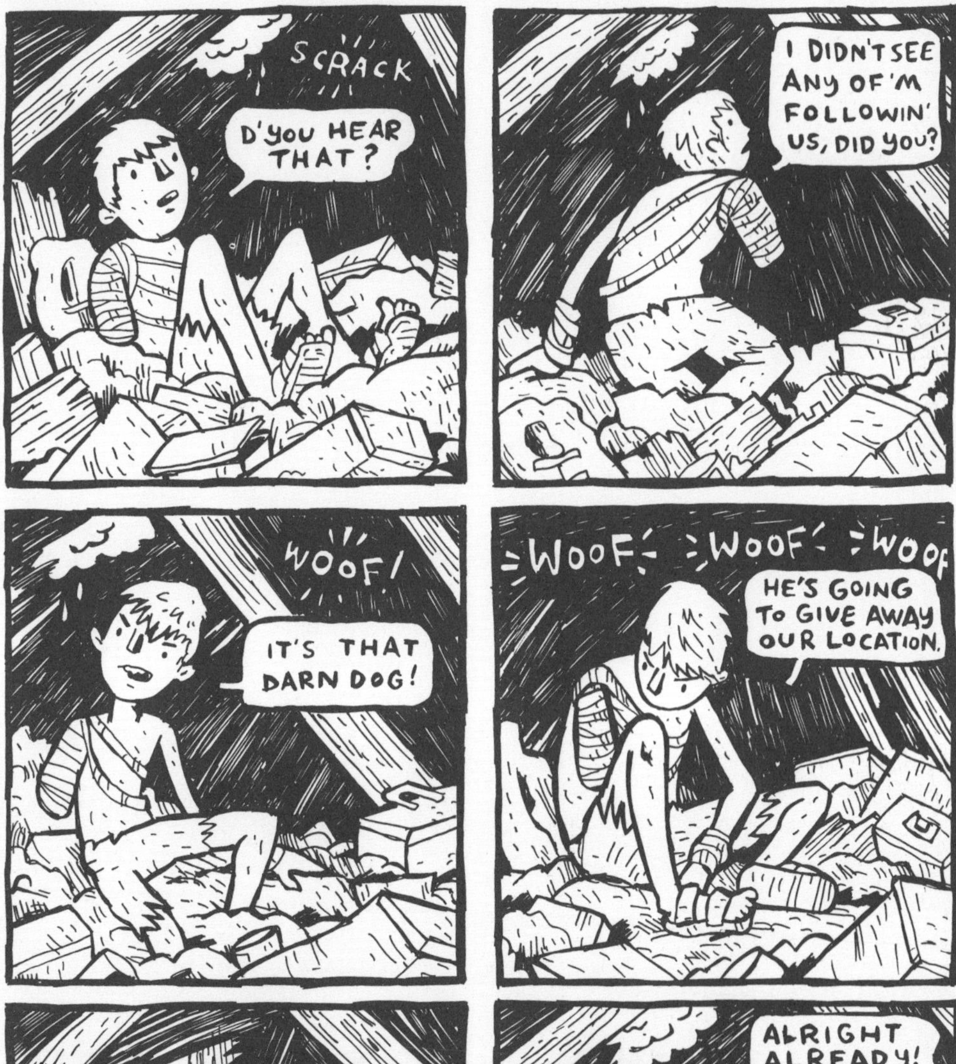
SCRACK
D'YOU HEAR THAT?
I DIDN'T SEE ANY OF 'M FOLLOWIN' US, DID YOU?
WOOF!
IT'S THAT DARN DOG!
WOOF WOOF WOOF
HE'S GOING TO GIVE AWAY OUR LOCATION.
ALRIGHT ALREADY! THAT'S ENOUGH BOY!

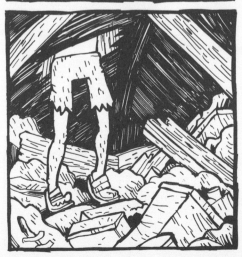

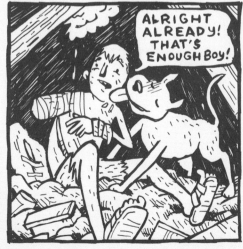

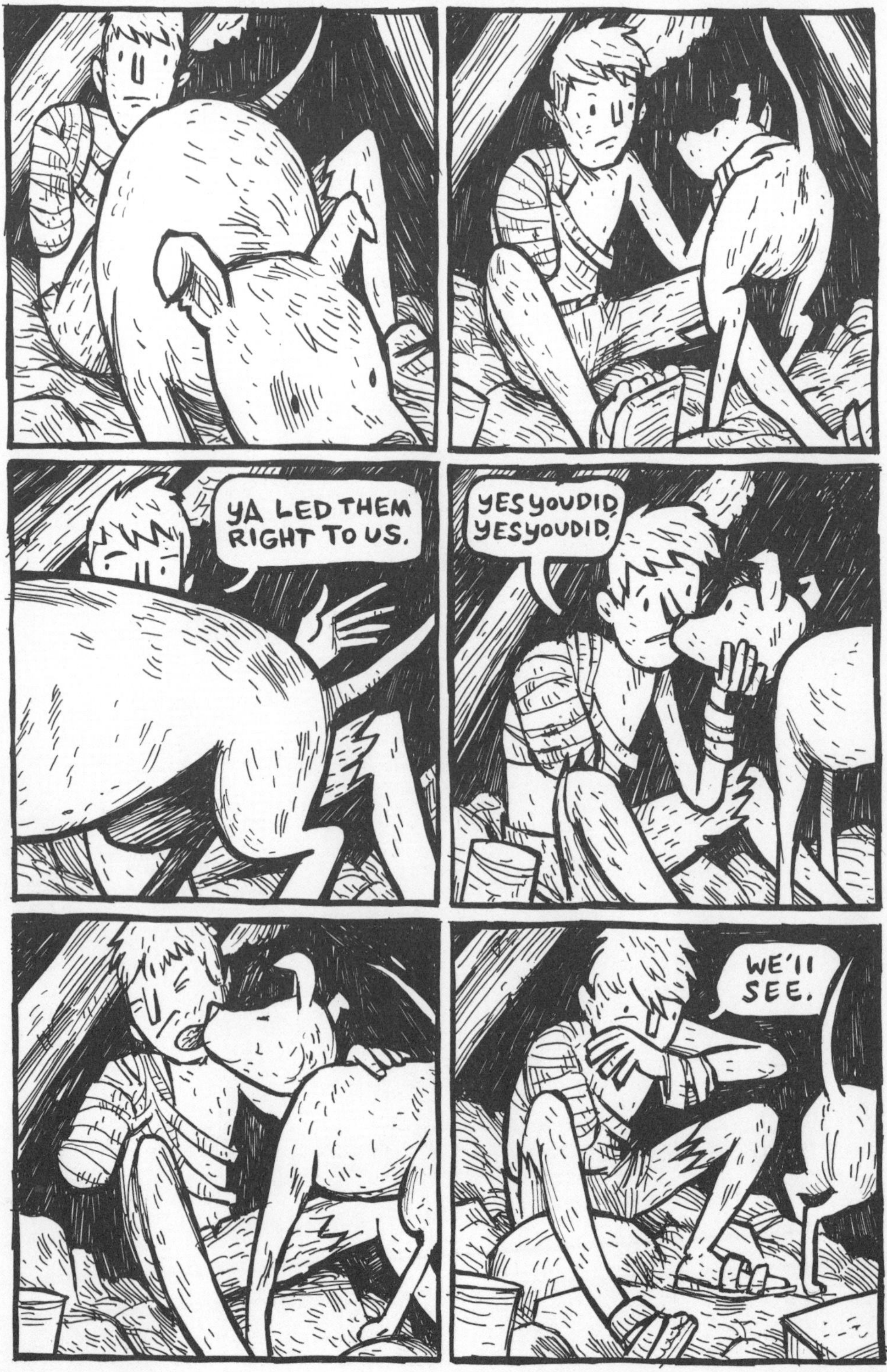
YA LED THEM RIGHT TO US.
YESYOUDID, YESYOUDID.
WE'll SEE.

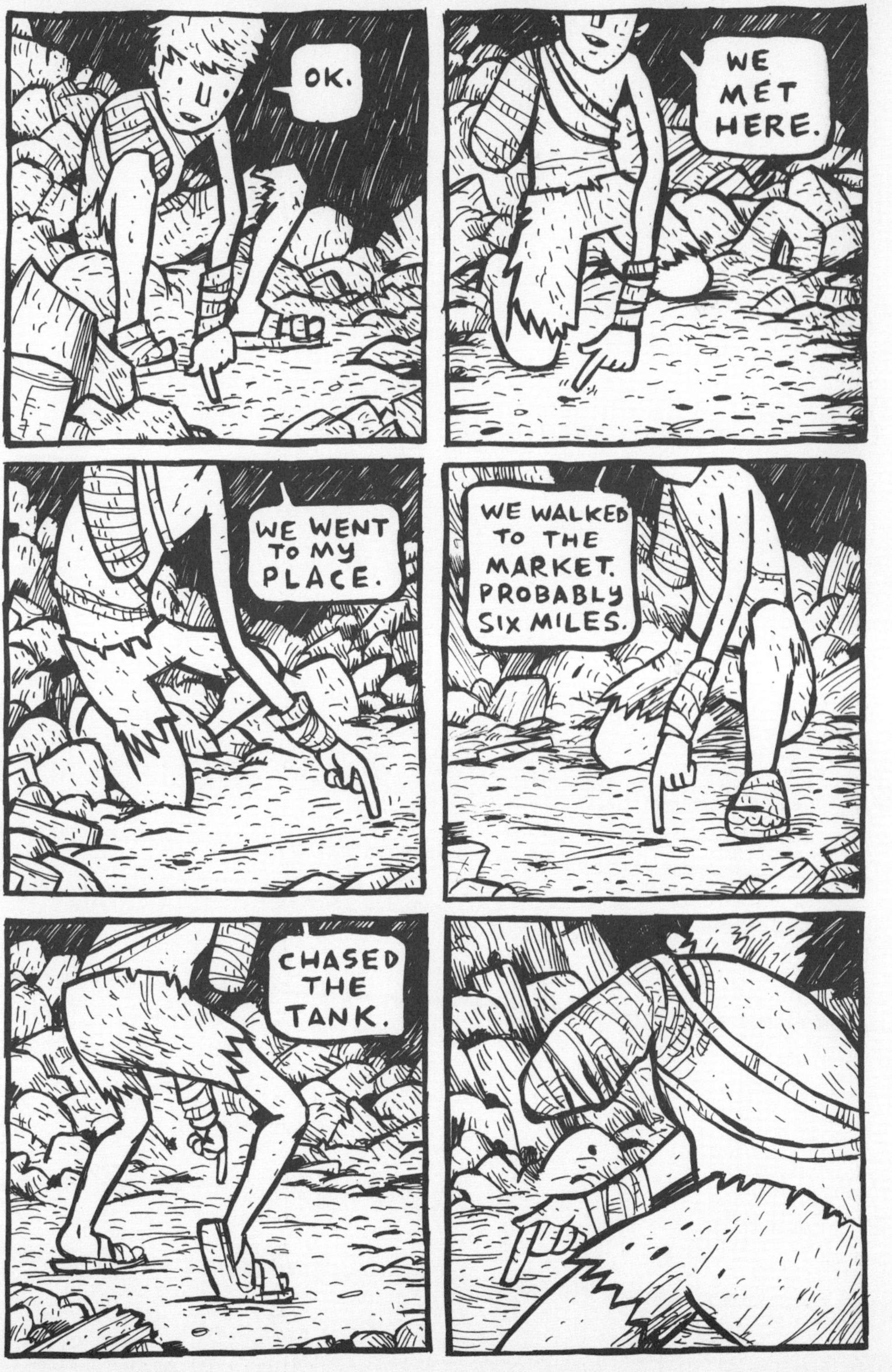
OK.
WE MET HERE.
WE WENT TO MY PLACE.
WE WALKED TO THE MARKET. PROBABLY SIX MILES.
CHASED THE TANK.

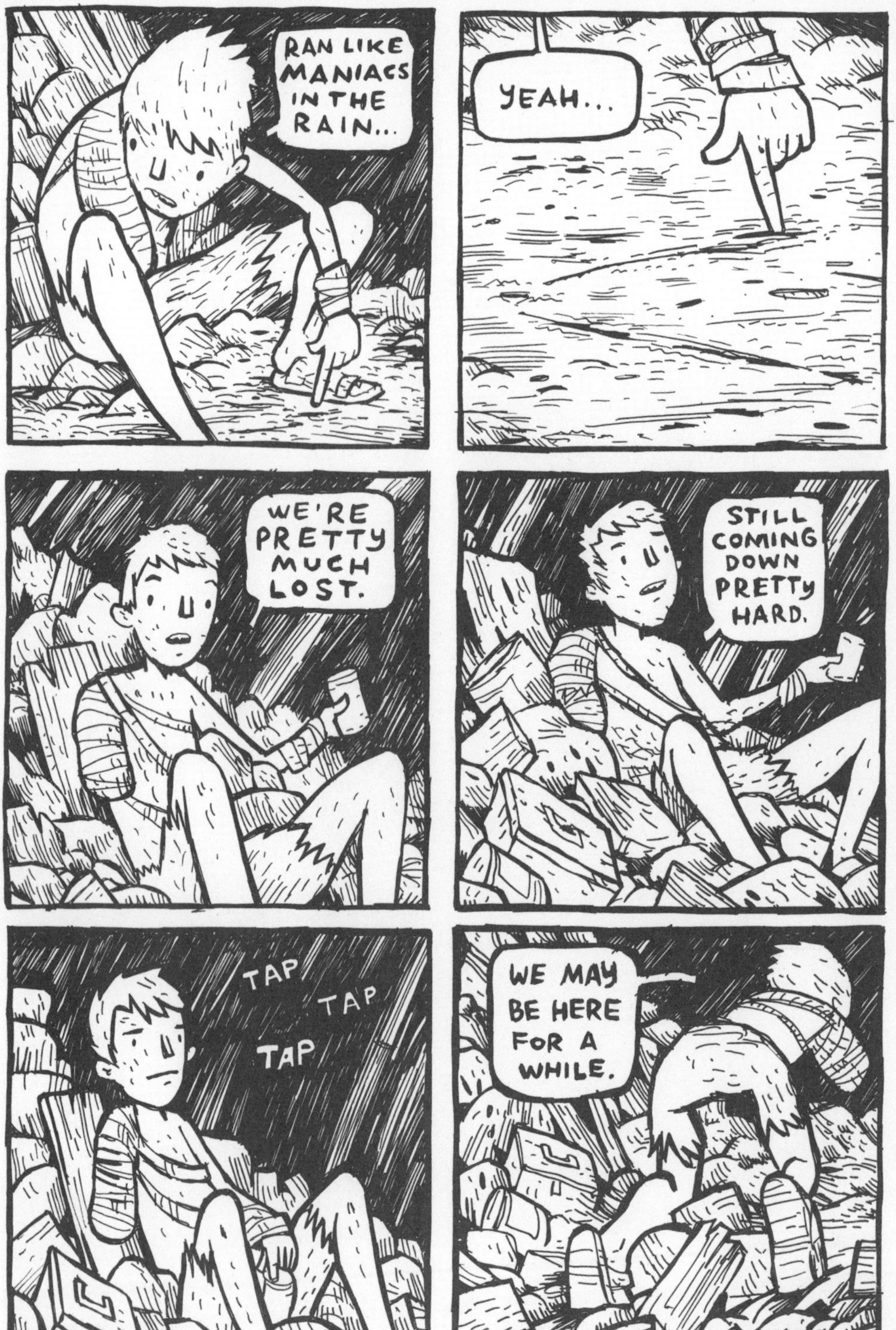
RAN LIKE MANIACS IN THE RAIN...
YEAH...
WE'RE PRETTY MUCH LOST.
STILL COMING DOWN PRETTY HARD.
TAP
TAP
TAP
WE MAY BE HERE FOR A WHILE.

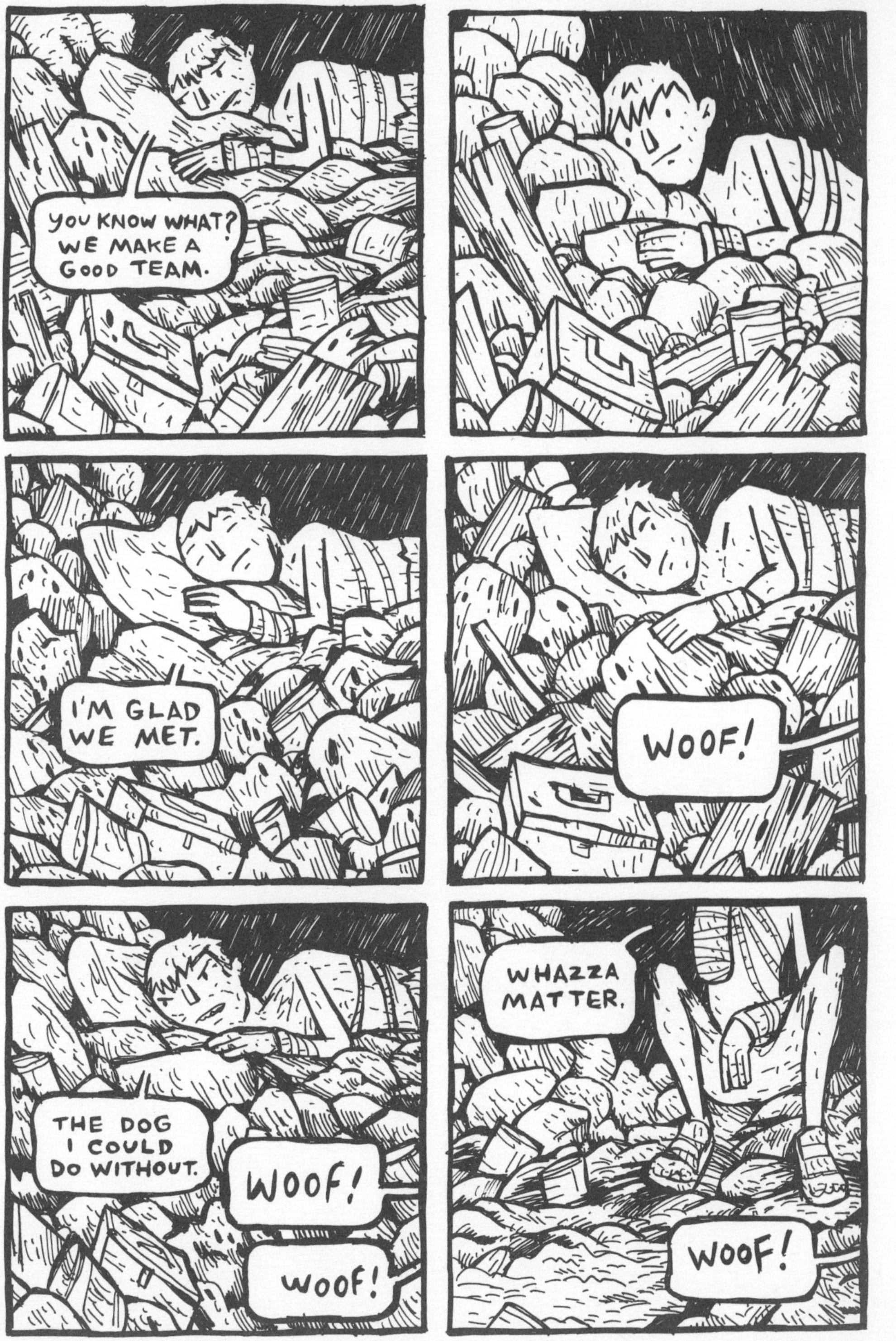
YOU KNOW WHAT? WE MAKE A GOOD TEAM.
I'M GLAD WE MET.
WOOF!
THE DOG I COULD DO WITHOUT.
WOOF!
WOOF!
WHAZZA MATTER.
WOOF!

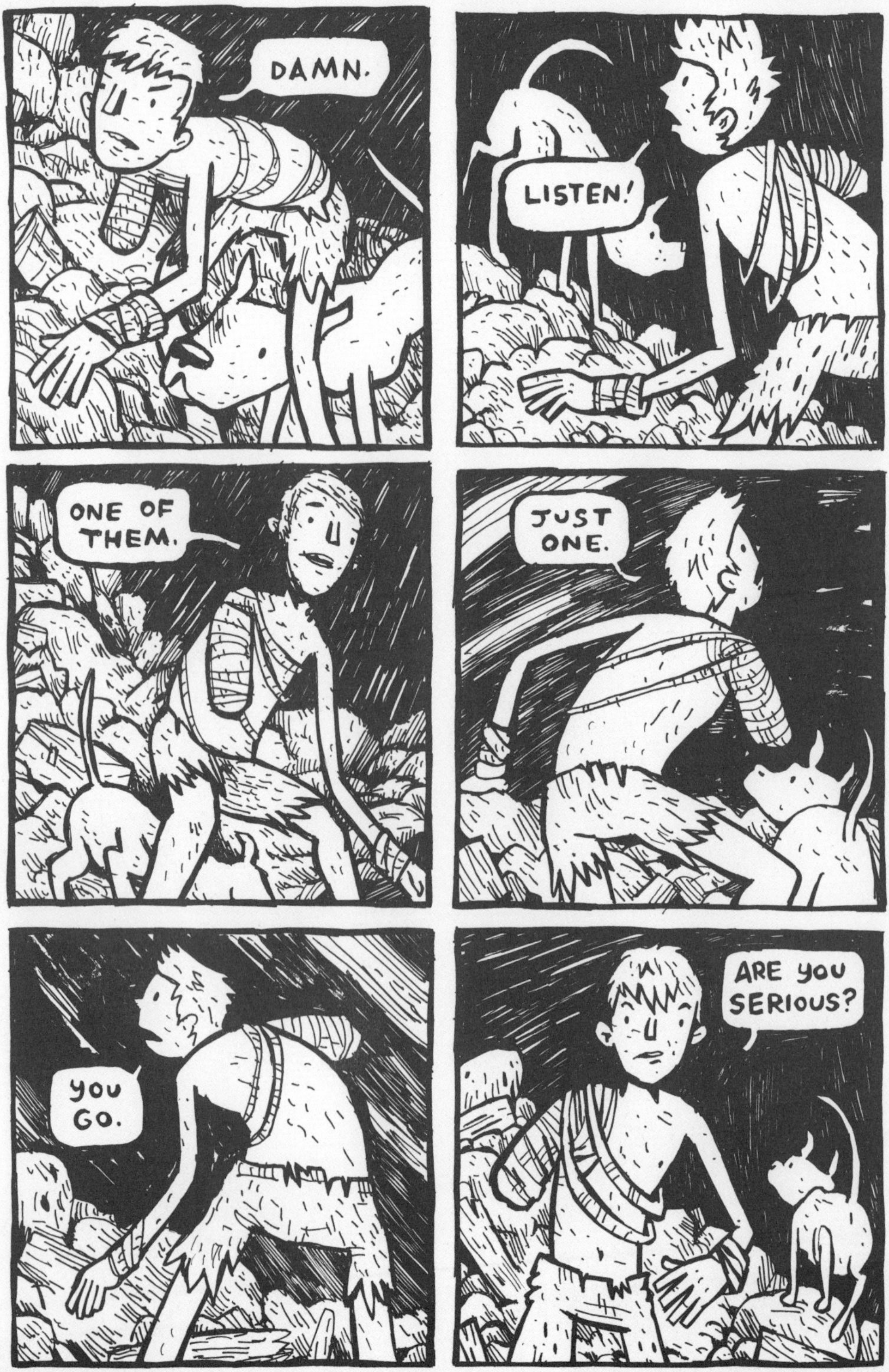
DAMN.
LISTEN!
ONE OF THEM.
JUST ONE.
YOU GO.
ARE YOU SERIOUS?

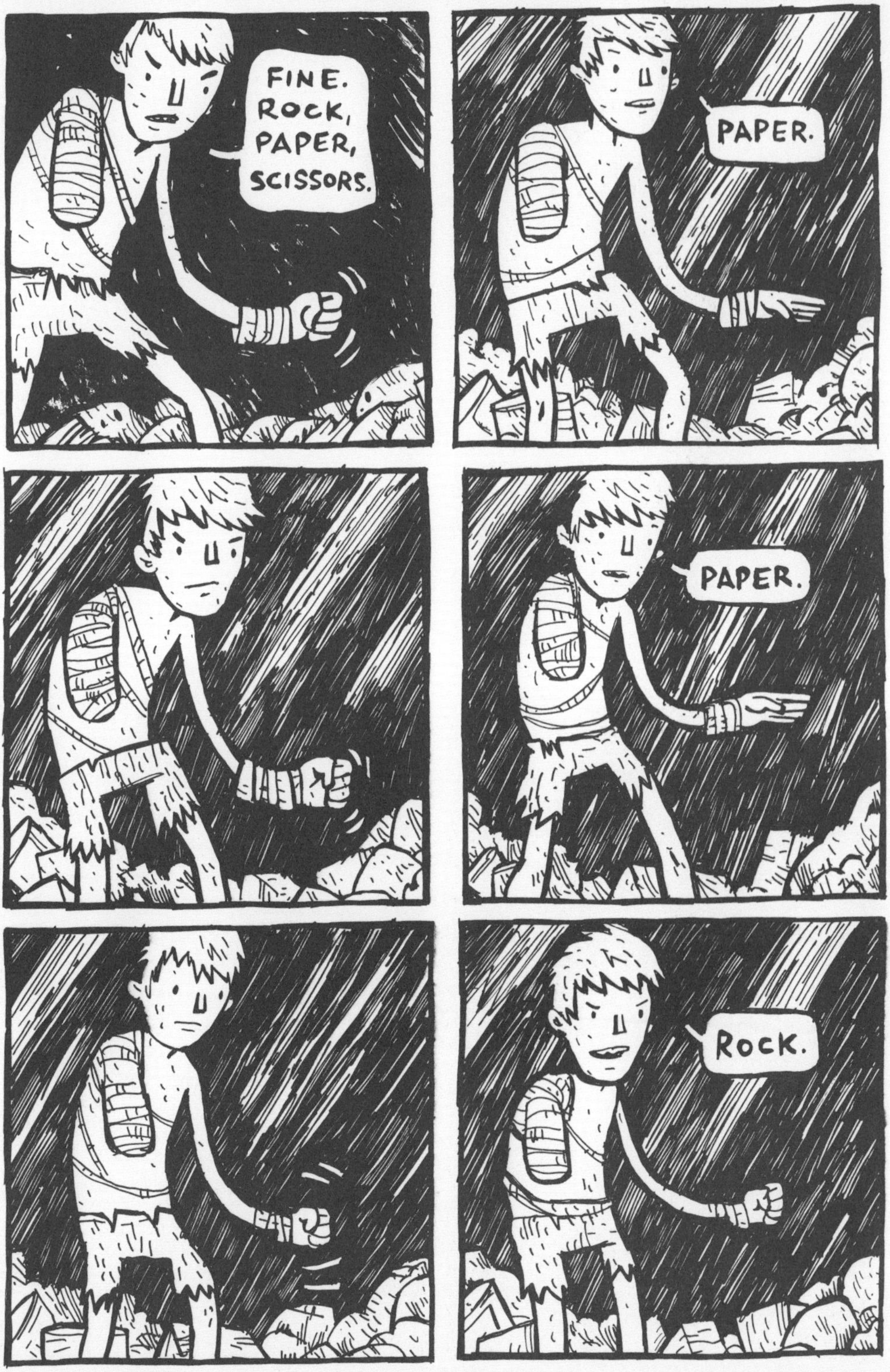
FINE. ROCK, PAPER, SCISSORS.
PAPER.
PAPER.
ROCK.

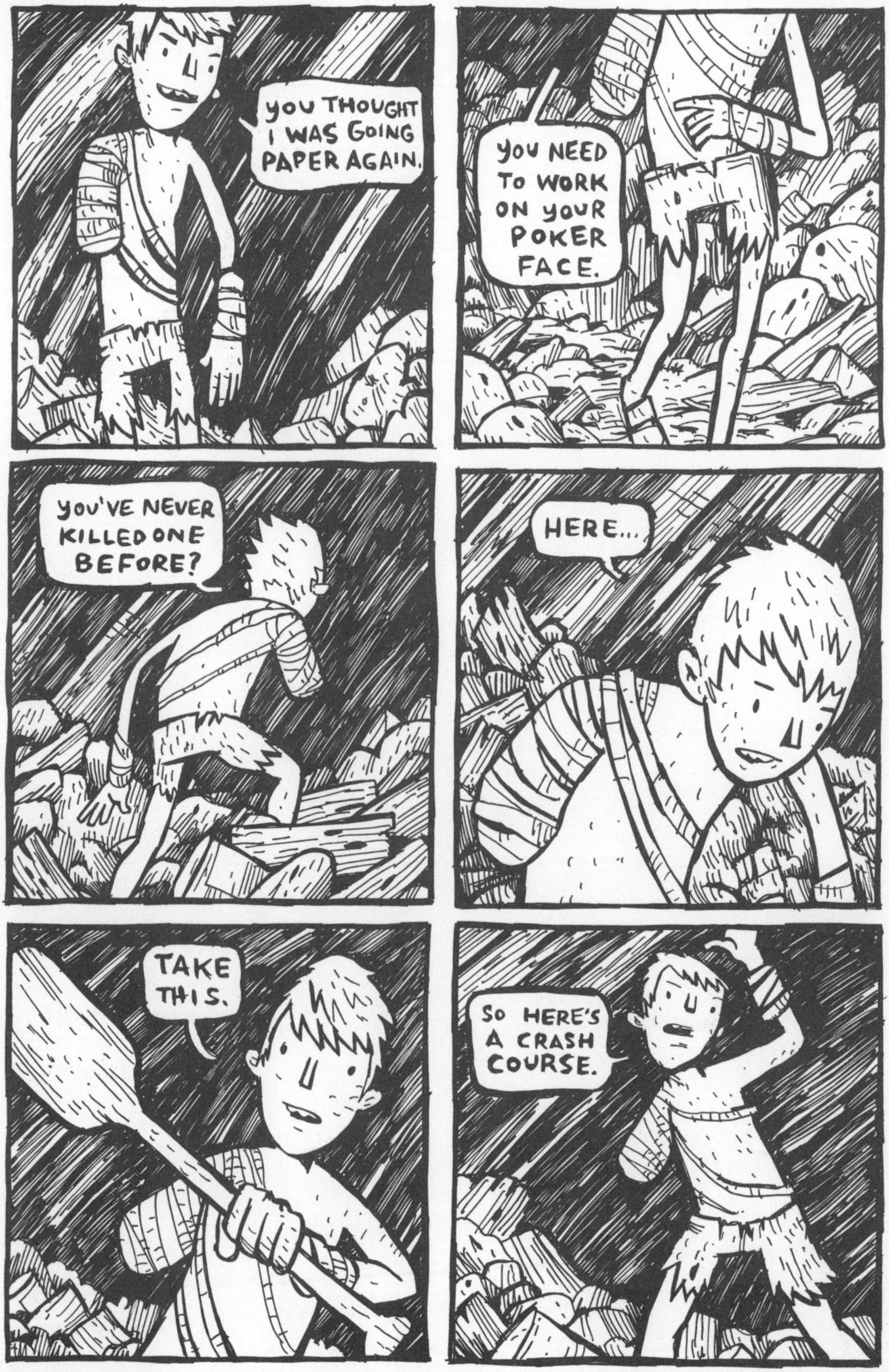
YOU THOUGHT I WAS GOING PAPER AGAIN.
YOU NEED TO WORK ON YOUR POKER FACE.
YOU'VE NEVER KILLED ONE BEFORE?
HERE...
TAKE THIS.
SO HERE'S A CRASH COURSE.

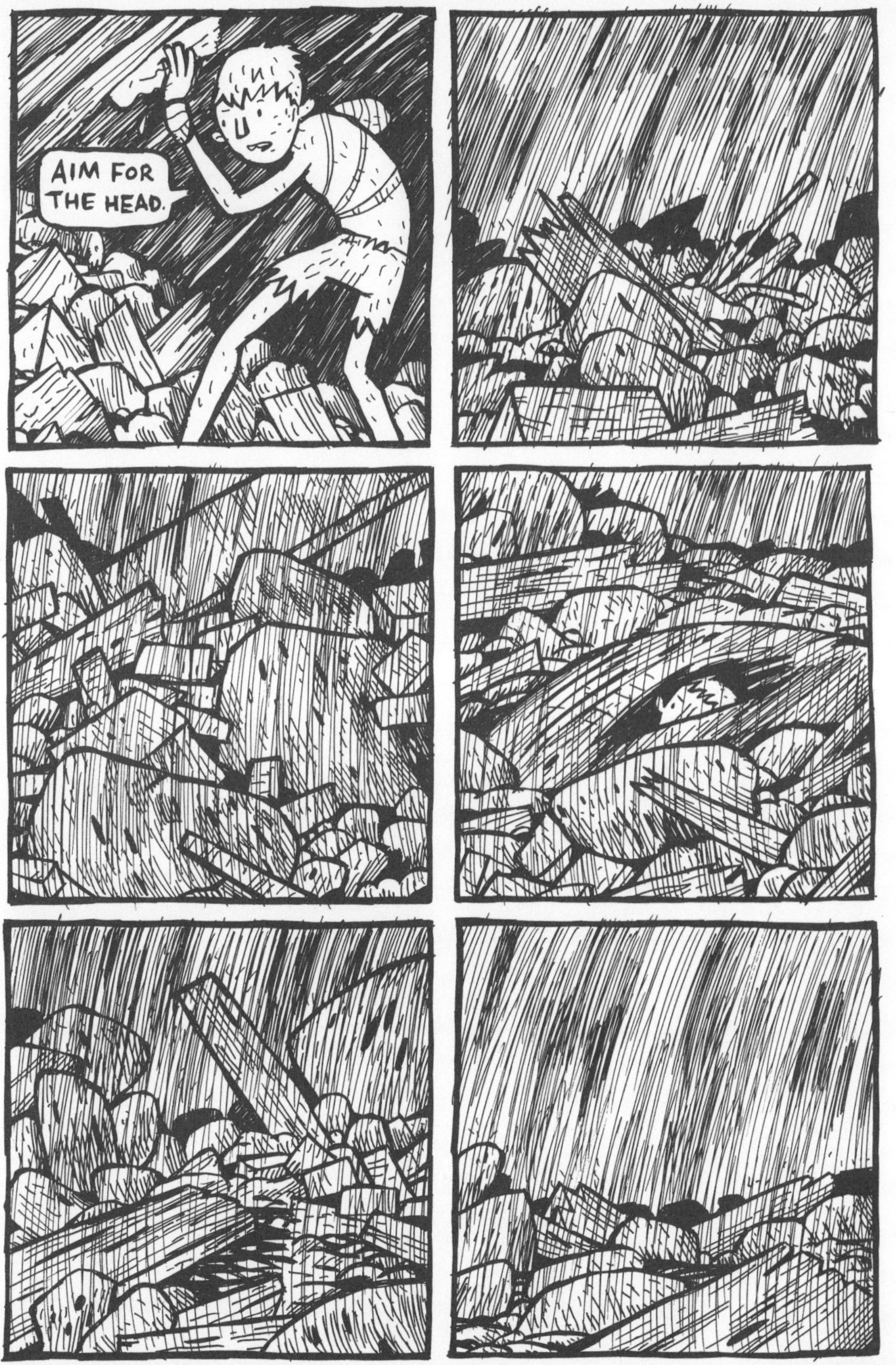
AIM FOR THE HEAD.

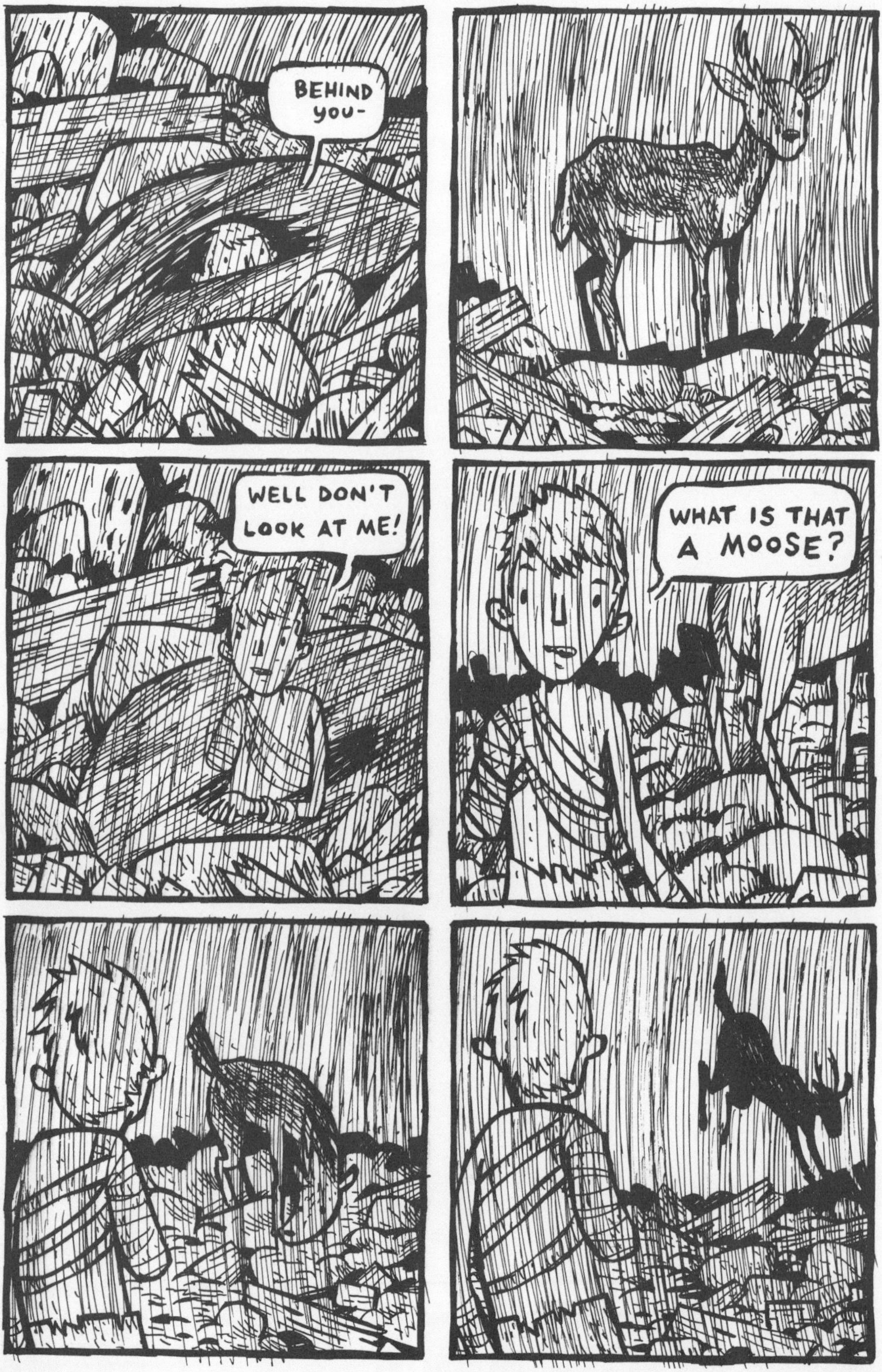
BEHIND you-
WELL DON'T LOOK AT ME!
WHAT IS THAT A MOOSE?

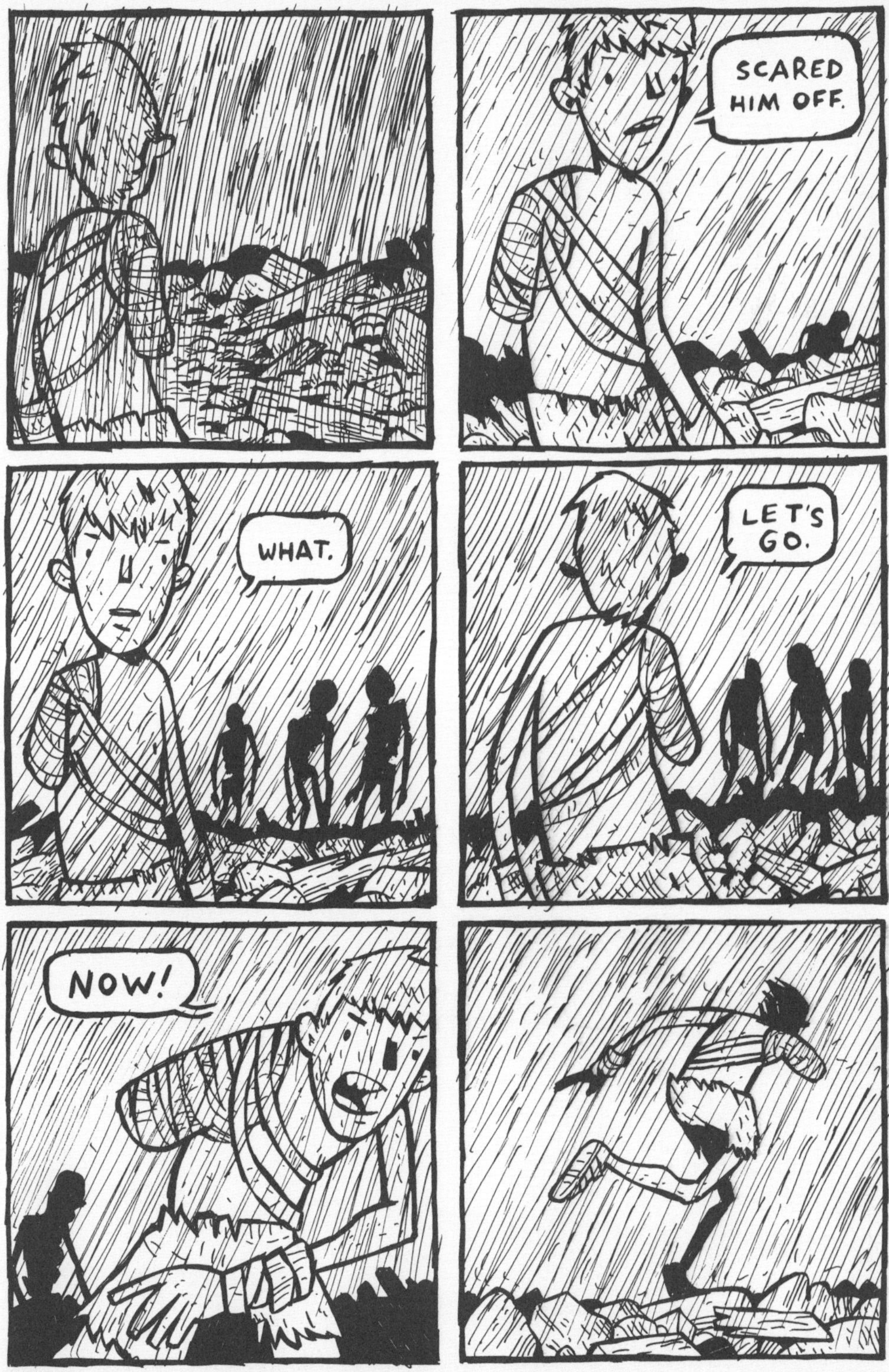
SCARED HIM OFF.
WHAT.
LET'S GO.
NOW!

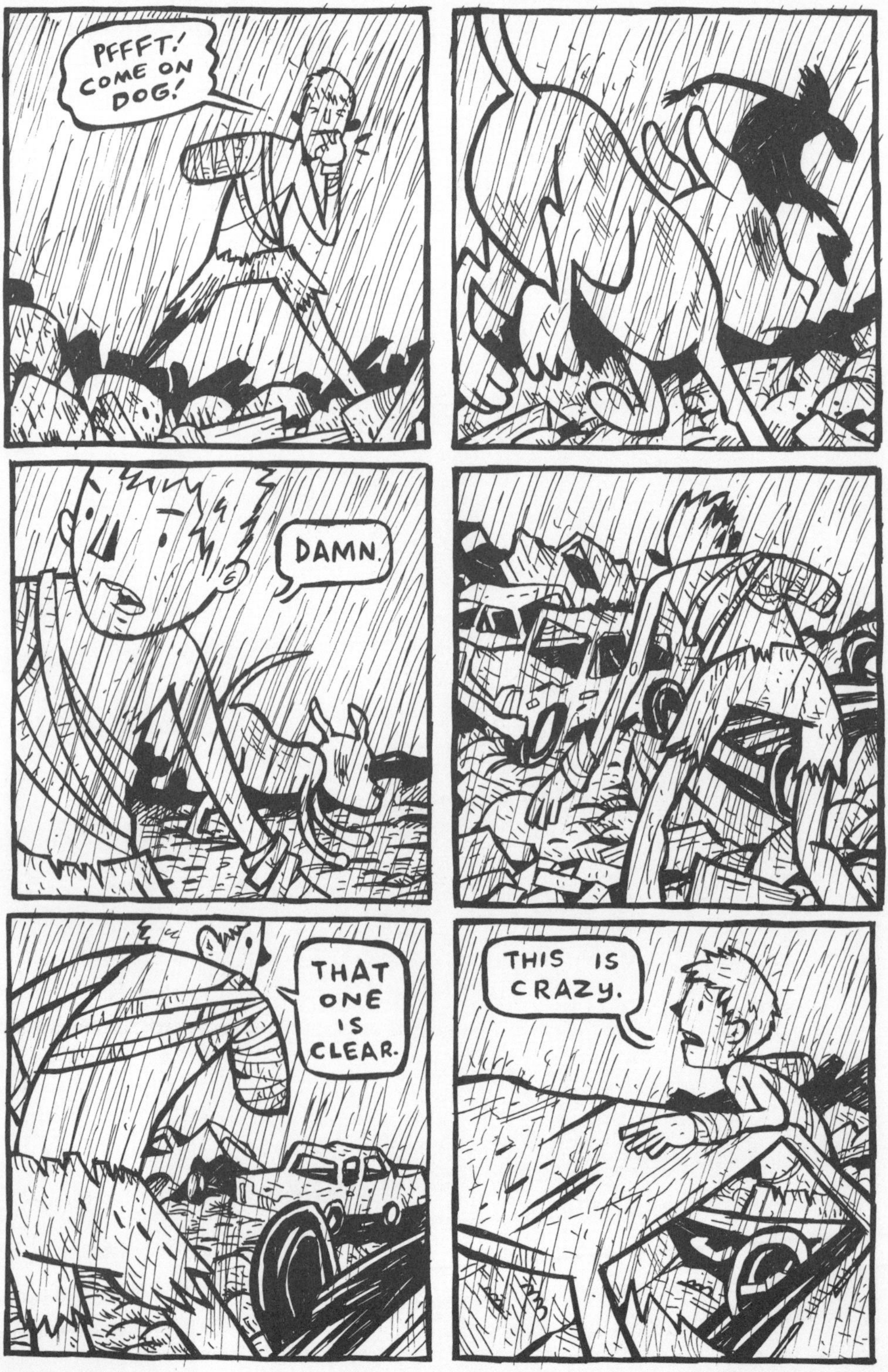
PFFFT! COME ON DOG!
DAMN.
THAT ONE IS CLEAR.
THIS IS CRAZY.

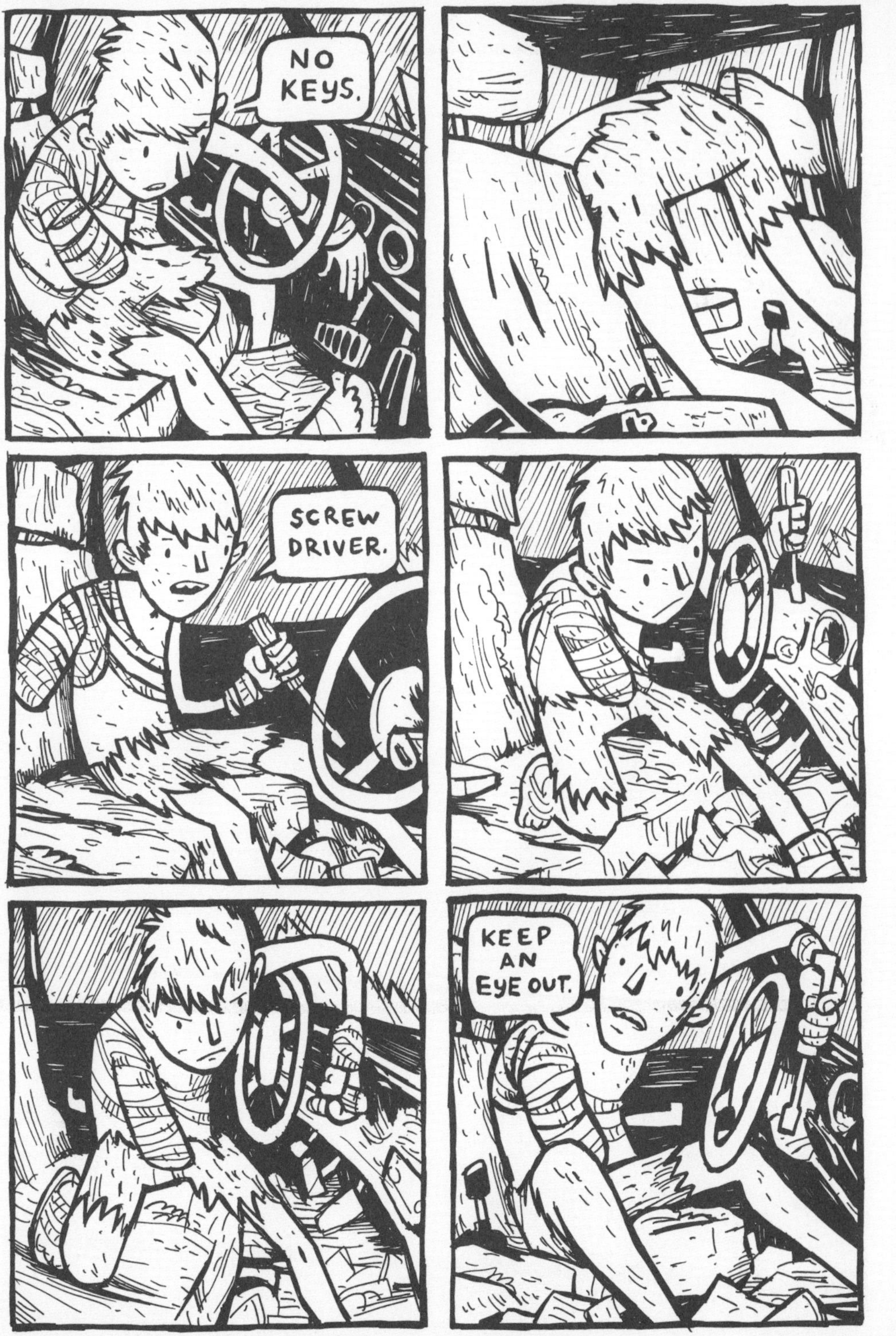
NO KEYS.
SCREW DRIVER.
KEEP AN EYE OUT.

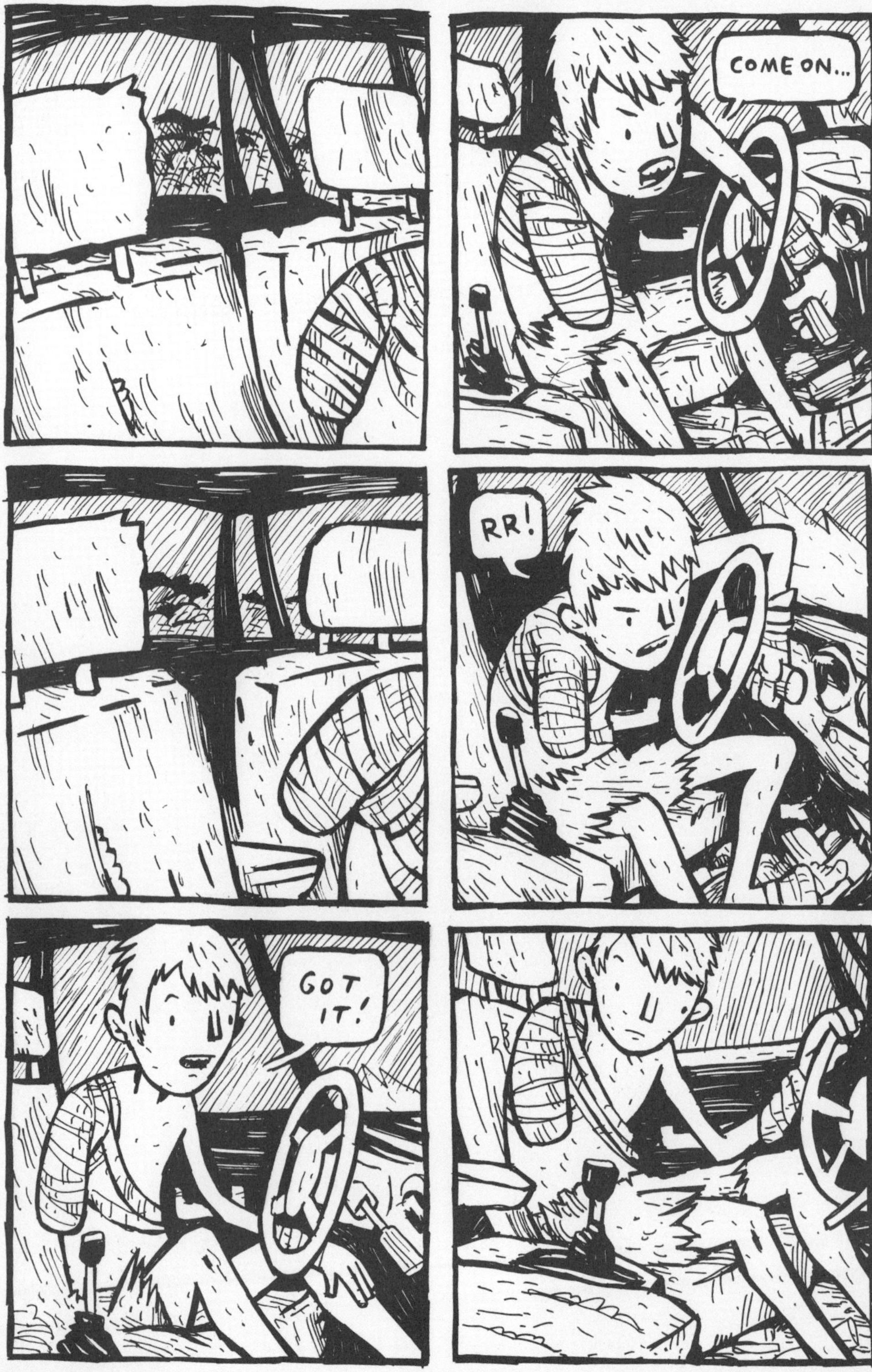
COME ON...
RR!
GOT IT!

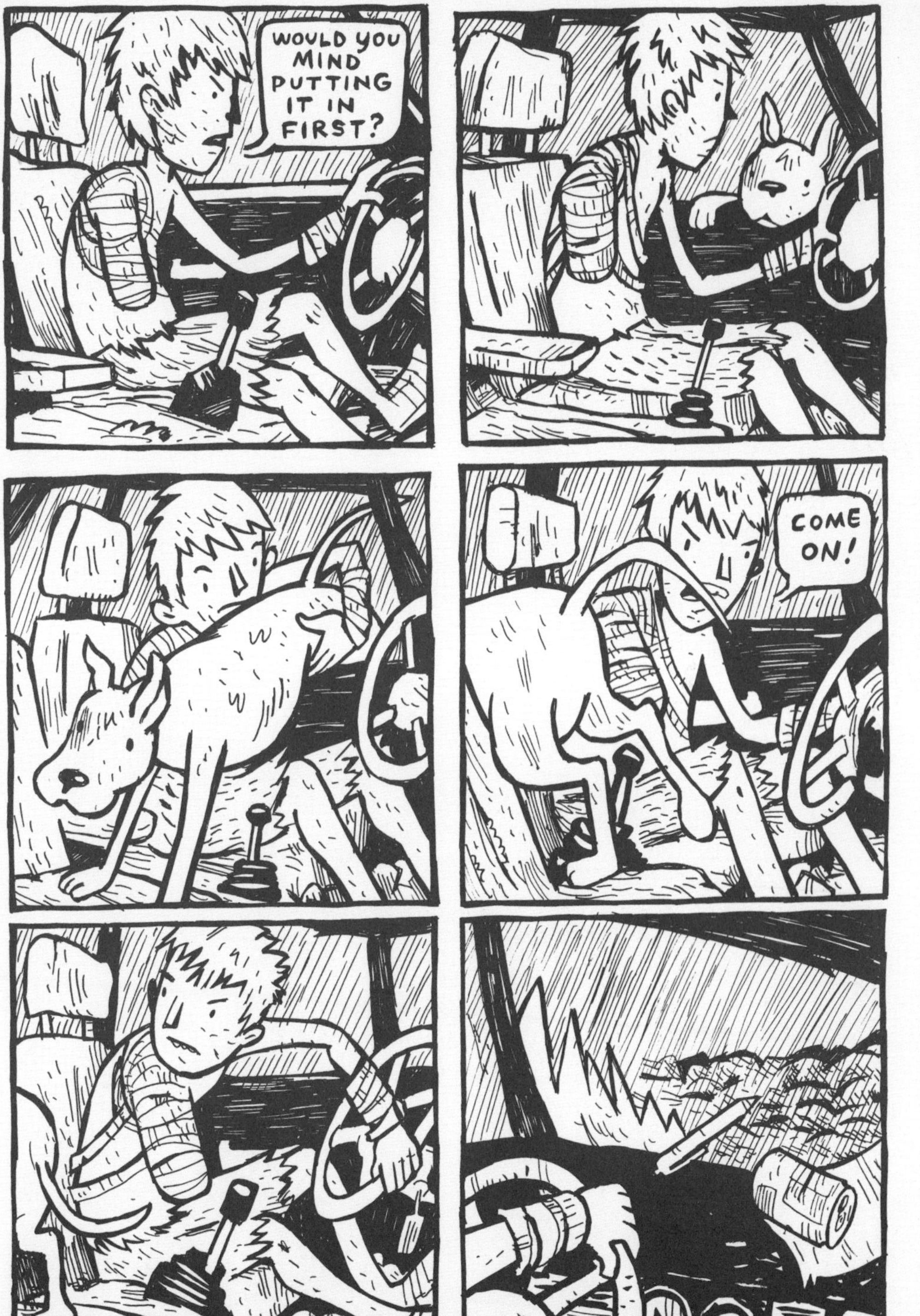
WOULD YOU MIND PUTTING IT IN FIRST?
COME ON!

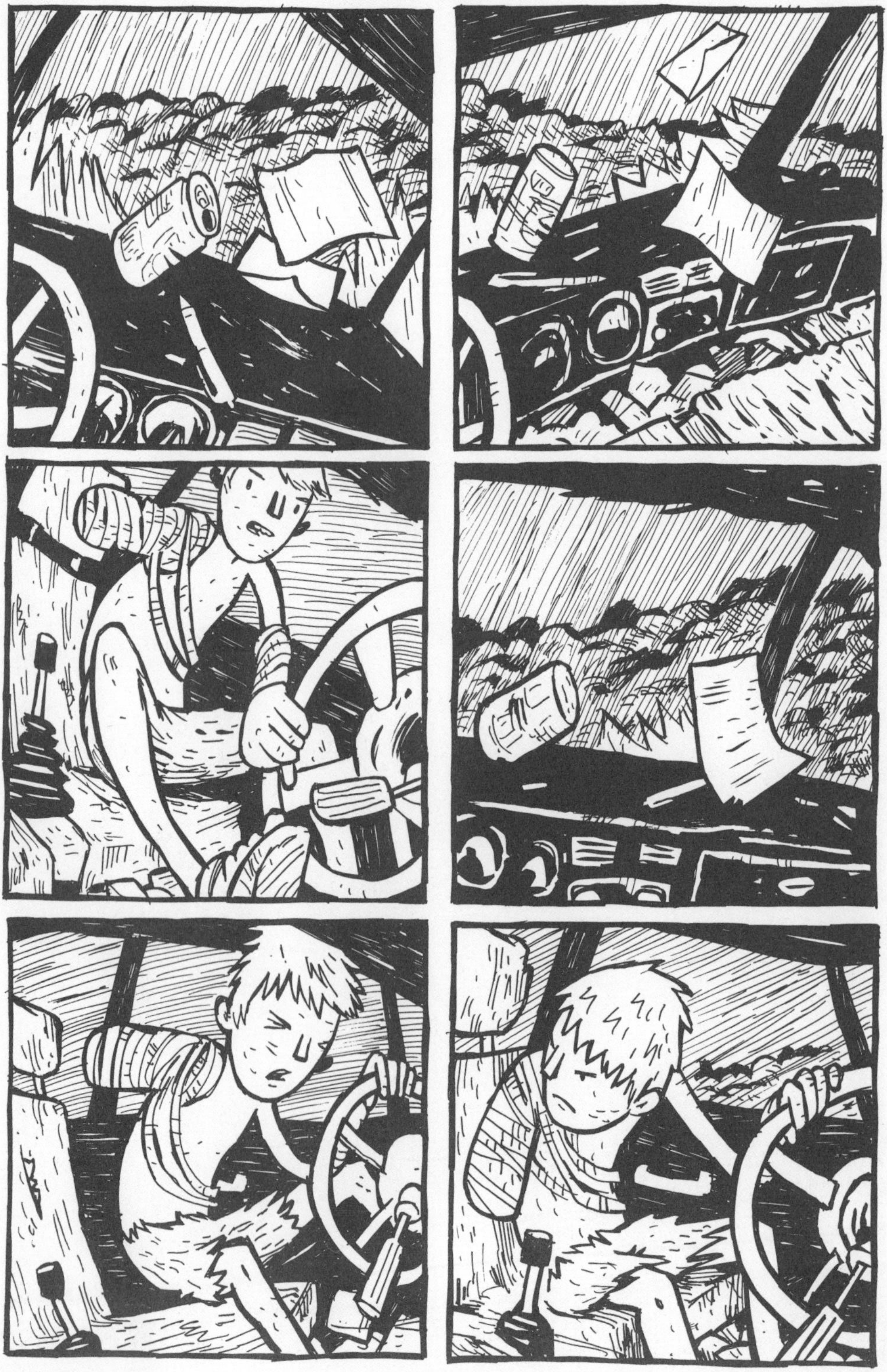

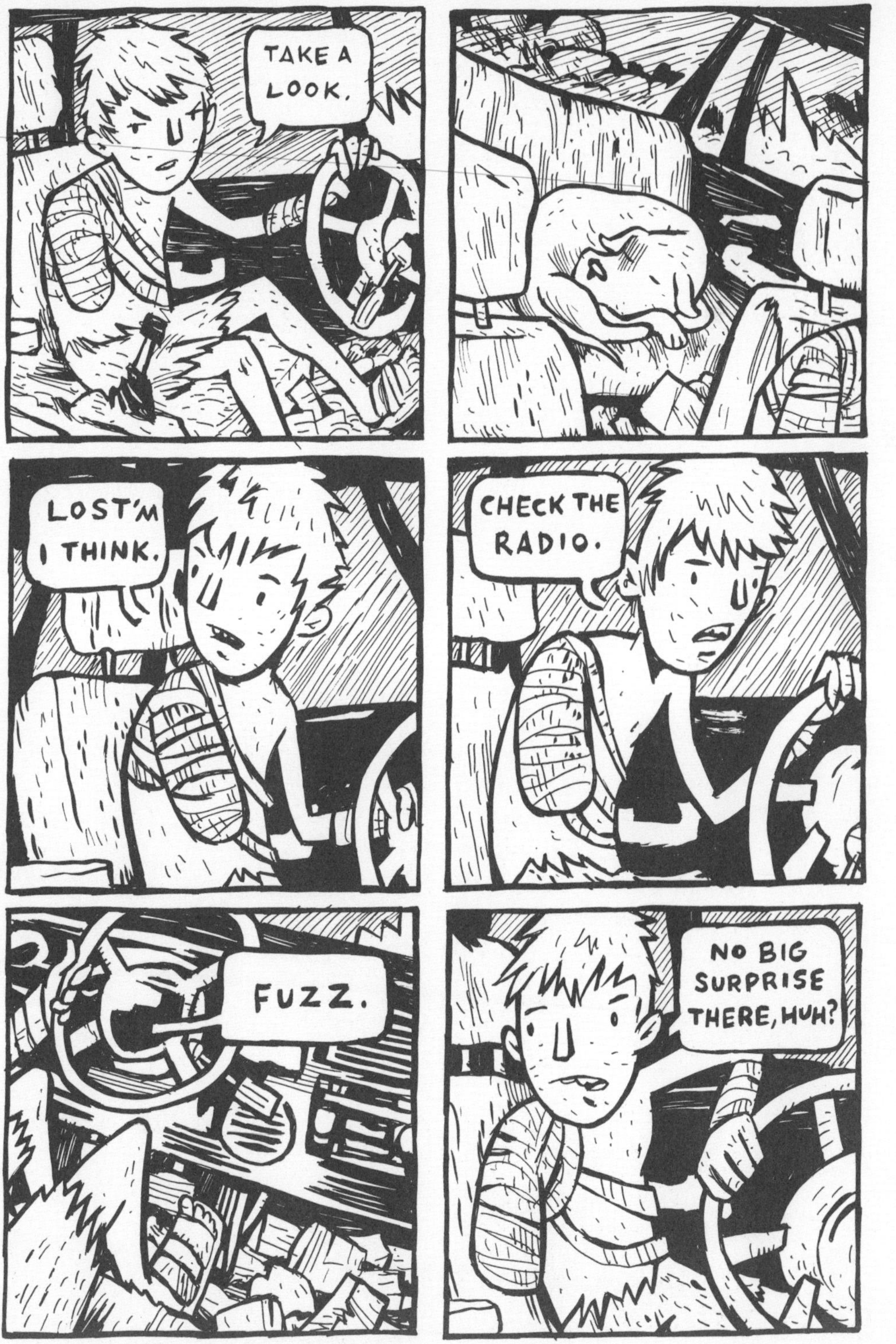
TAKE A LOOK.
LOST'M I THINK.
CHECK THE RADIO.
FUZZ.
NO BIG SURPRISE THERE, HUH?

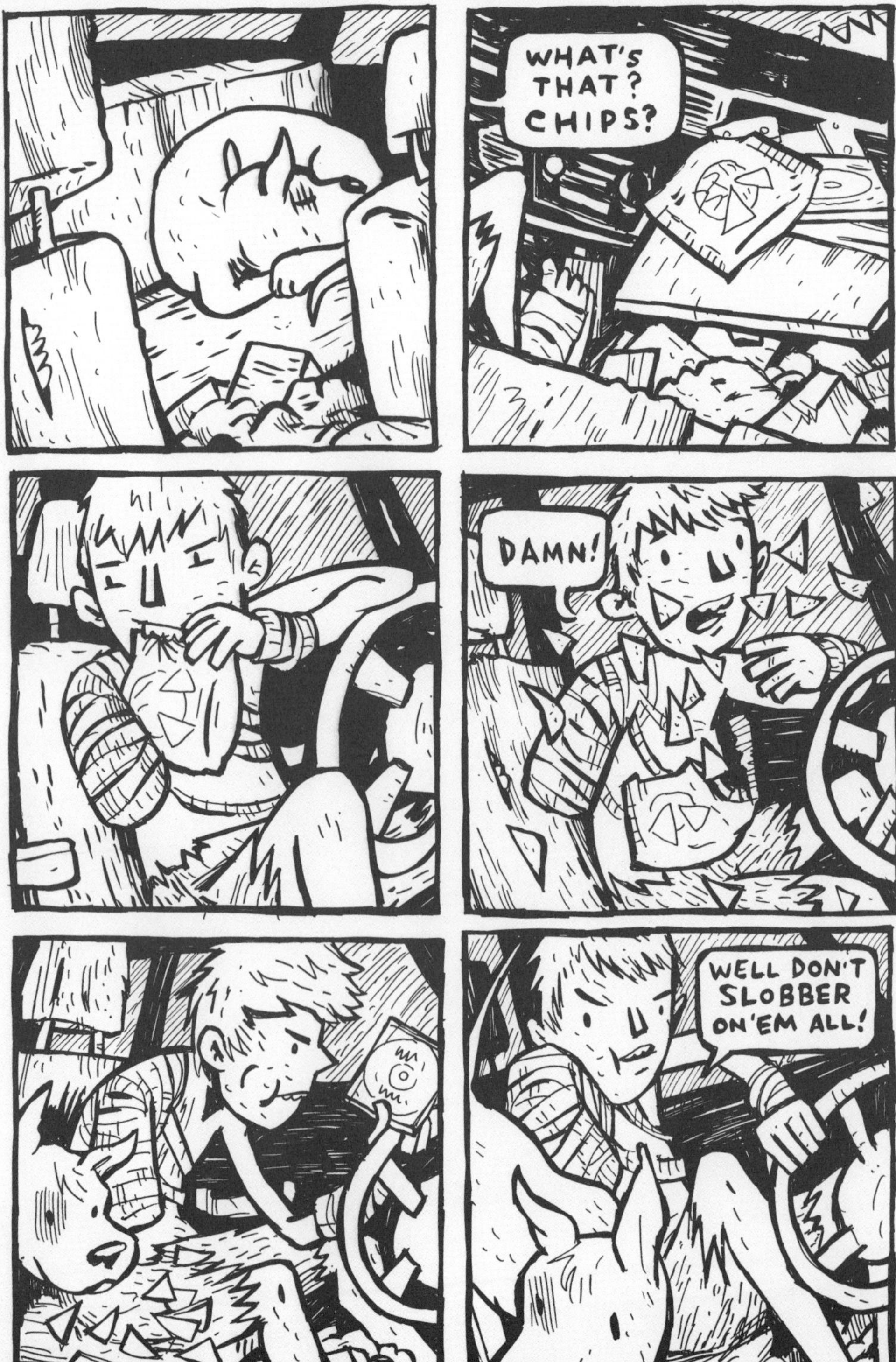
WHAT'S THAT? CHIPS?
DAMN!
WELL DON'T SLOBBER ON'EM ALL!

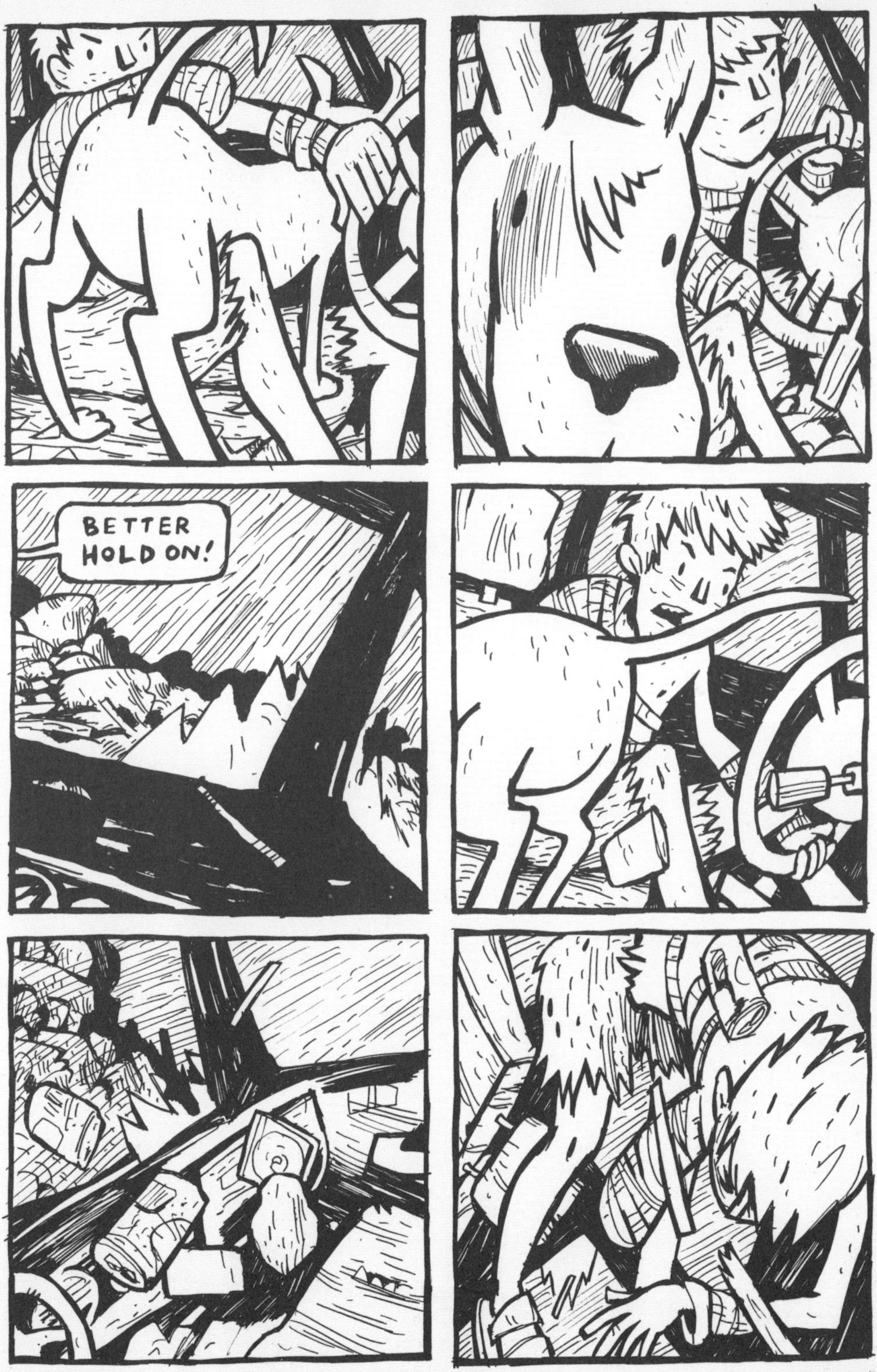
BETTER HOLD ON!

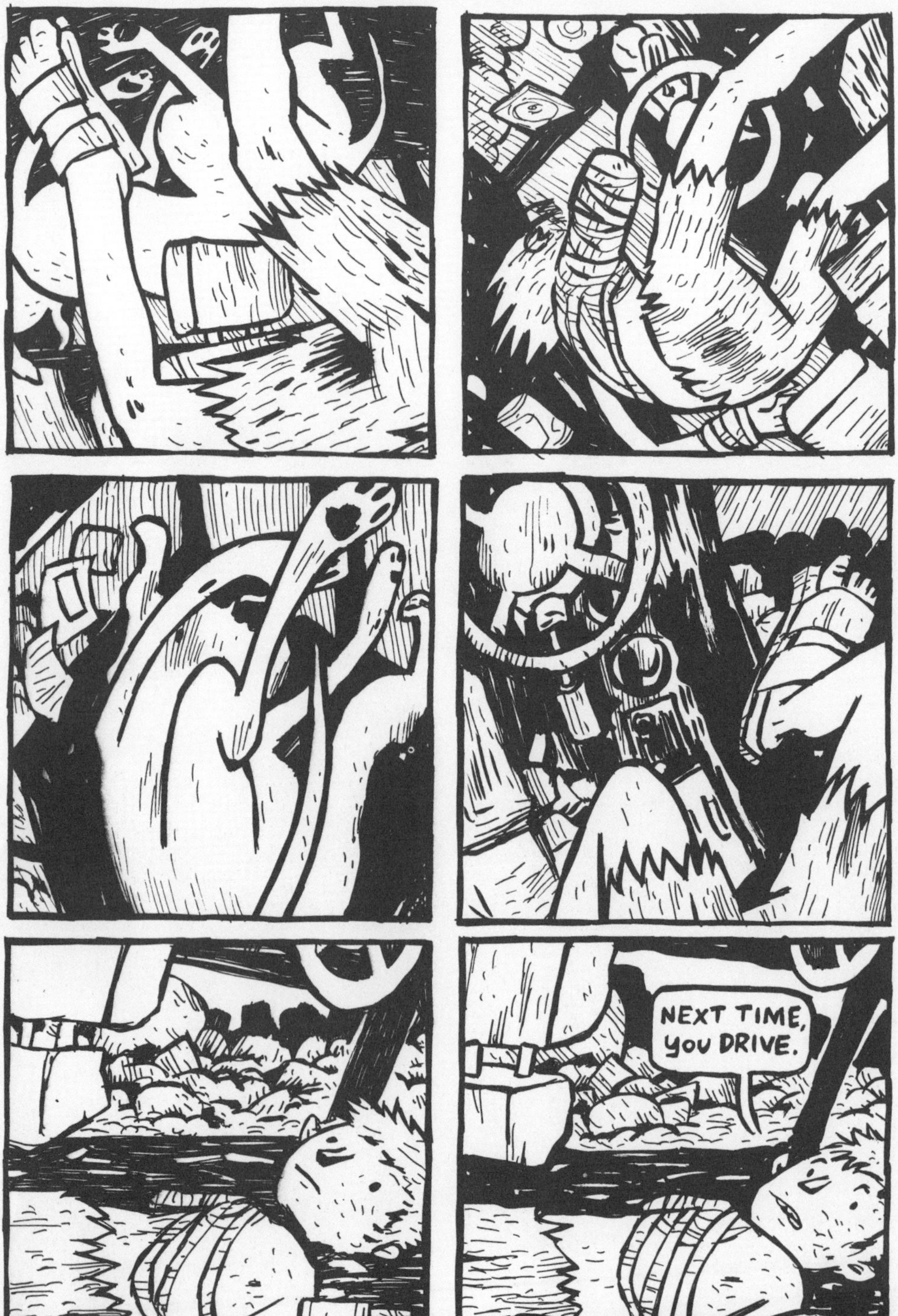
NEXT TIME,
you DRIVE.

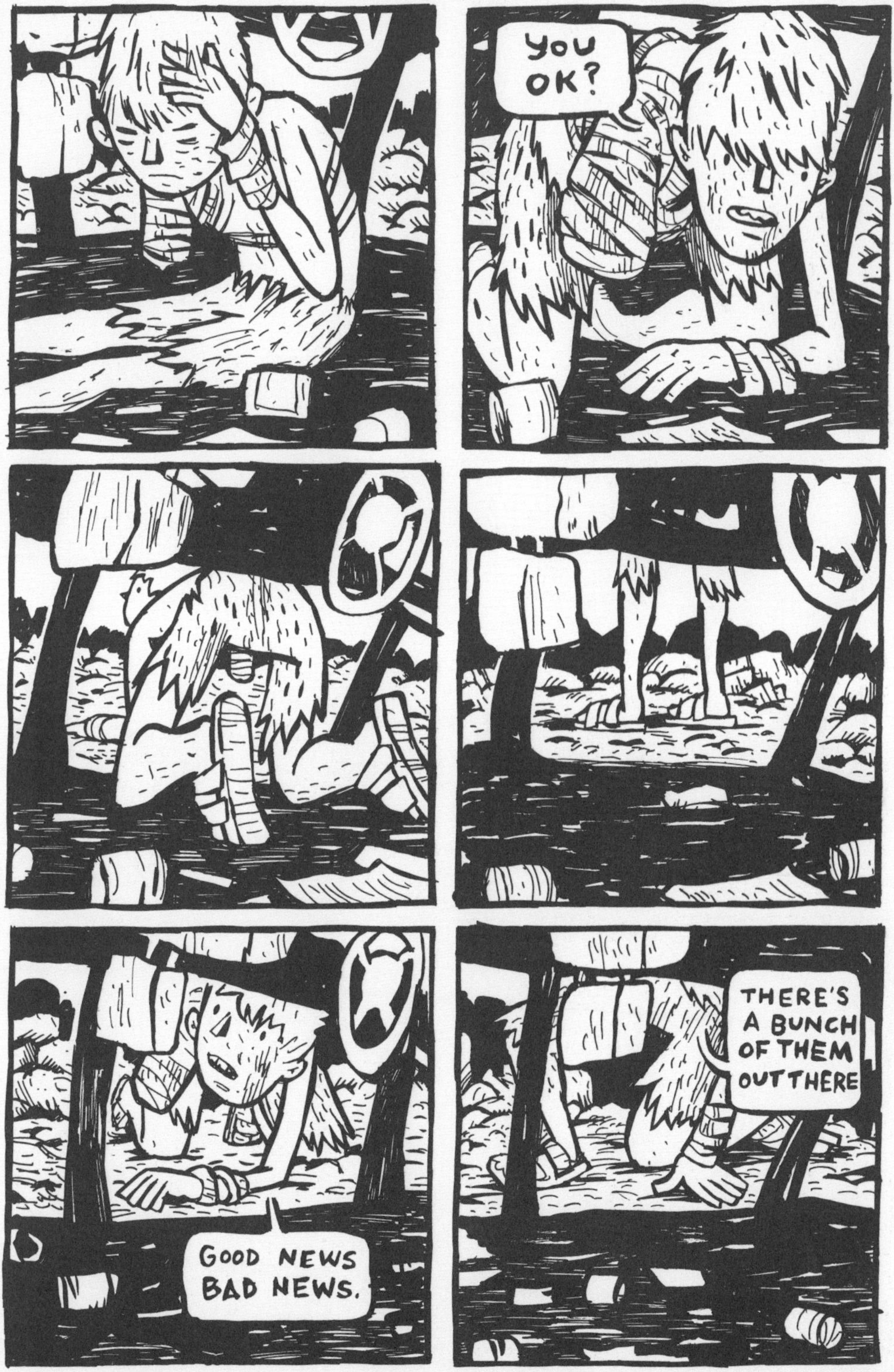
YOU OK?
GOOD NEWS BAD NEWS.
THERE'S A BUNCH OF THEM OUT THERE

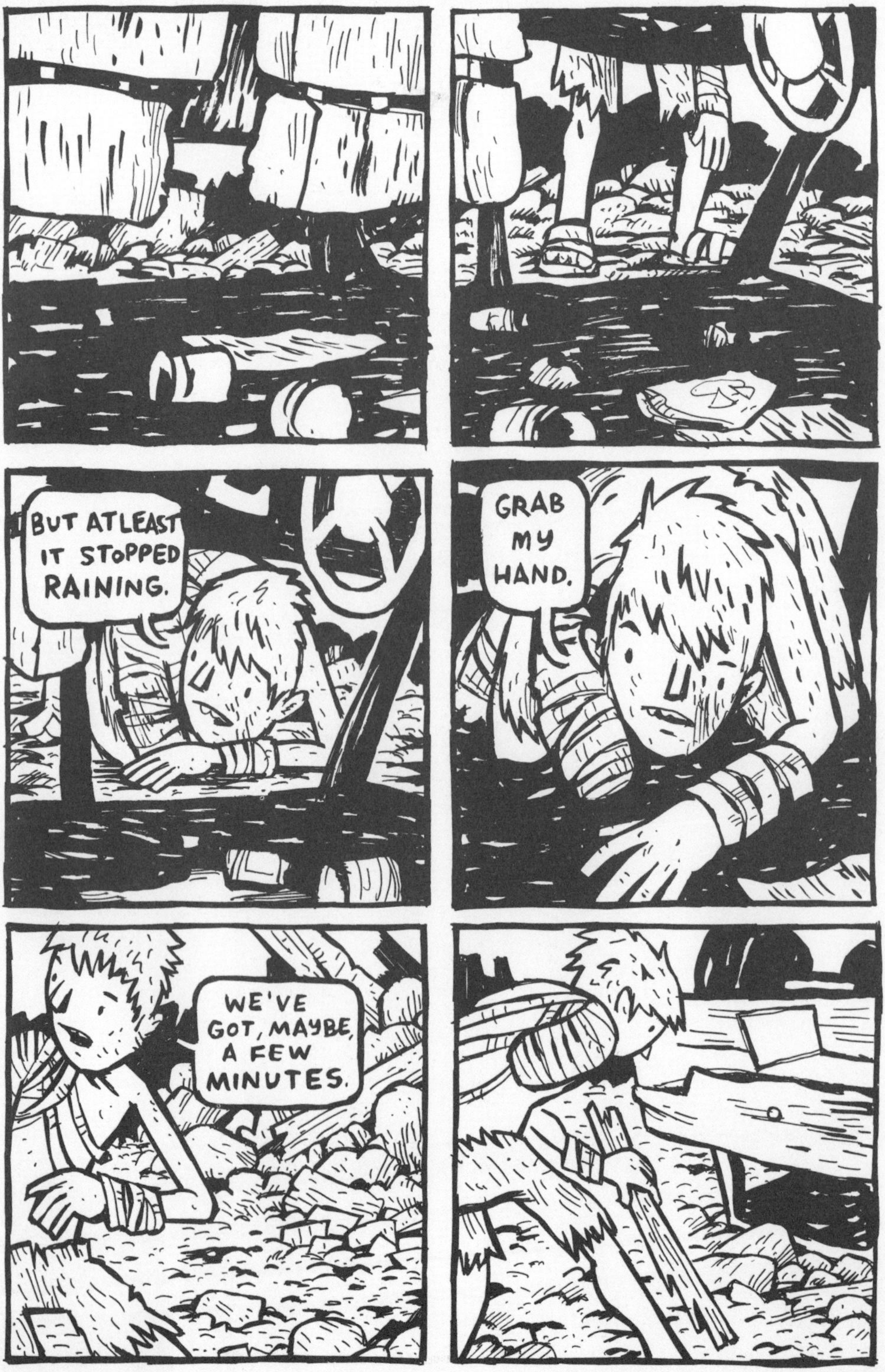
BUT ATLEAST IT STOPPED RAINING.
GRAB MY HAND.
WE'VE GOT, MAYBE, A FEW MINUTES.

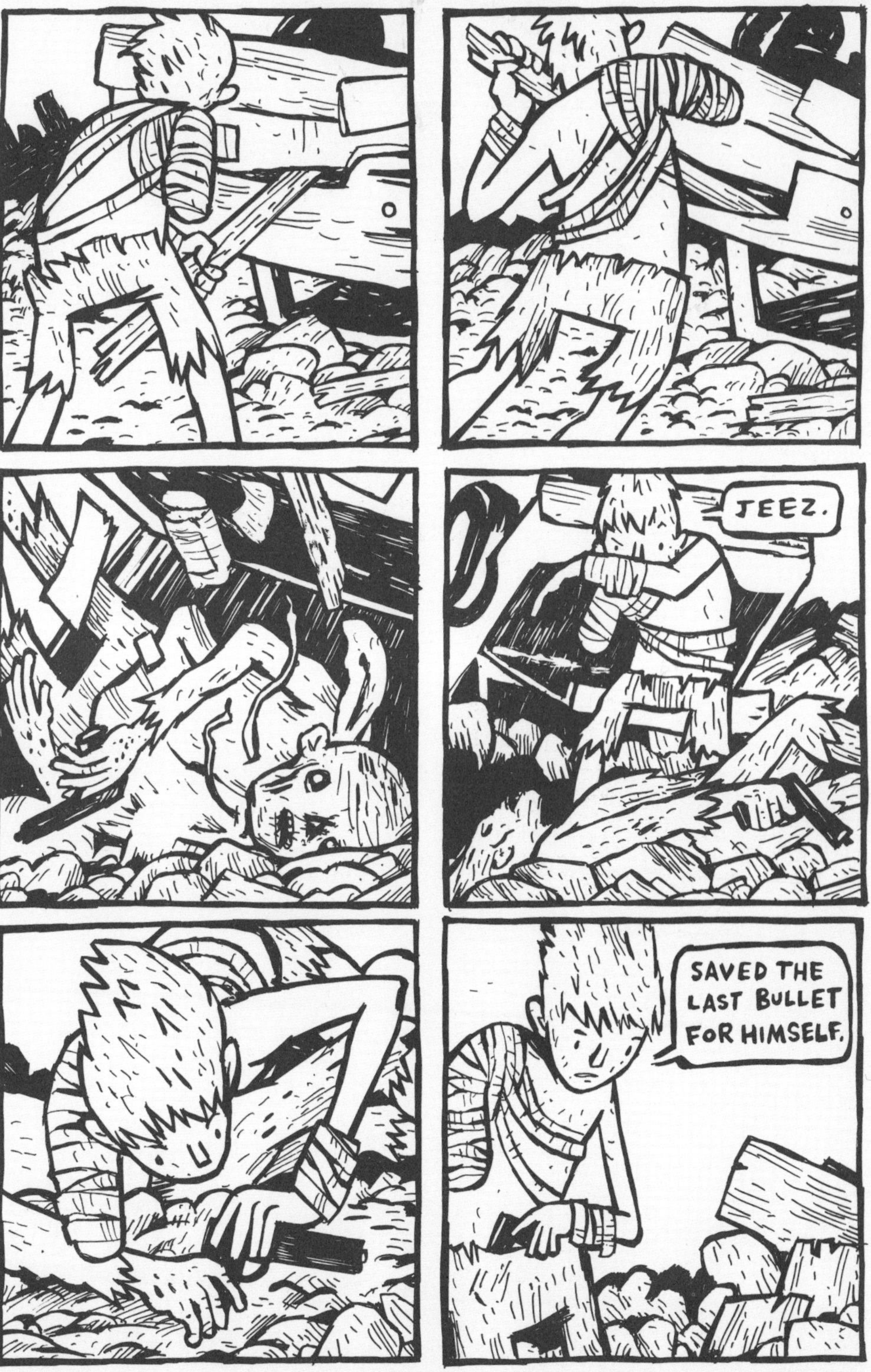
JEEZ.
SAVED THE LAST BULLET FOR HIMSELF.

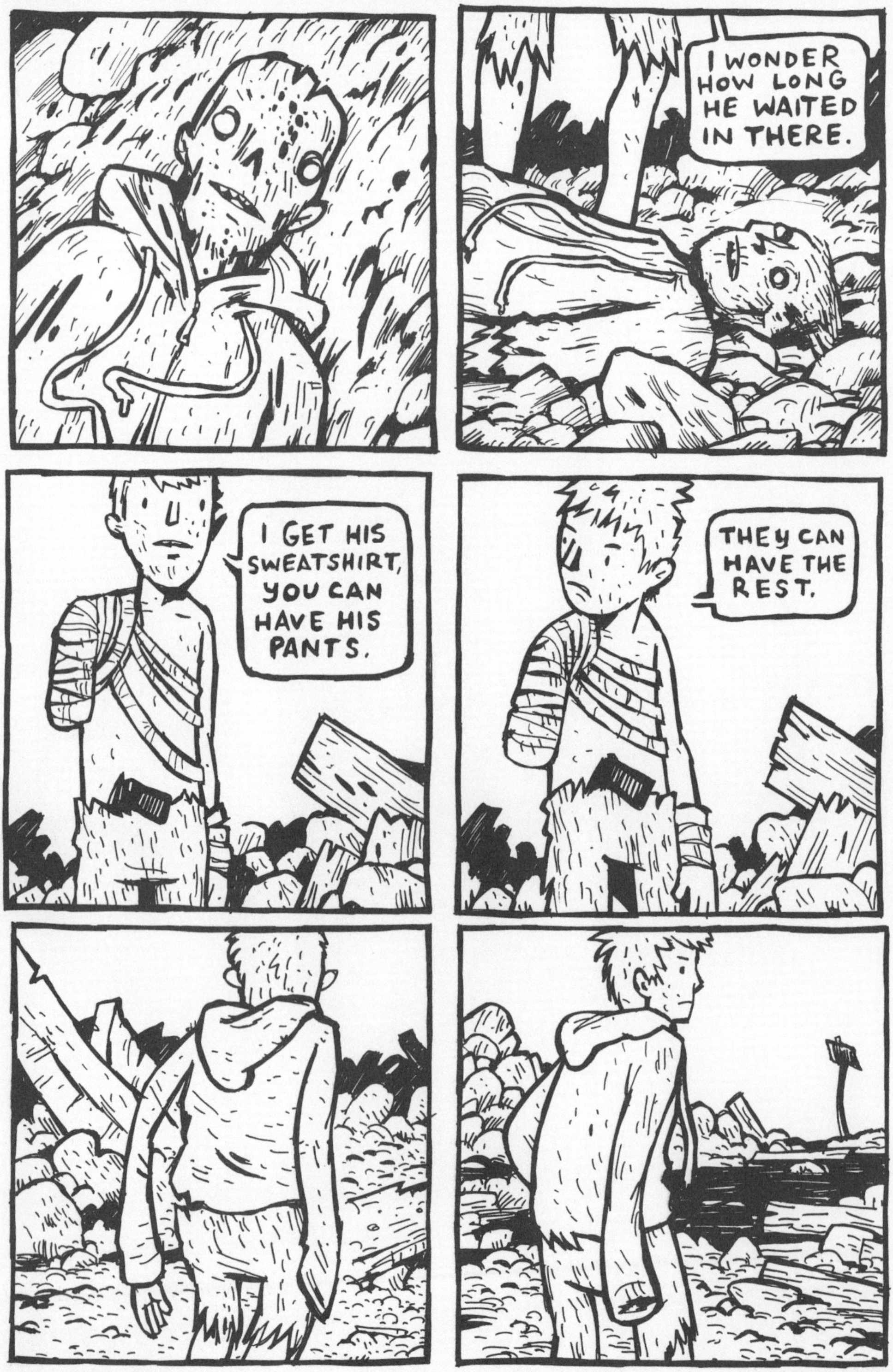
I WONDER HOW LONG HE WAITED IN THERE.
I GET HIS SWEATSHIRT, YOU CAN HAVE HIS PANTS.
THEY CAN HAVE THE REST.

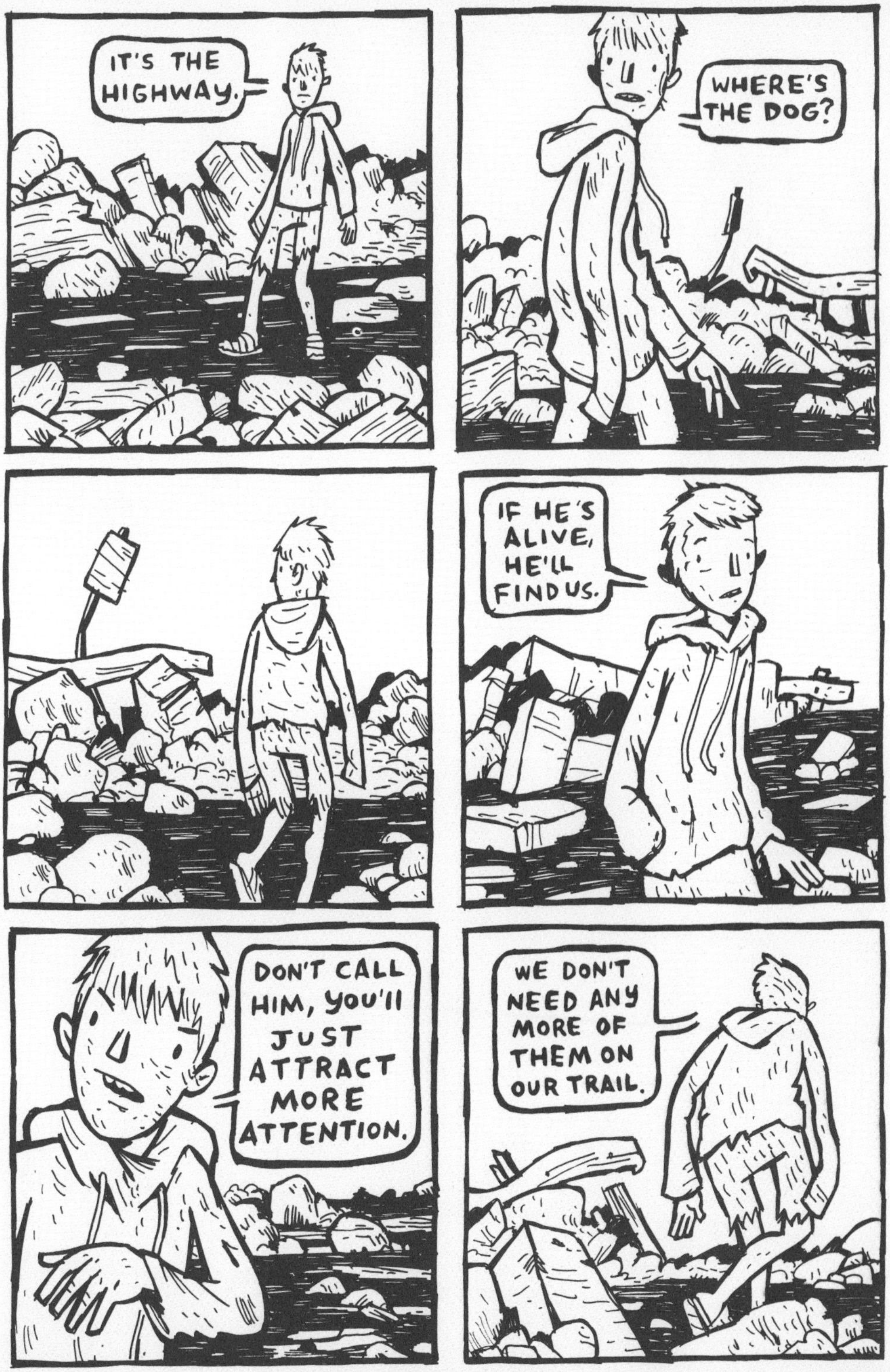
IT'S THE HIGHWAY.
WHERE'S THE DOG?
IF HE'S ALIVE, HE'LL FIND US.
DON'T CALL HIM, YOU'll JUST ATTRACT MORE ATTENTION.
WE DON'T NEED ANY MORE OF THEM ON OUR TRAIL.

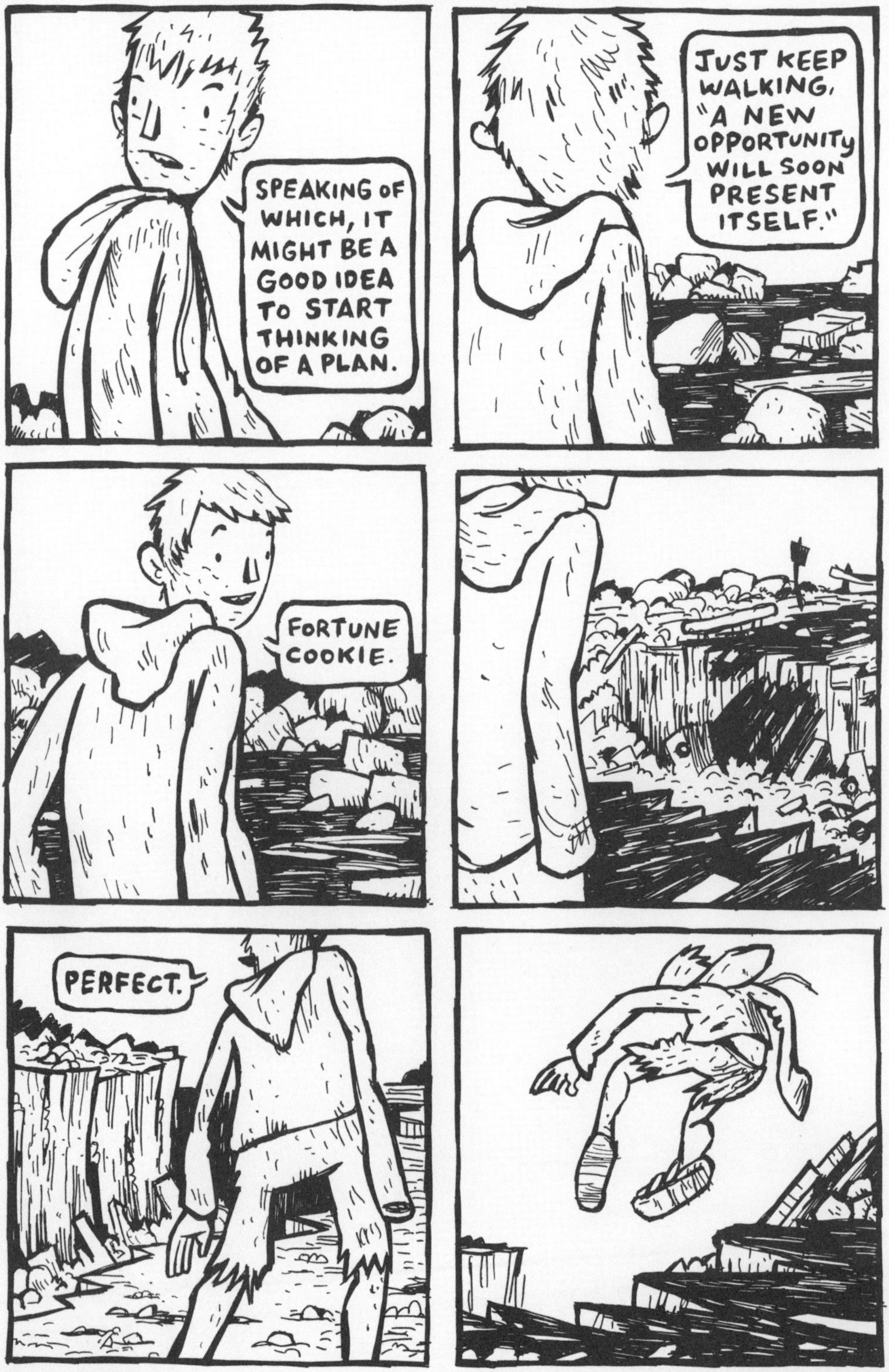
SPEAKING OF WHICH, IT MIGHT BE A GOOD IDEA TO START THINKING OF A PLAN.
JUST KEEP WALKING, "A NEW OPPORTUNITY WILL SOON PRESENT ITSELF."
FORTUNE COOKIE.
PERFECT.

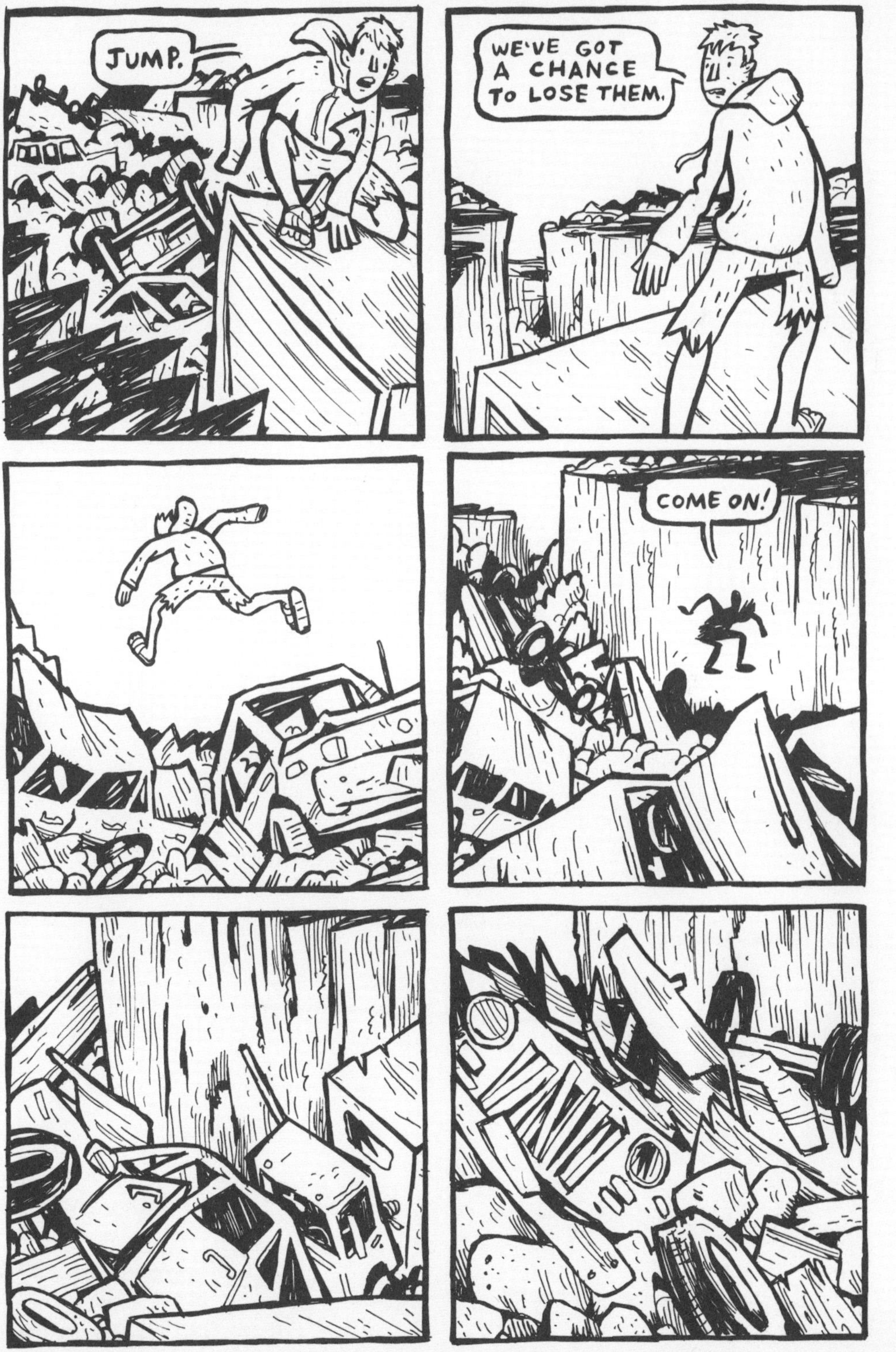
JUMP.
WE'VE GOT A CHANCE TO LOSE THEM.
COME ON!

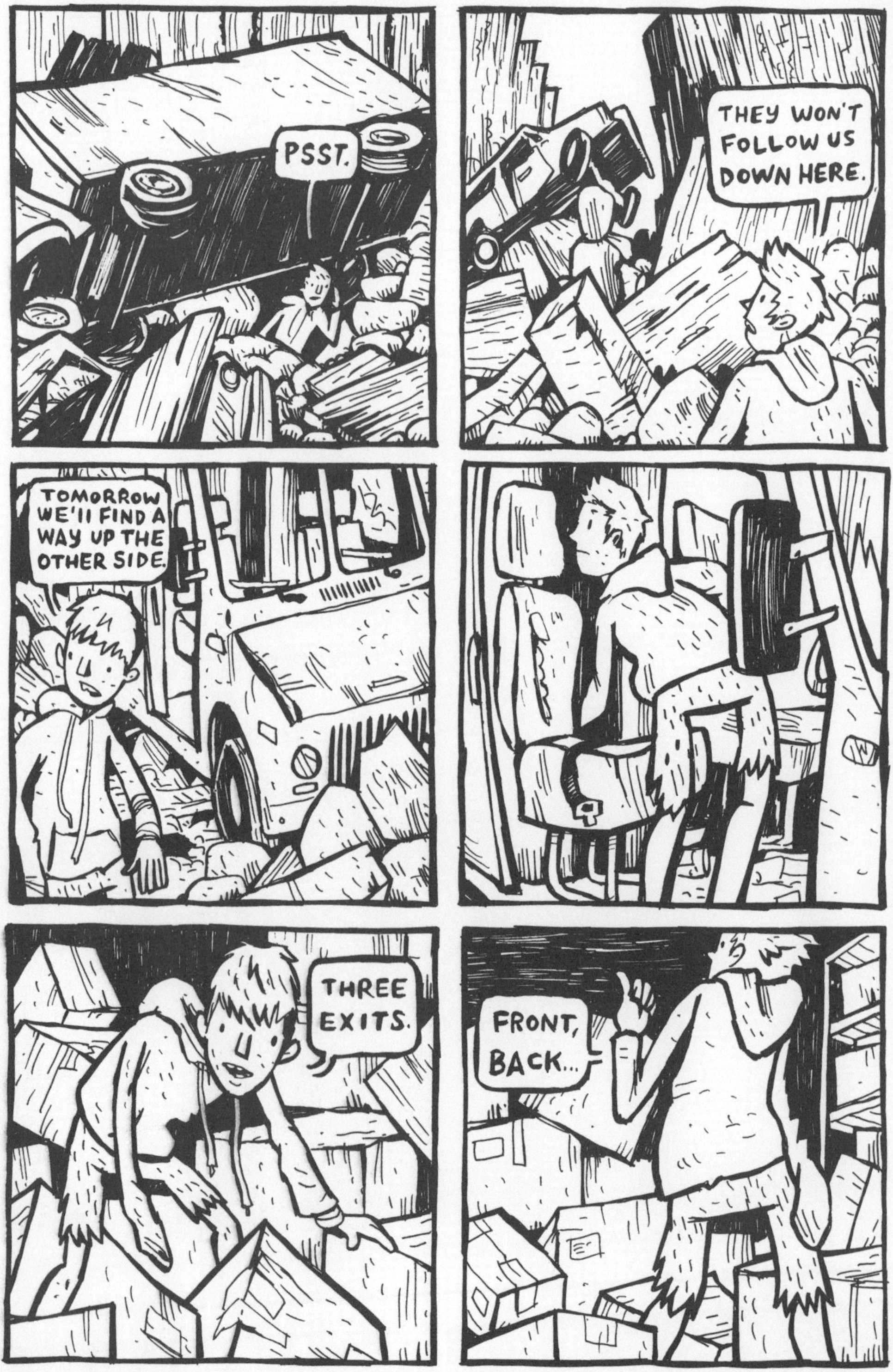
PSST.
THEY WON'T FOLLOW US DOWN HERE.
TOMORROW WE'll FIND A WAY UP THE OTHER SIDE.
THREE EXITS.
FRONT, BACK...

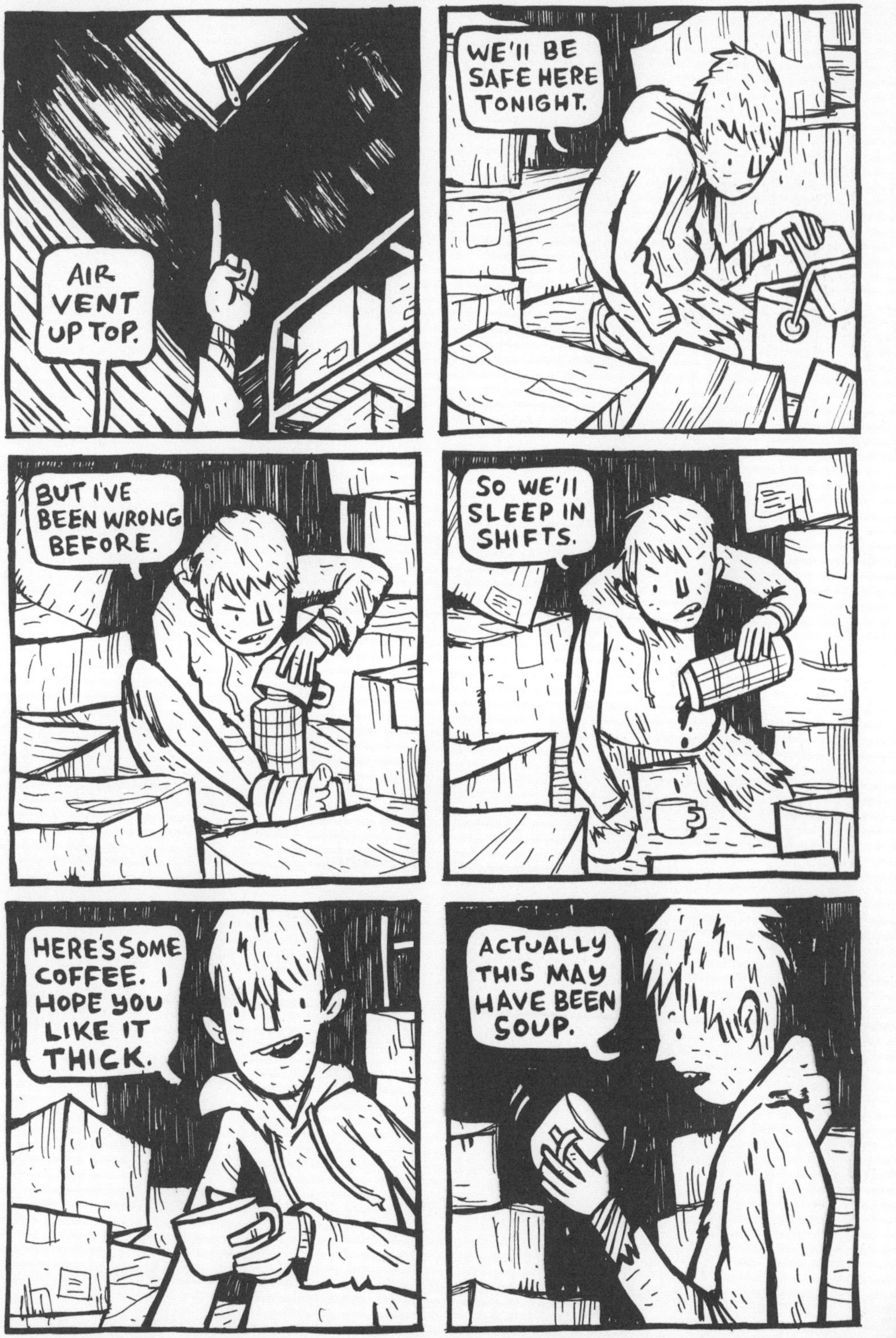
AIR VENT UP TOP.
WE'll BE SAFE HERE TONIGHT.
BUT I'VE BEEN WRONG BEFORE.
SO WE'll SLEEP IN SHIFTS.
HERE'S SOME COFFEE. I HOPE YOU LIKE IT THICK.
ACTUALLY THIS MAY HAVE BEEN SOUP.

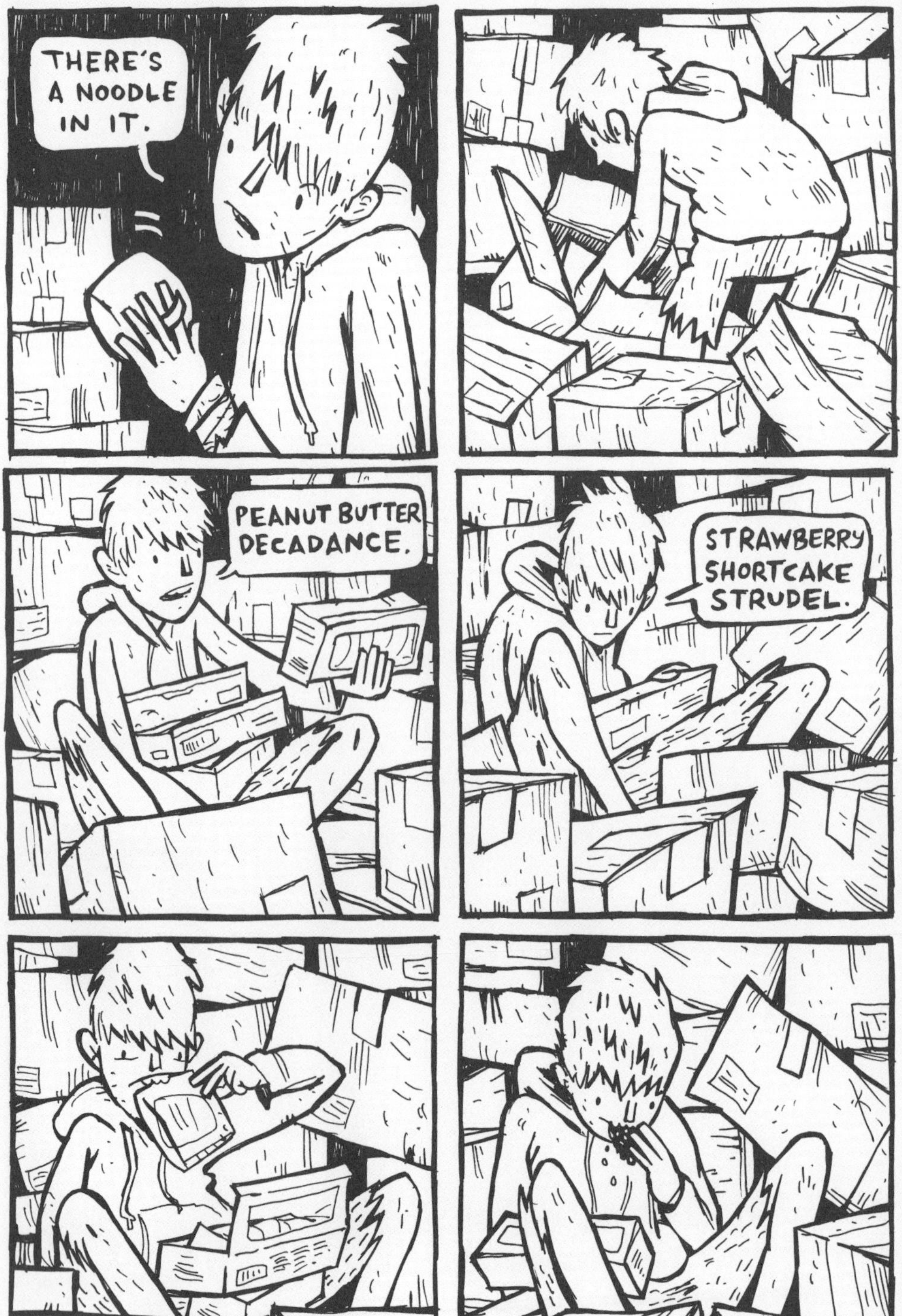
THERE'S A NOODLE IN IT.
PEANUT BUTTER DECADANCE.
STRAWBERRY SHORTCAKE STRUDEL.

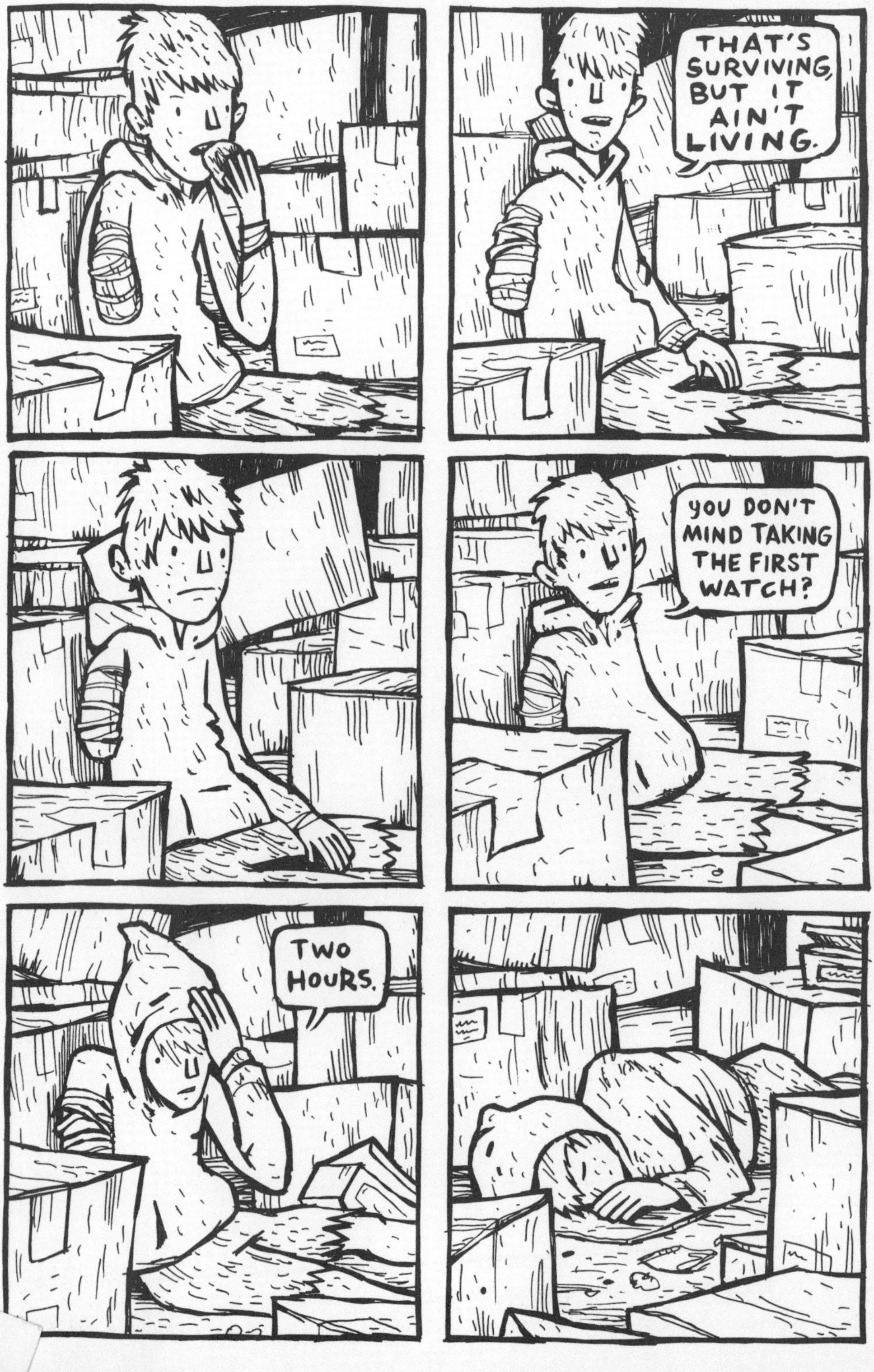
THAT'S SURVIVING, BUT IT AIN'T LIVING.
YOU DON'T MIND TAKING THE FIRST WATCH?
TWO HOURS.

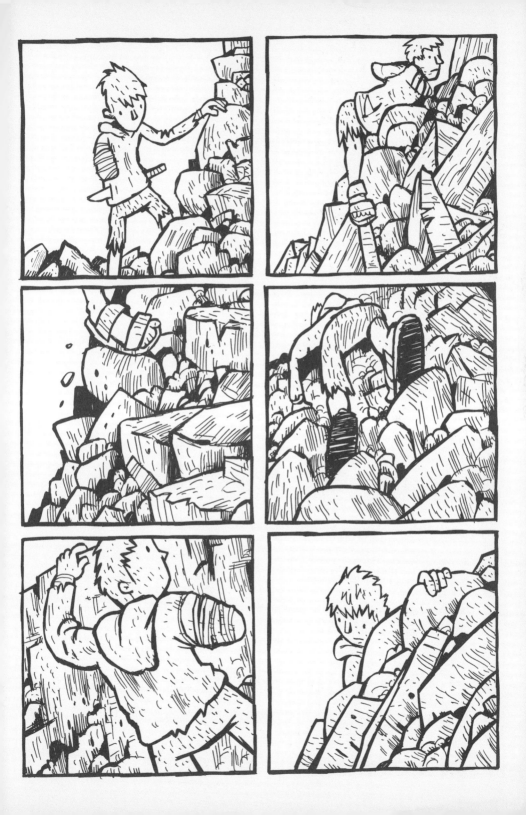

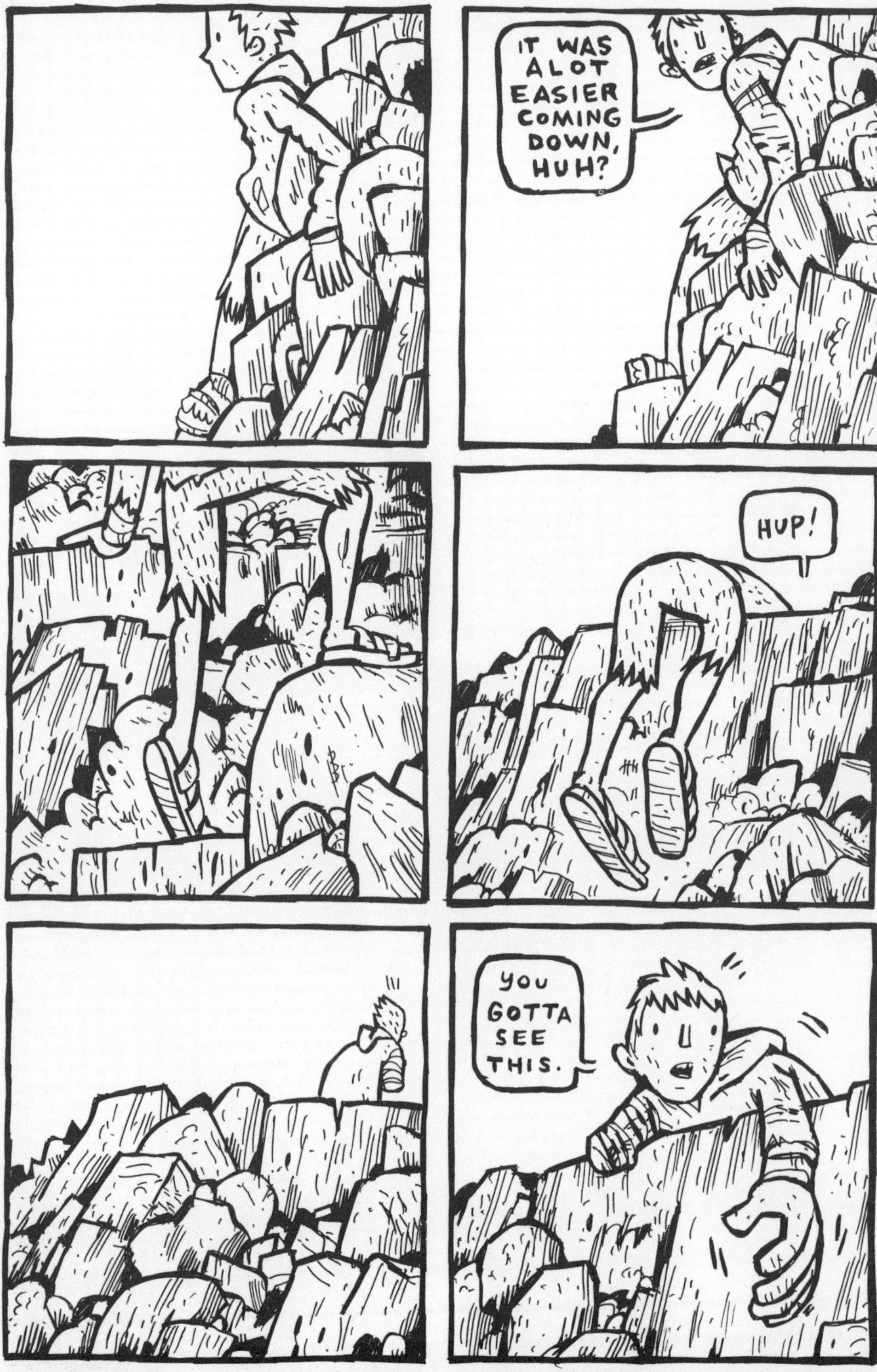
IT WAS ALOT EASIER COMING DOWN, HUH?
HUP!
YOU GOTTA SEE THIS.

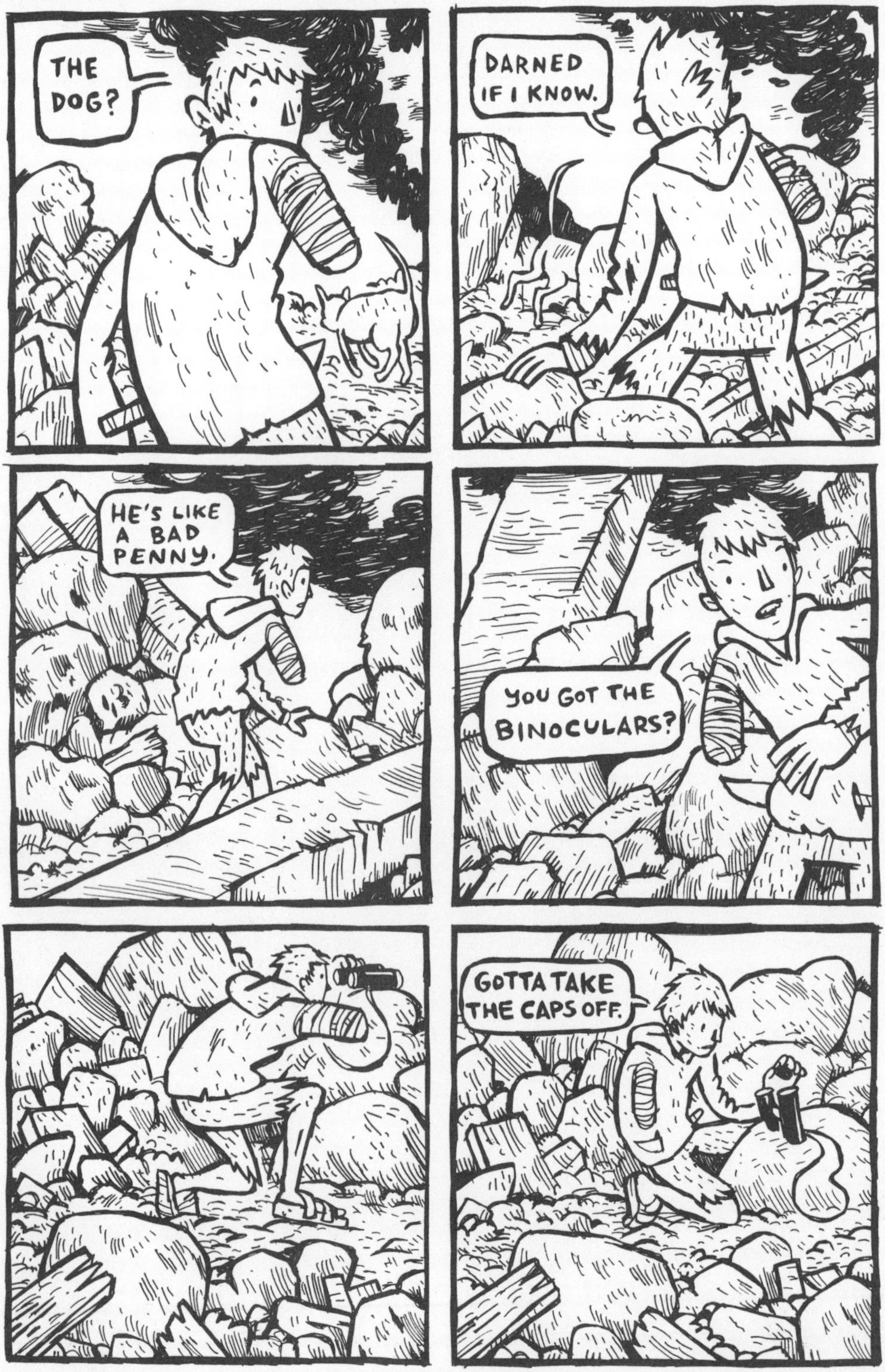
THE DOG?
DARNED IF I KNOW.
HE'S LIKE A BAD PENNY.
YOU GOT THE BINOCULARS?
GOTTA TAKE THE CAPS OFF.

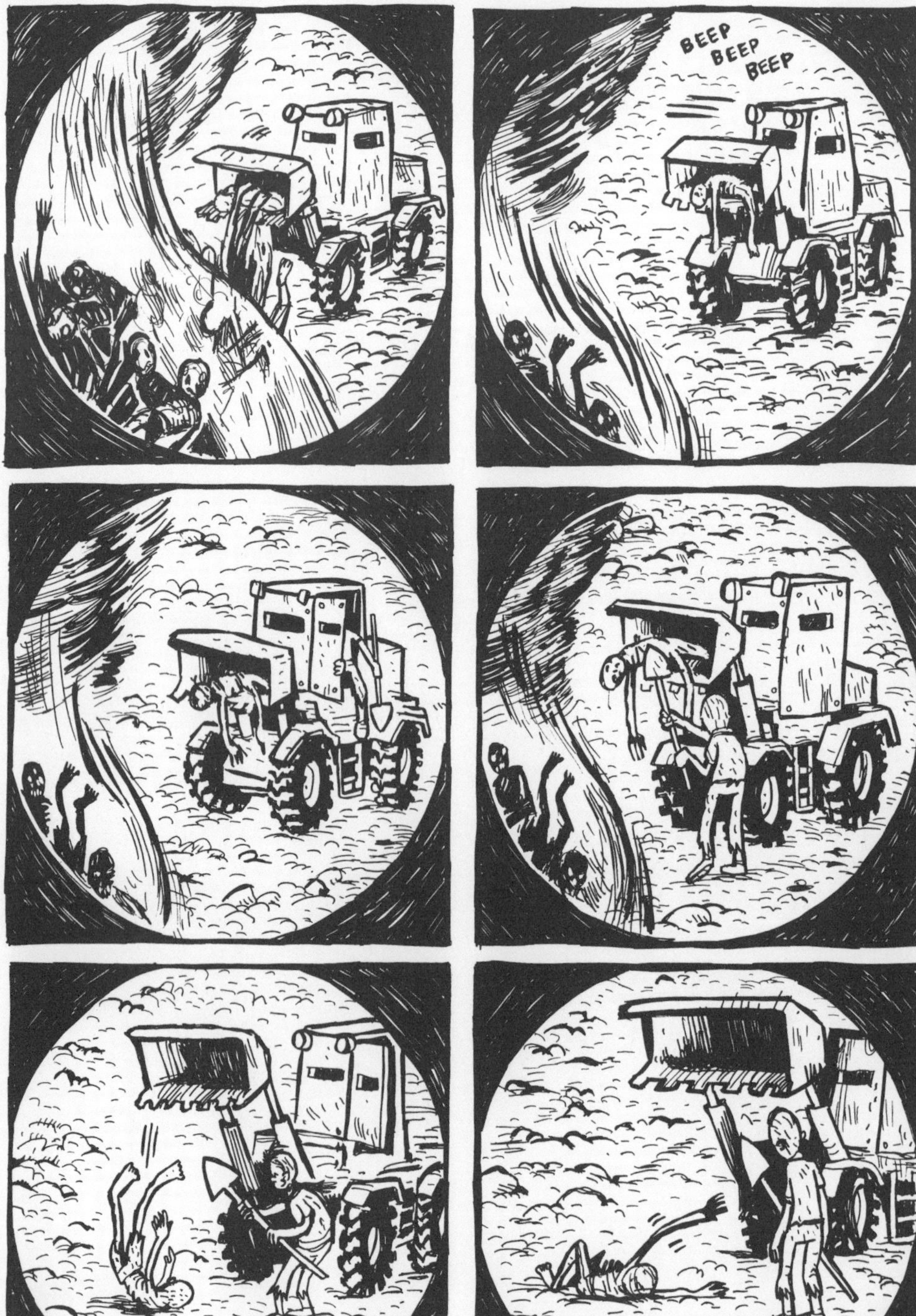
BEEP
BEEP
BEEP

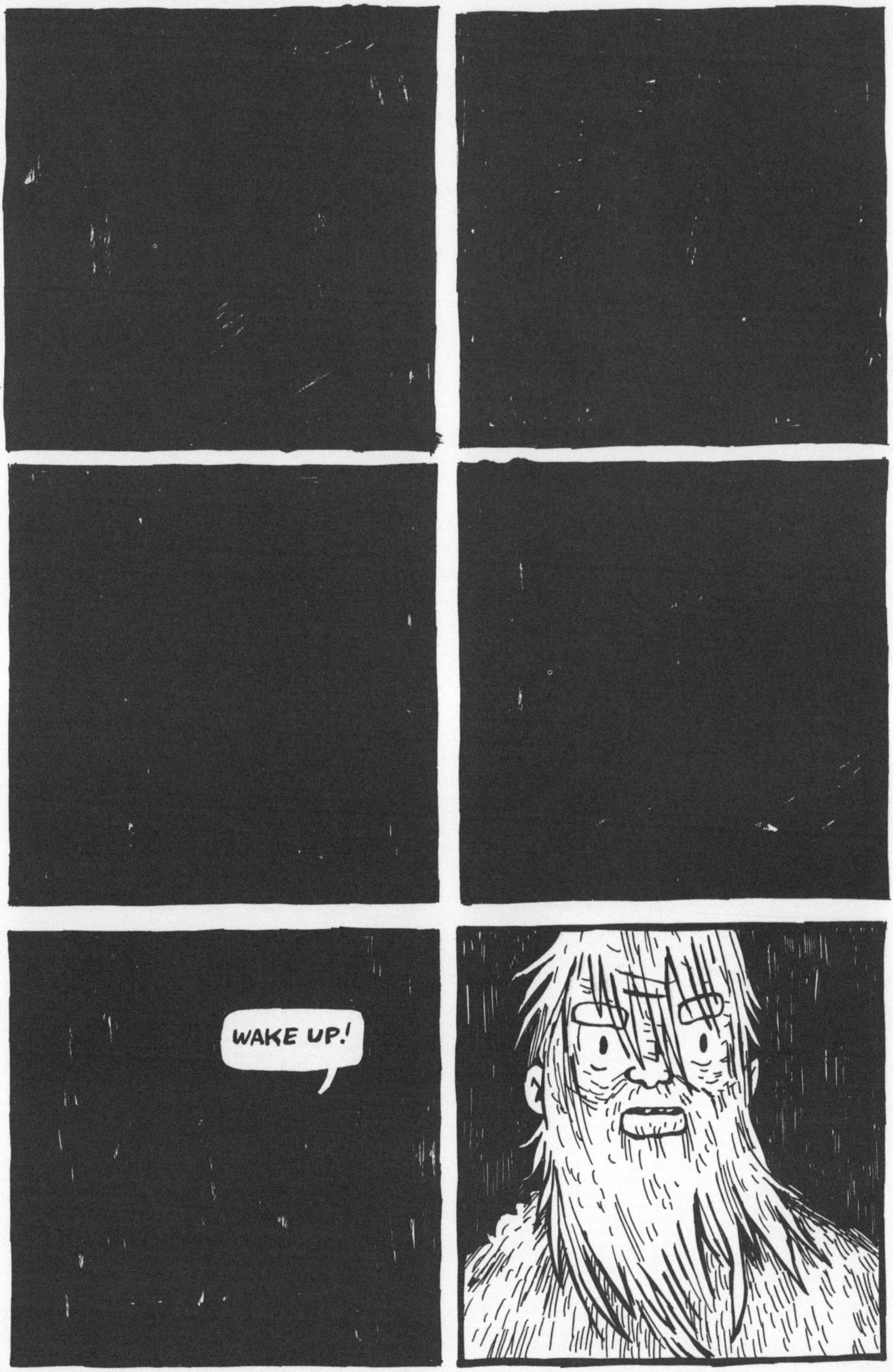
WAKE UP!

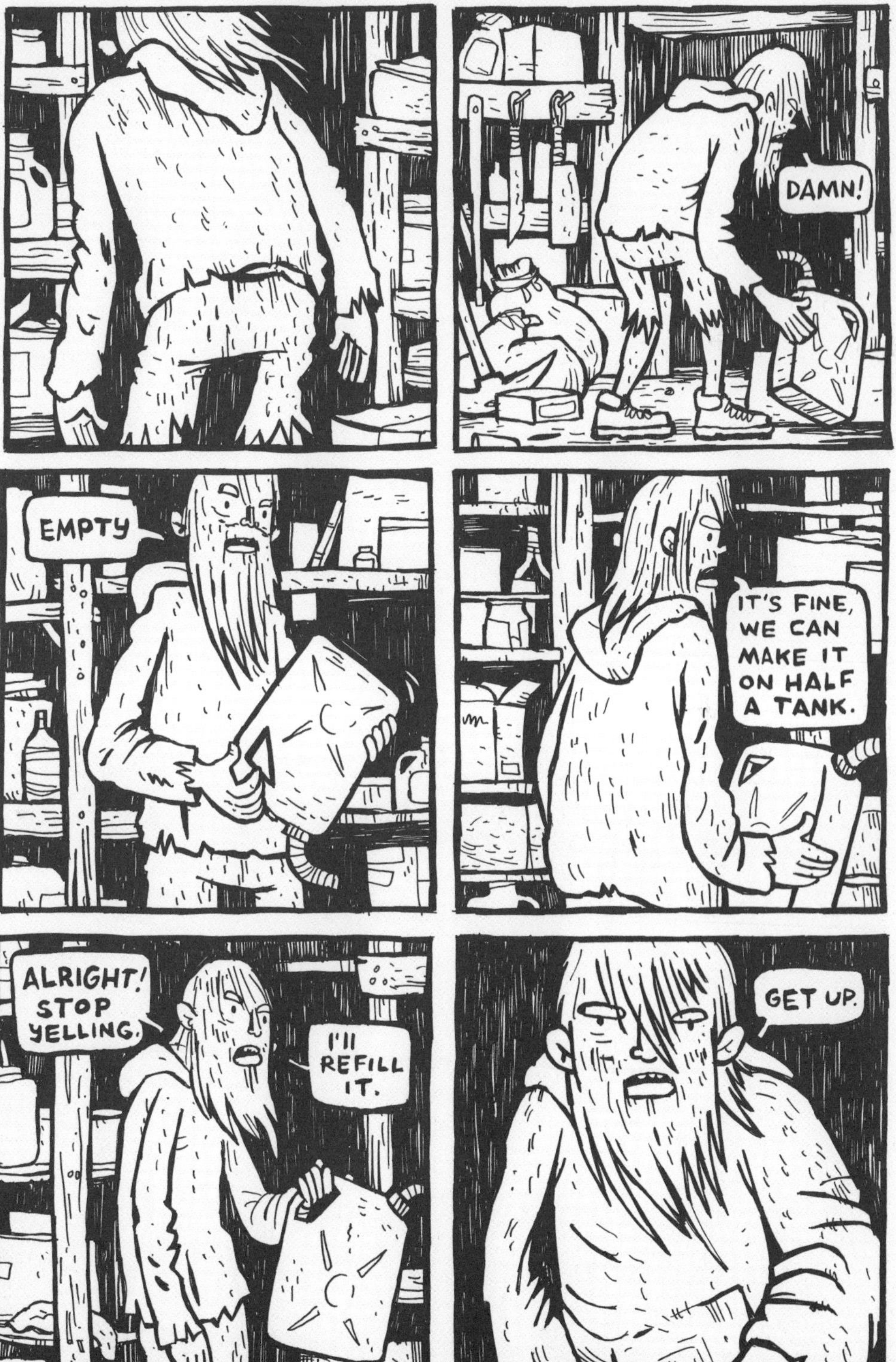
DAMN!
EMPTY
IT'S FINE, WE CAN MAKE IT ON HALF A TANK.
ALRIGHT! STOP YELLING.
I'LL REFILL IT.
GET UP.

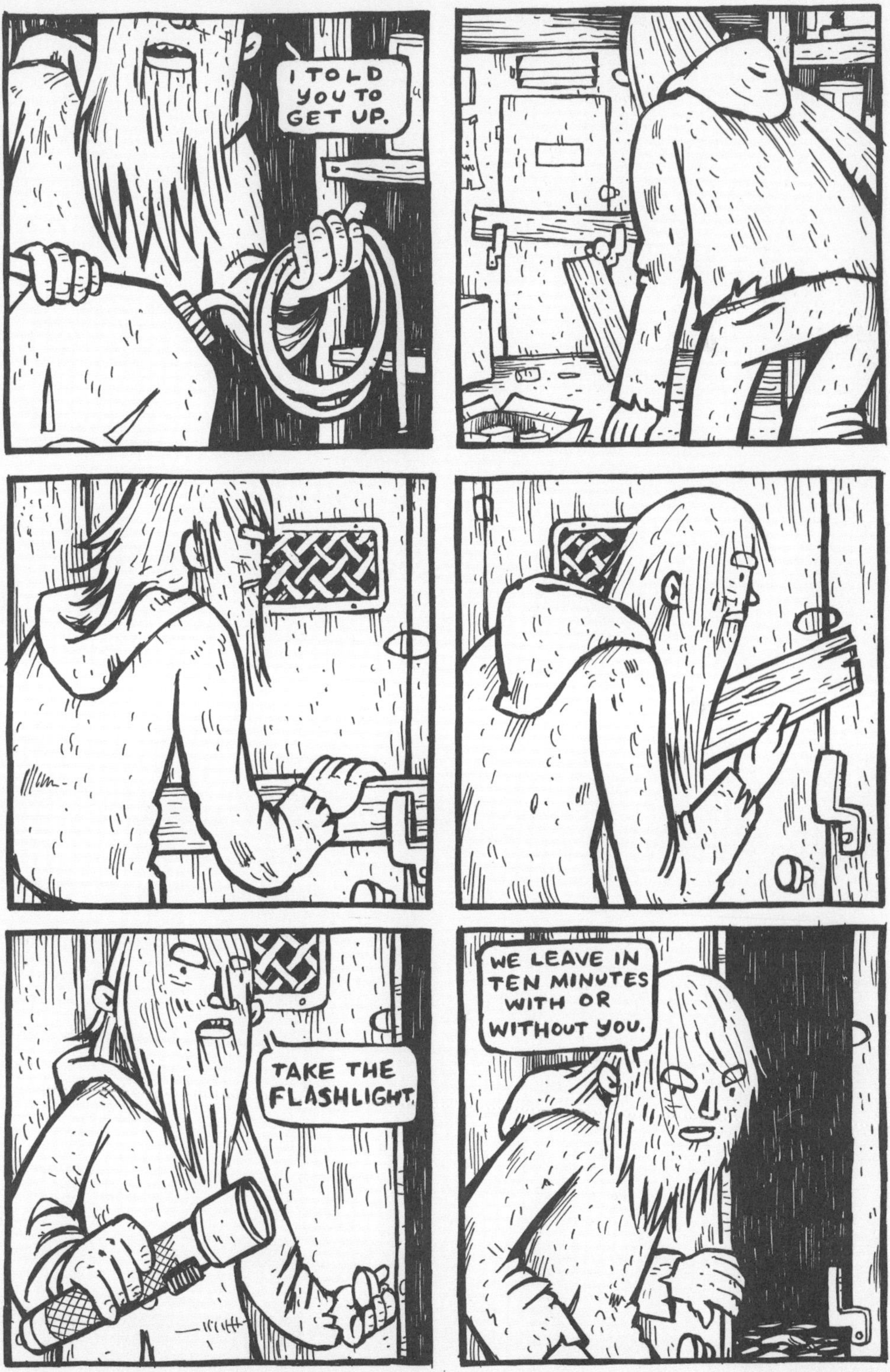
I TOLD YOU TO GET UP.
TAKE THE FLASHLIGHT.
WE LEAVE IN TEN MINUTES WITH OR WITHOUT YOU.

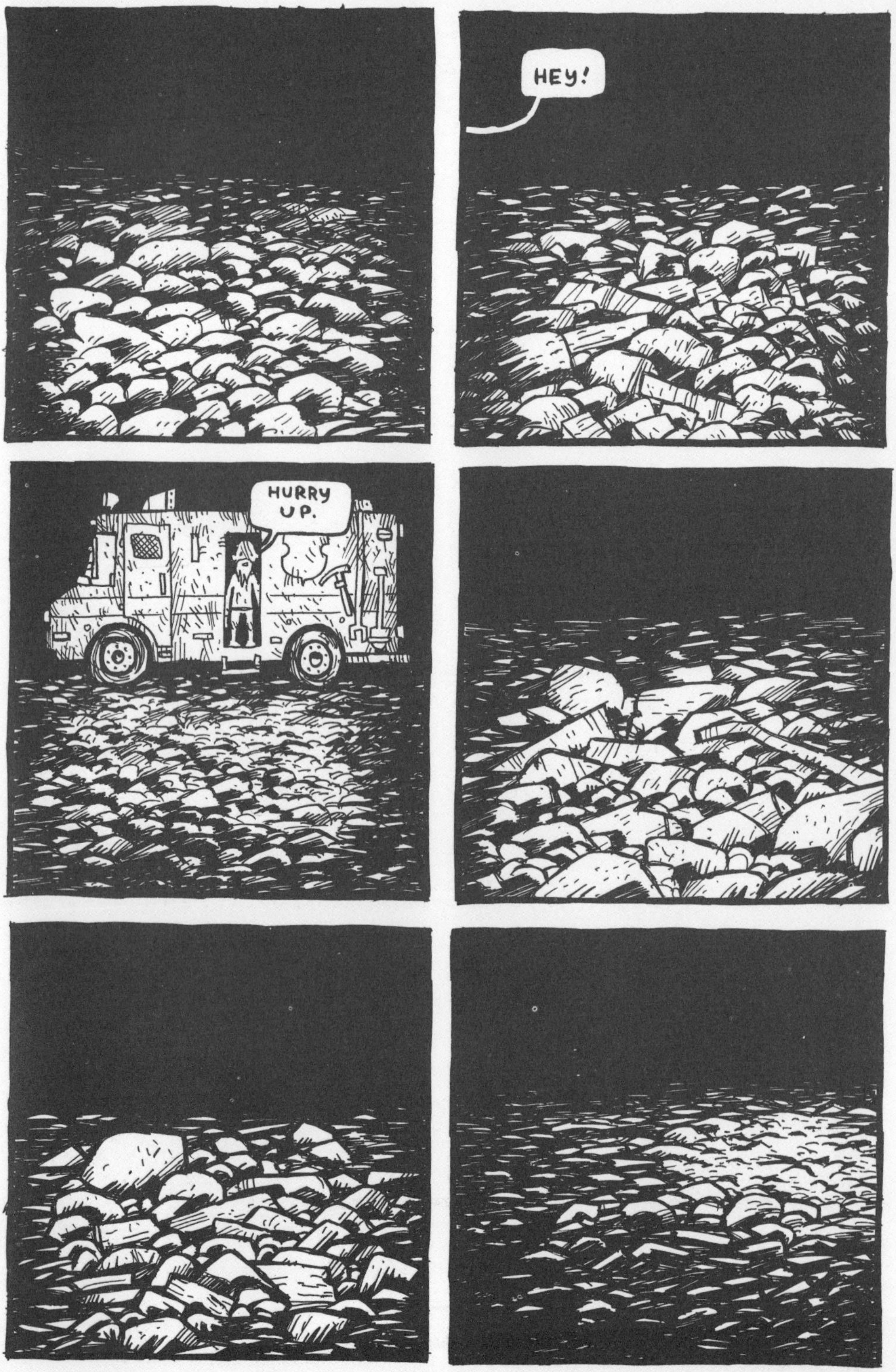
HEY!
HURRY UP.

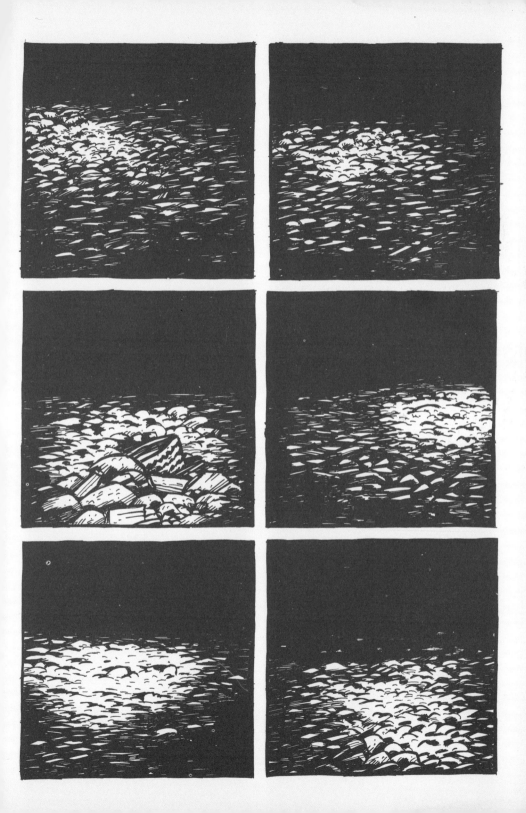

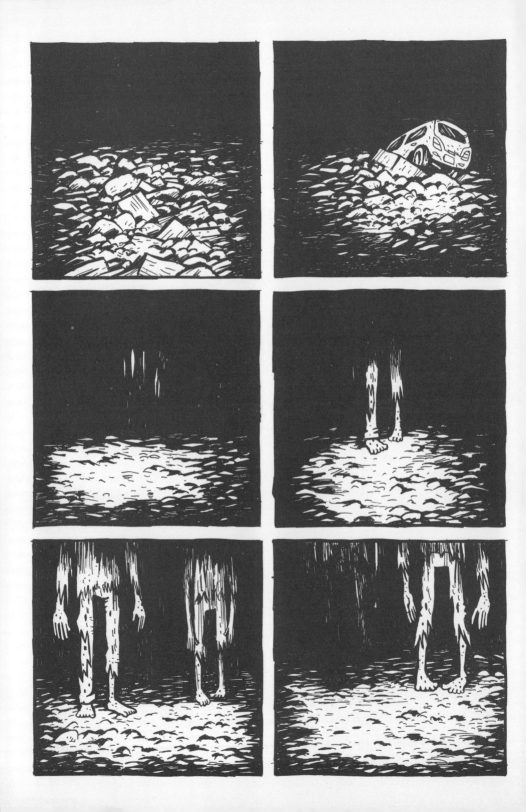

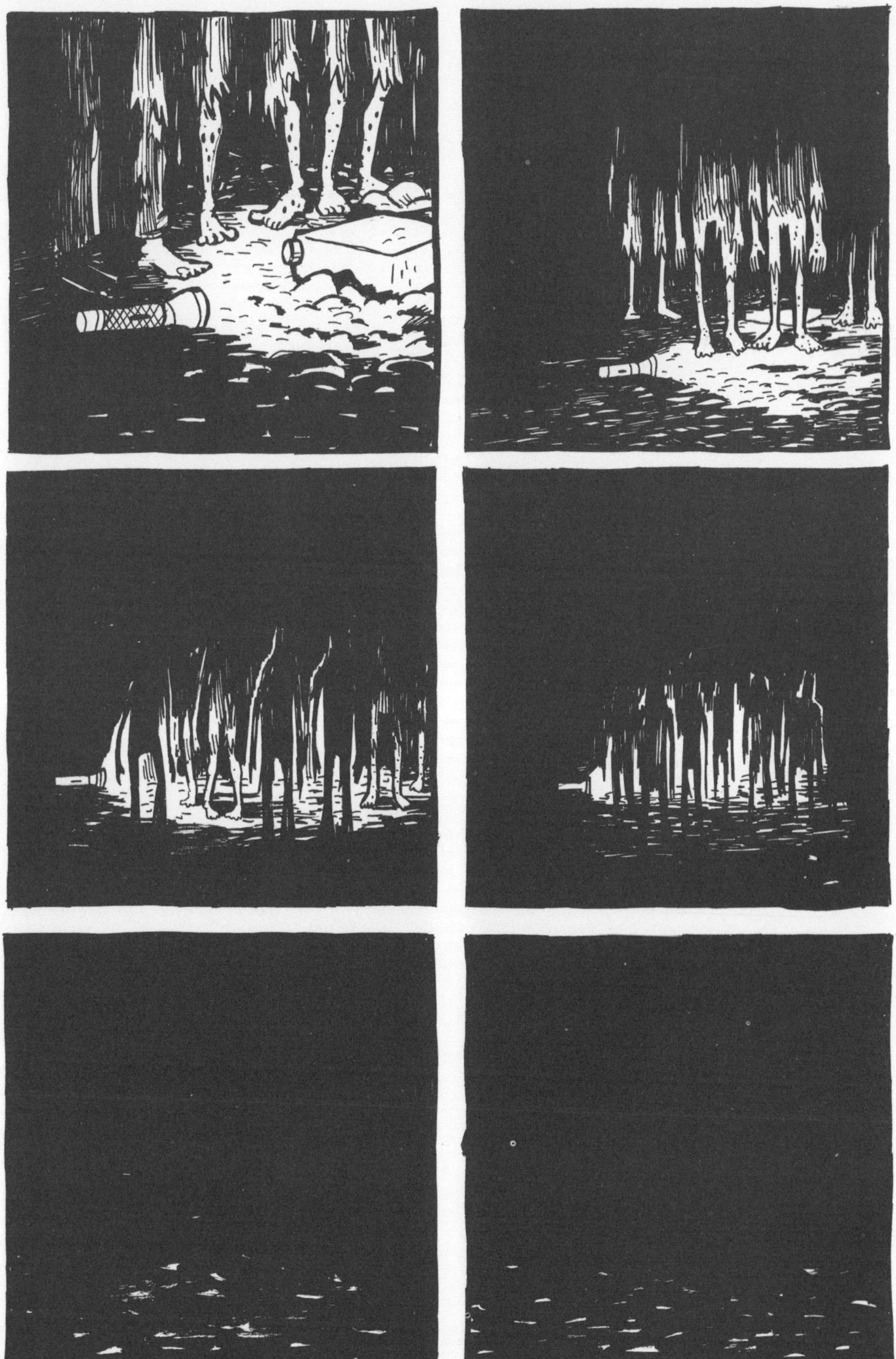

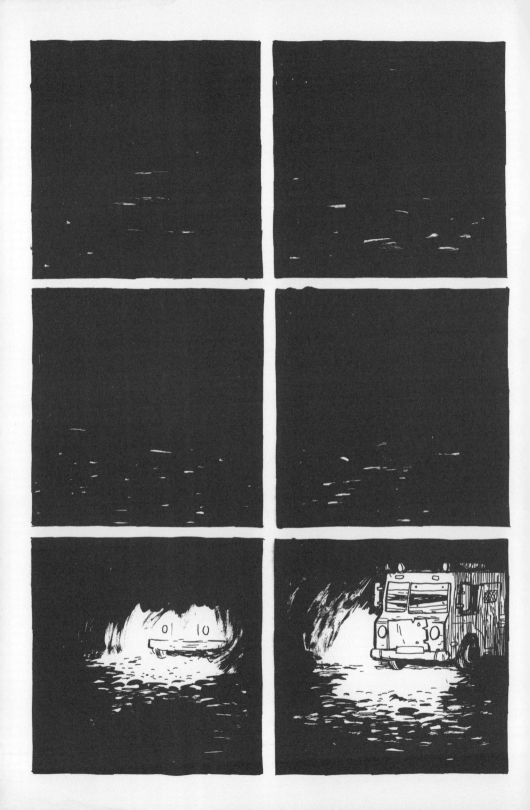

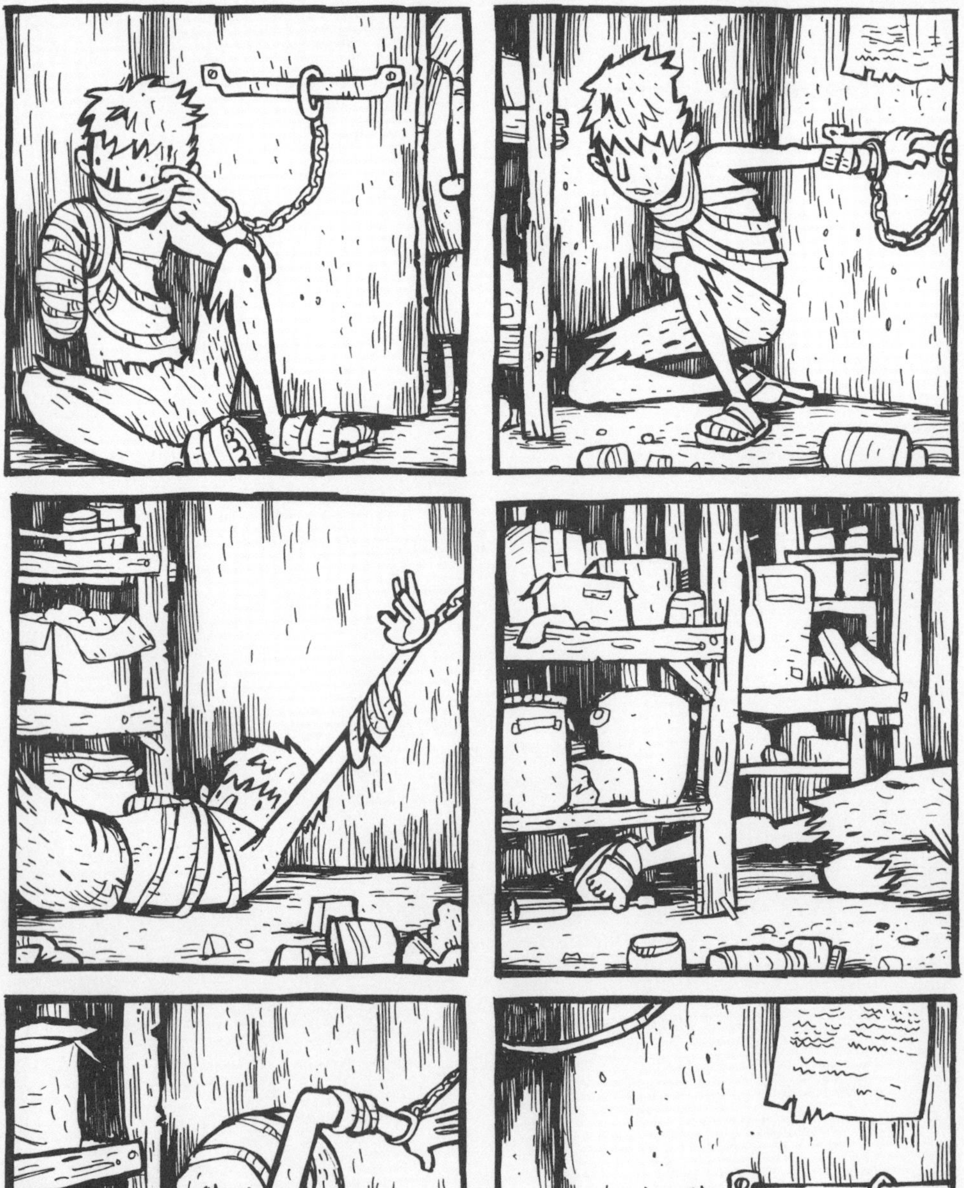

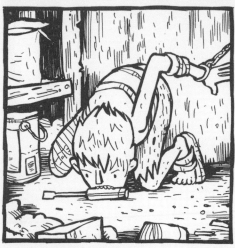

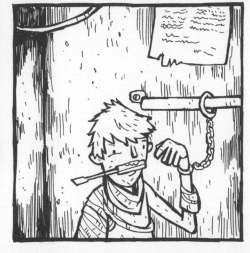

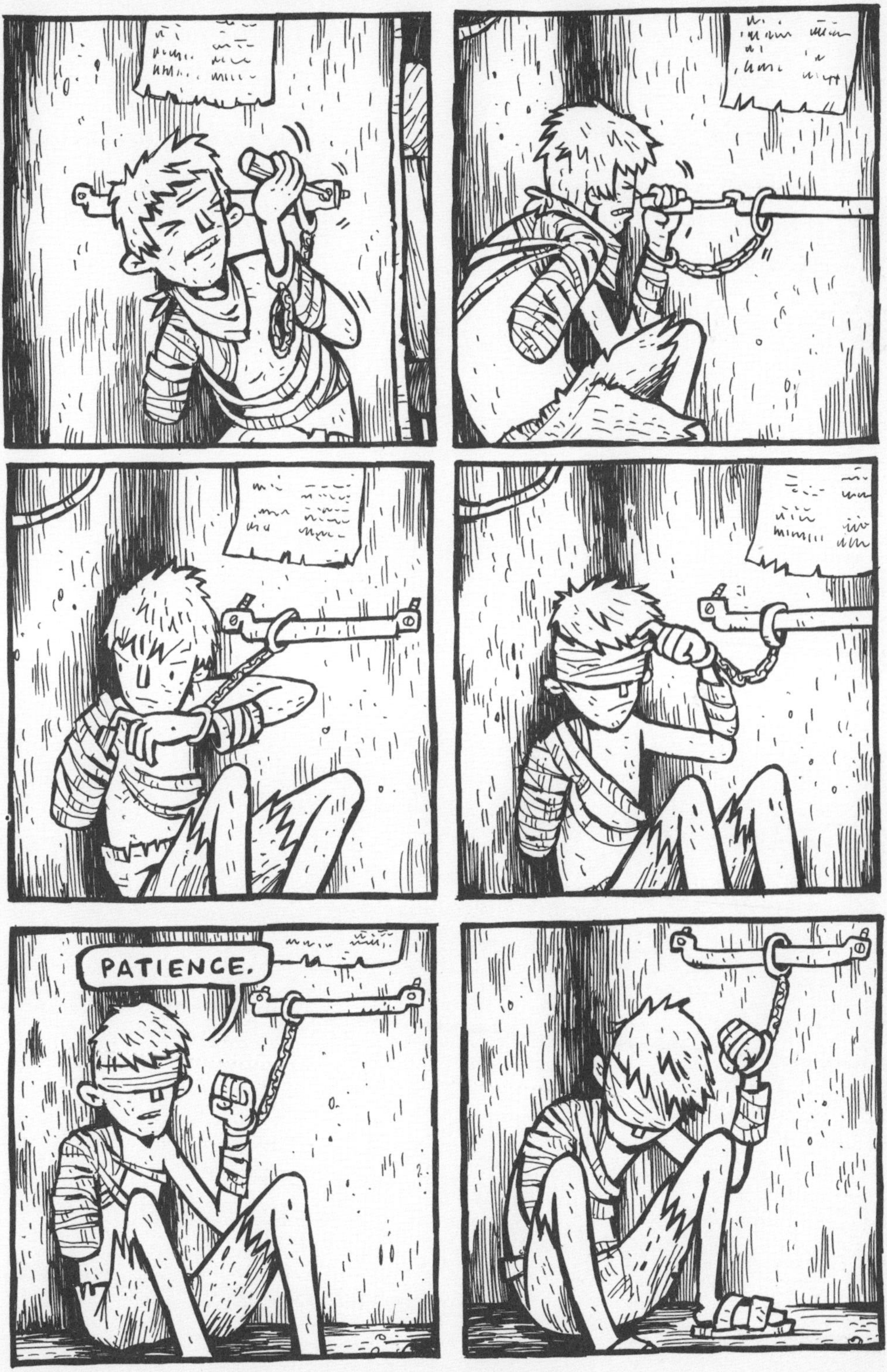
PATIENCE.

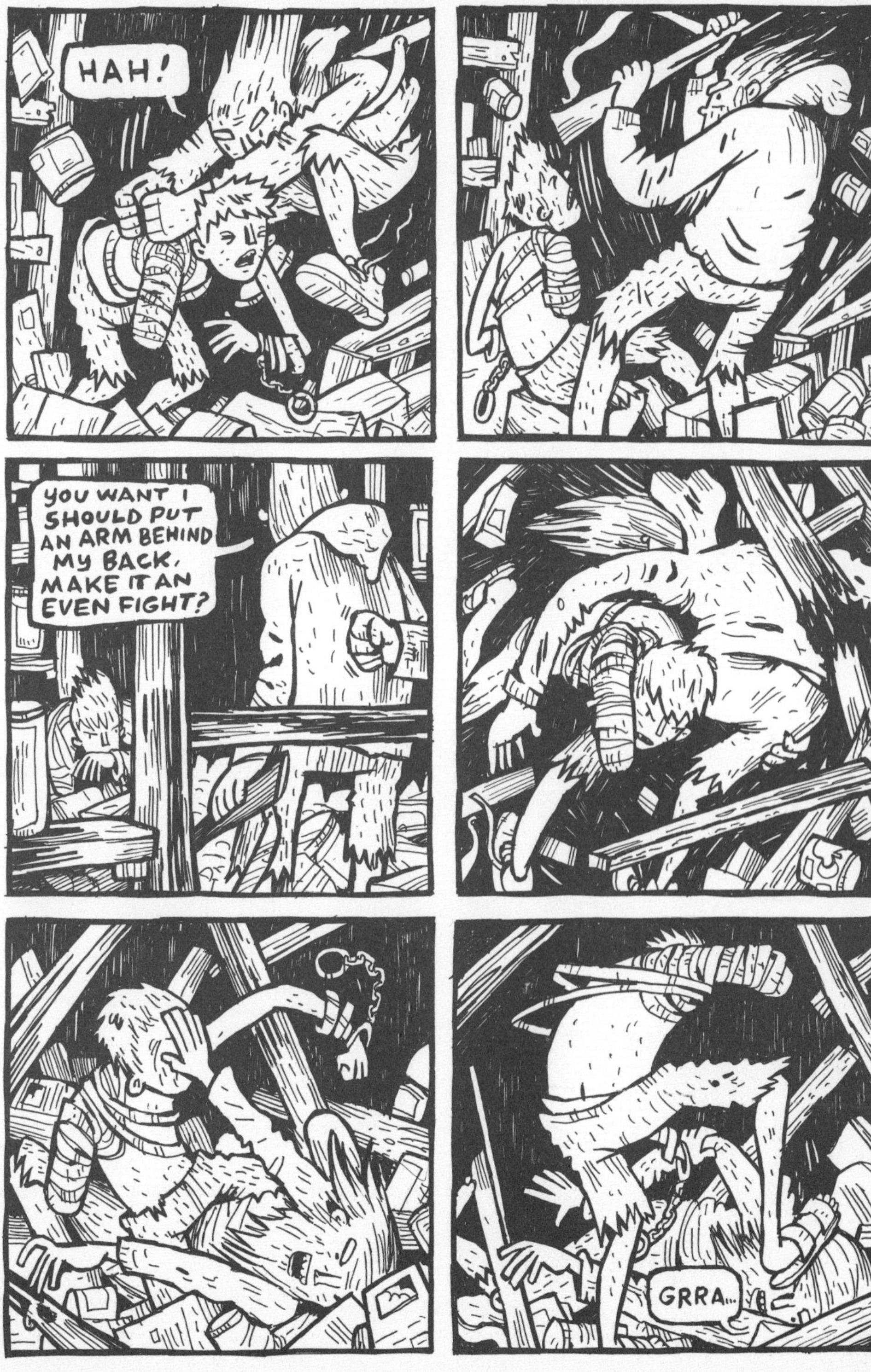
HAH!
YOU WANT I SHOULD PUT AN ARM BEHIND MY BACK, MAKE IT AN EVEN FIGHT?
GRRA...

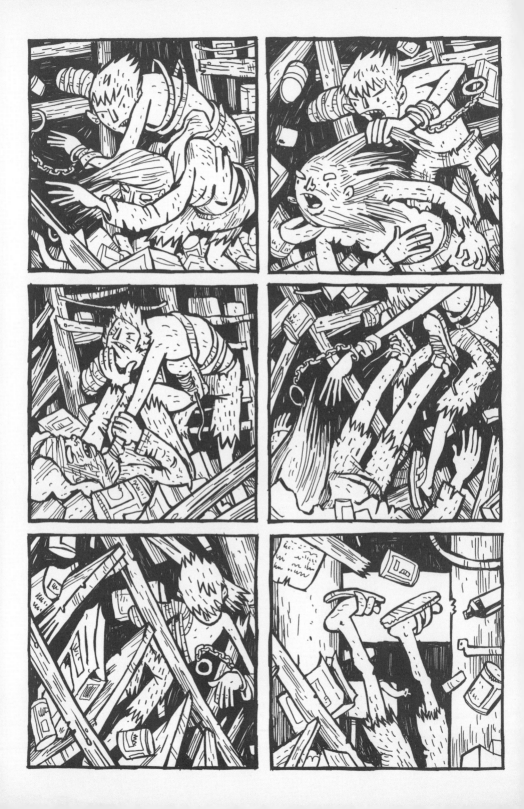

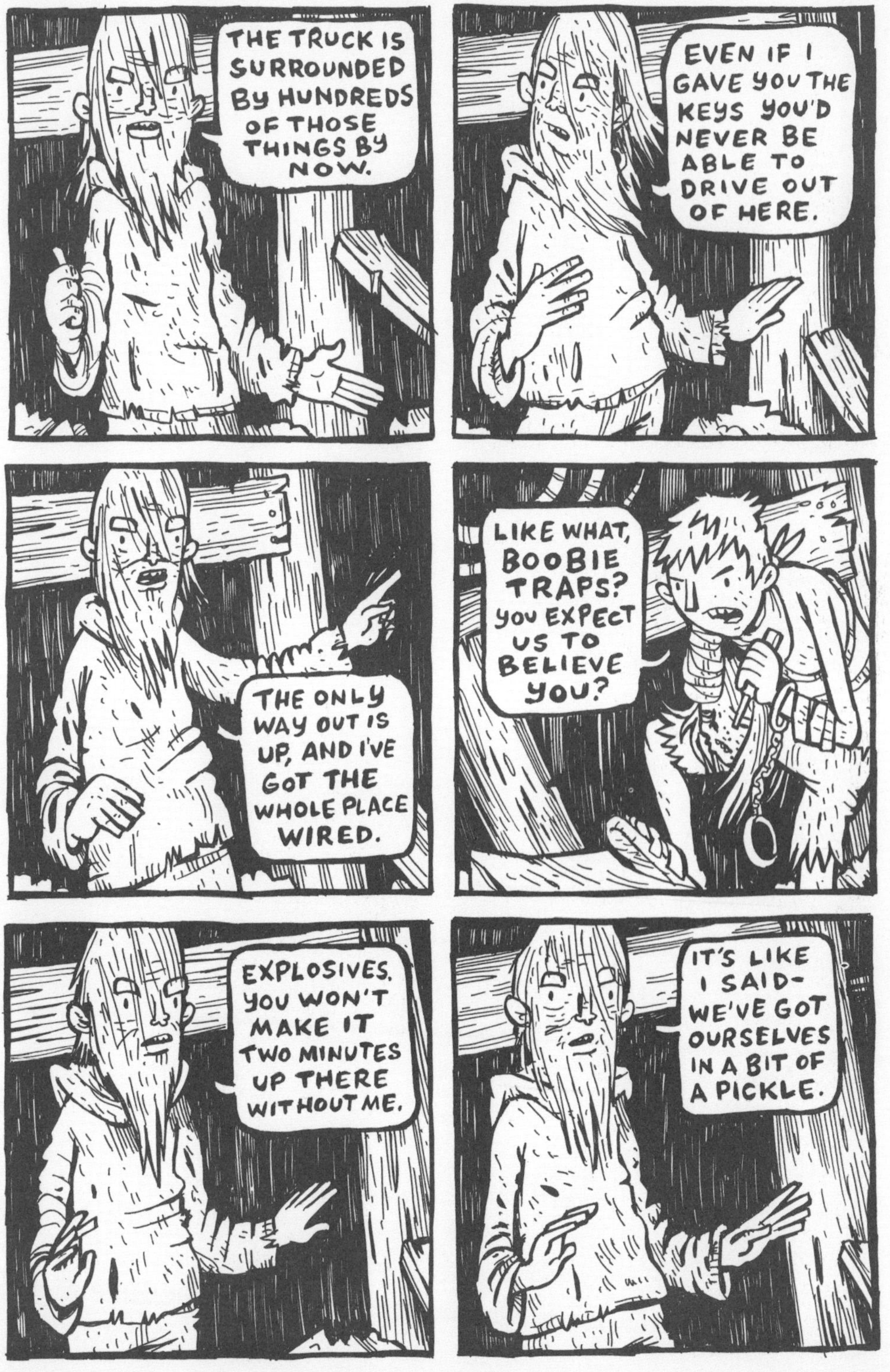
THE TRUCK IS SURROUNDED BY HUNDREDS OF THOSE THINGS BY NOW.
EVEN IF I GAVE YOU THE KEYS YOU'D NEVER BE ABLE TO DRIVE OUT OF HERE.
THE ONLY WAY OUT IS UP, AND I'VE GOT THE WHOLE PLACE WIRED.
LIKE WHAT, BOOBIE TRAPS? YOU EXPECT US TO BELIEVE YOU?
EXPLOSIVES. YOU WON'T MAKE IT TWO MINUTES UP THERE WITHOUT ME.
IT'S LIKE I SAID- WE'VE GOT OURSELVES IN A BIT OF A PICKLE.

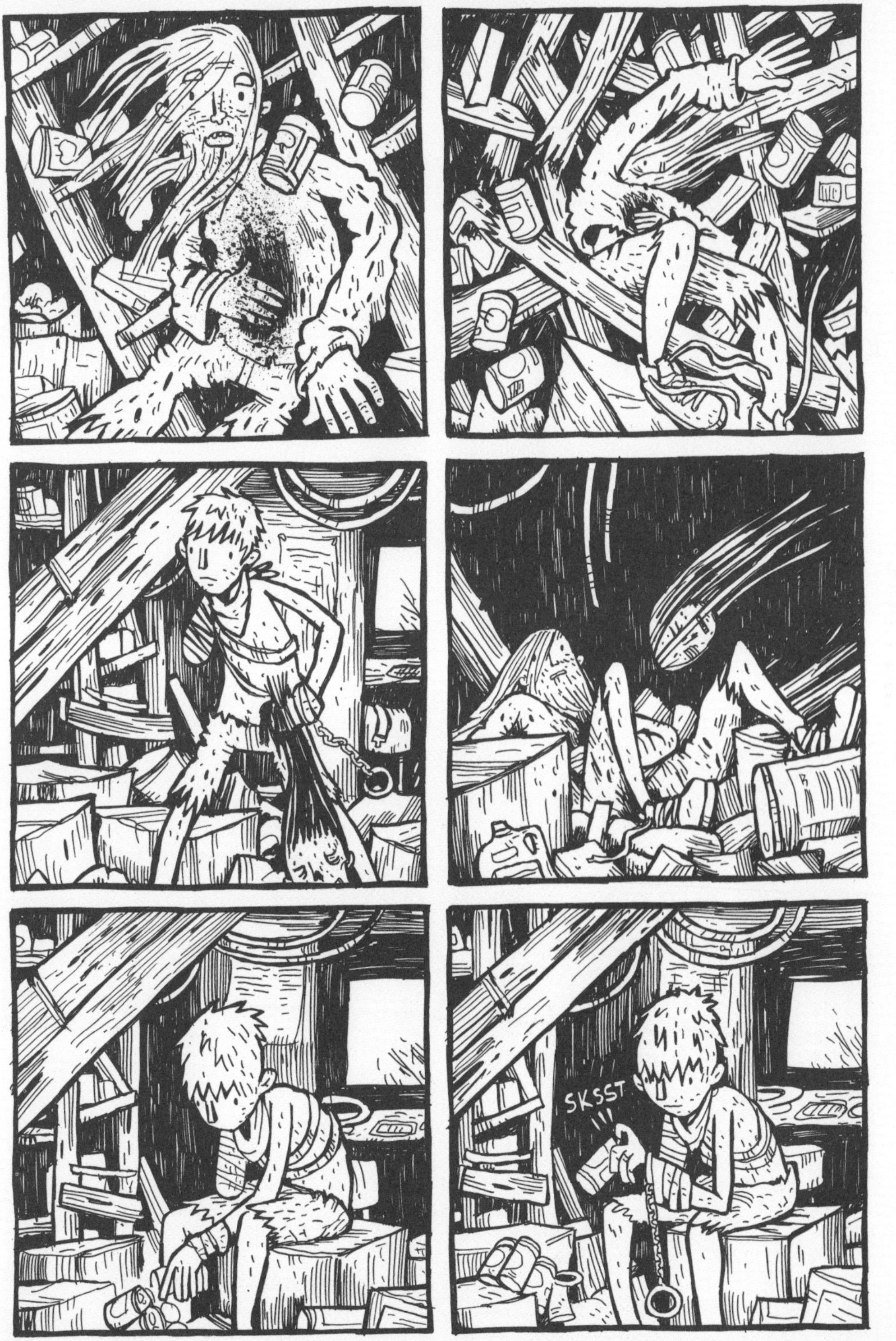
SKSST

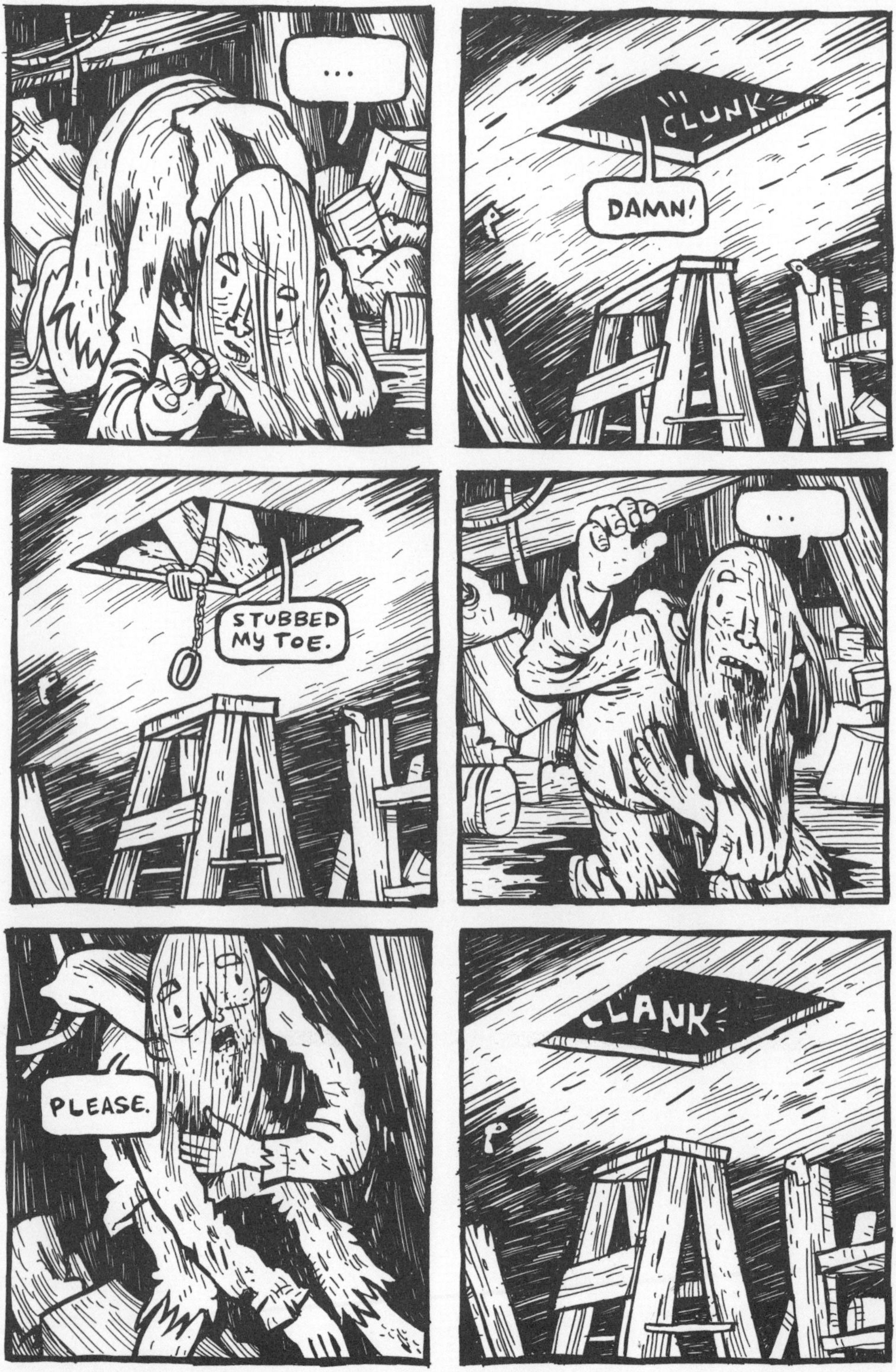
...
CLUNK
DAMN!
STUBBED MY TOE.
...
PLEASE.
CLANK

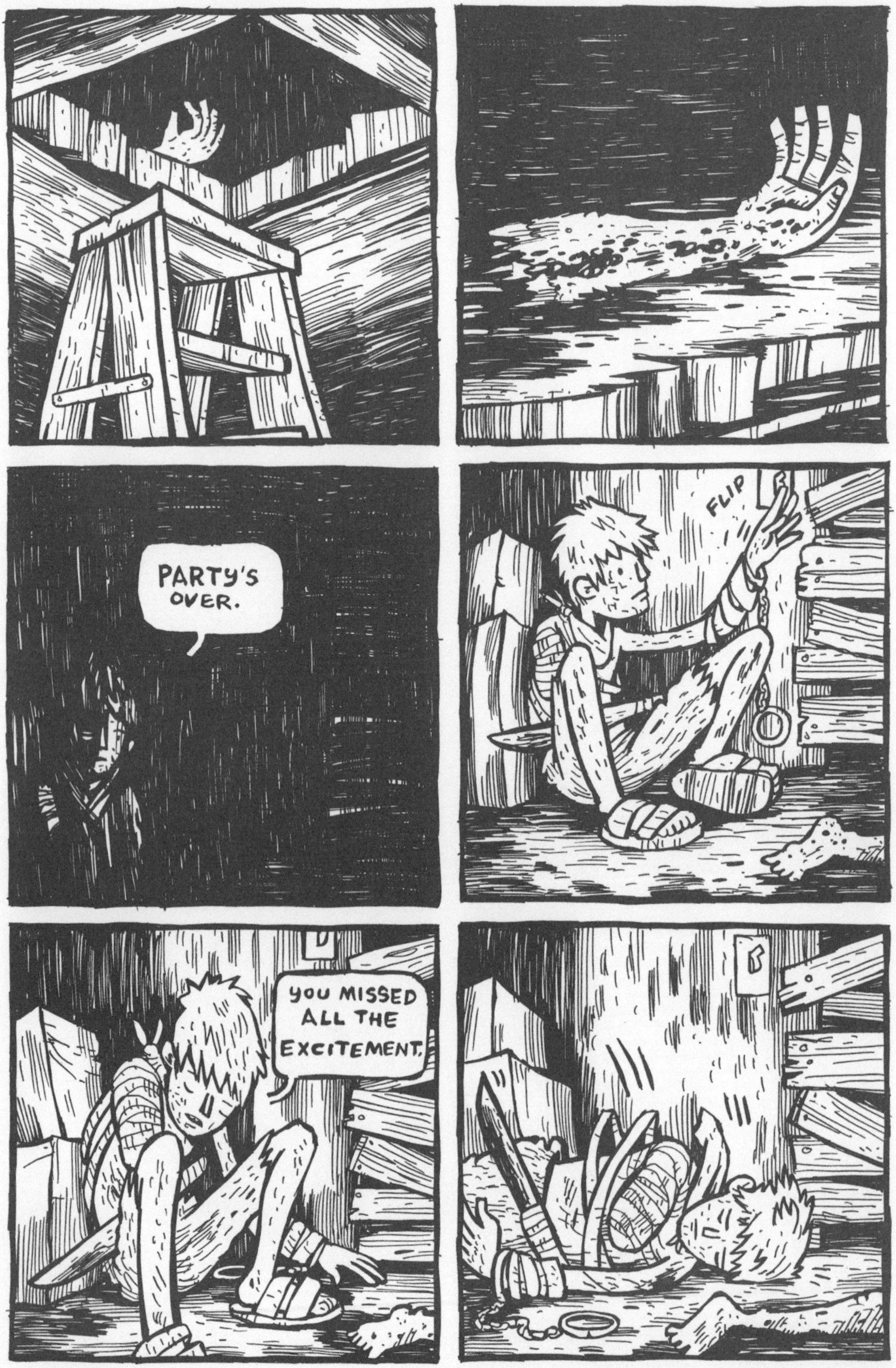
PARTY'S OVER.
FLIP
YOU MISSED ALL THE EXCITEMENT.

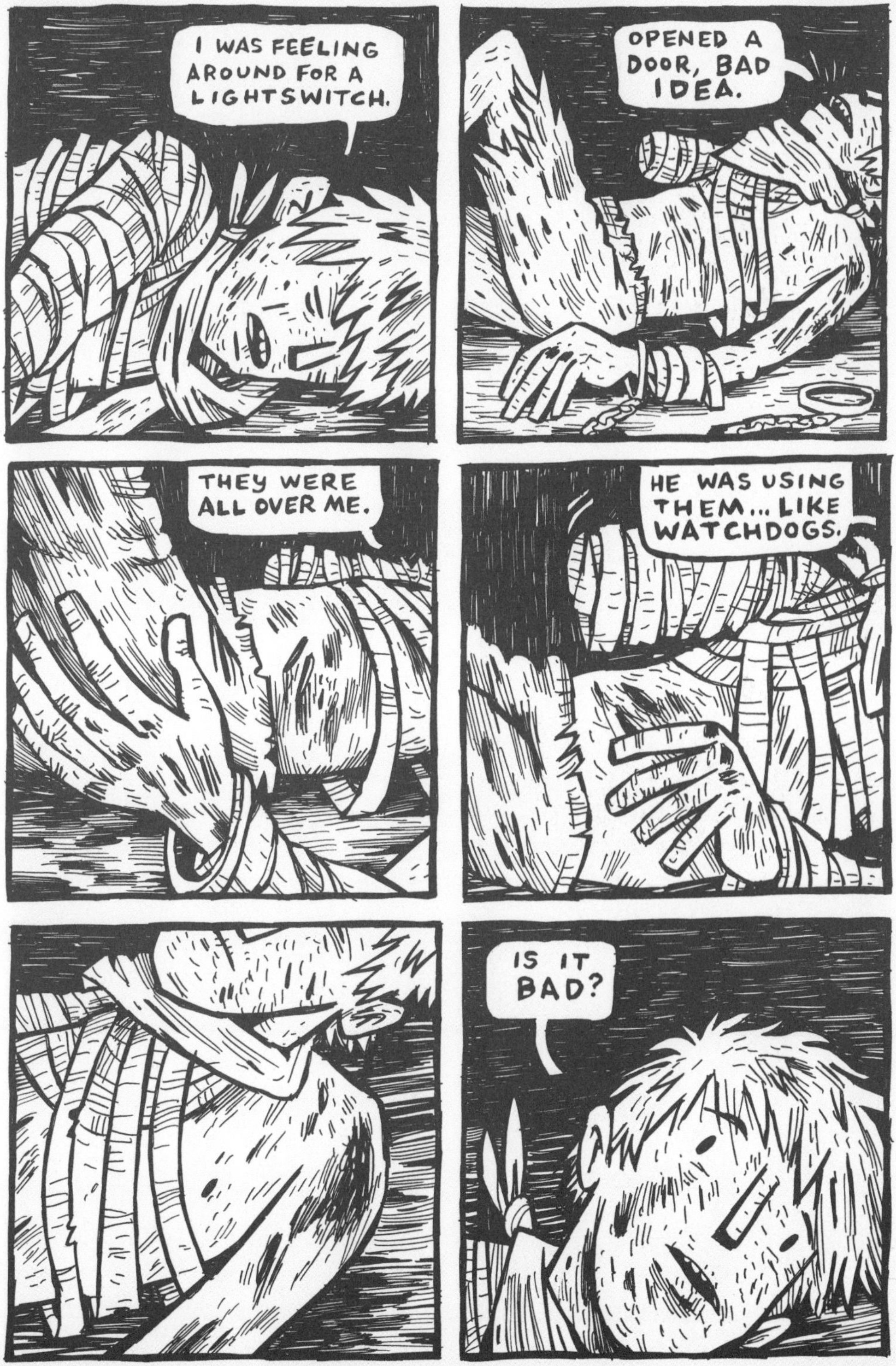
I WAS FEELING AROUND FOR A LIGHTSWITCH.
OPENED A DOOR, BAD IDEA.
THEY WERE ALL OVER ME.
HE WAS USING THEM... LIKE WATCHDOGS.
IS IT BAD?

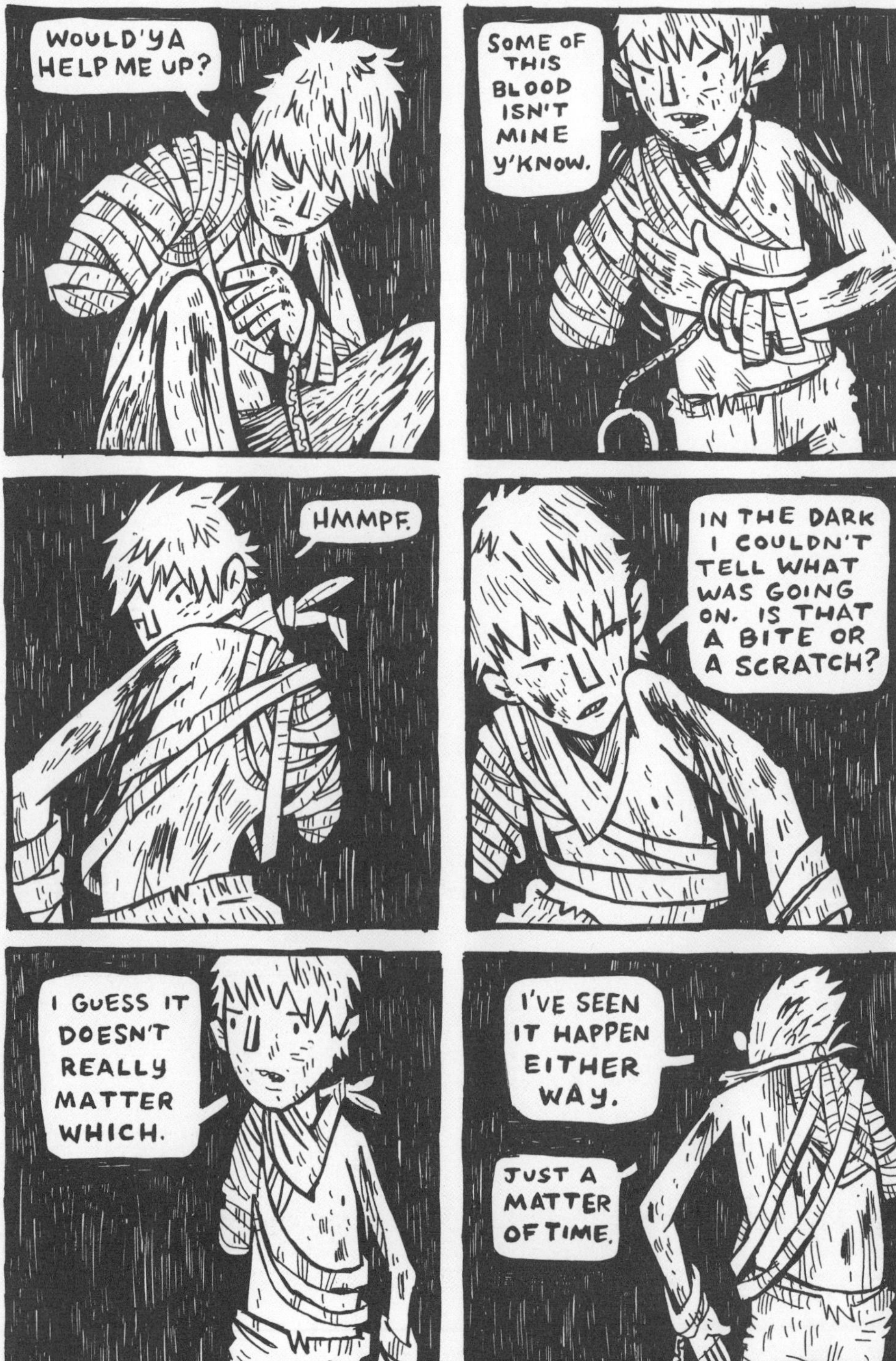
WOULD'YA HELP ME UP?
SOME OF THIS BLOOD ISN'T MINE Y'KNOW.
HMMPF.
IN THE DARK I COULDN'T TELL WHAT WAS GOING ON. IS THAT A BITE OR A SCRATCH?
I GUESS IT DOESN'T REALLY MATTER WHICH.
I'VE SEEN IT HAPPEN EITHER WAY.
JUST A MATTER OF TIME.

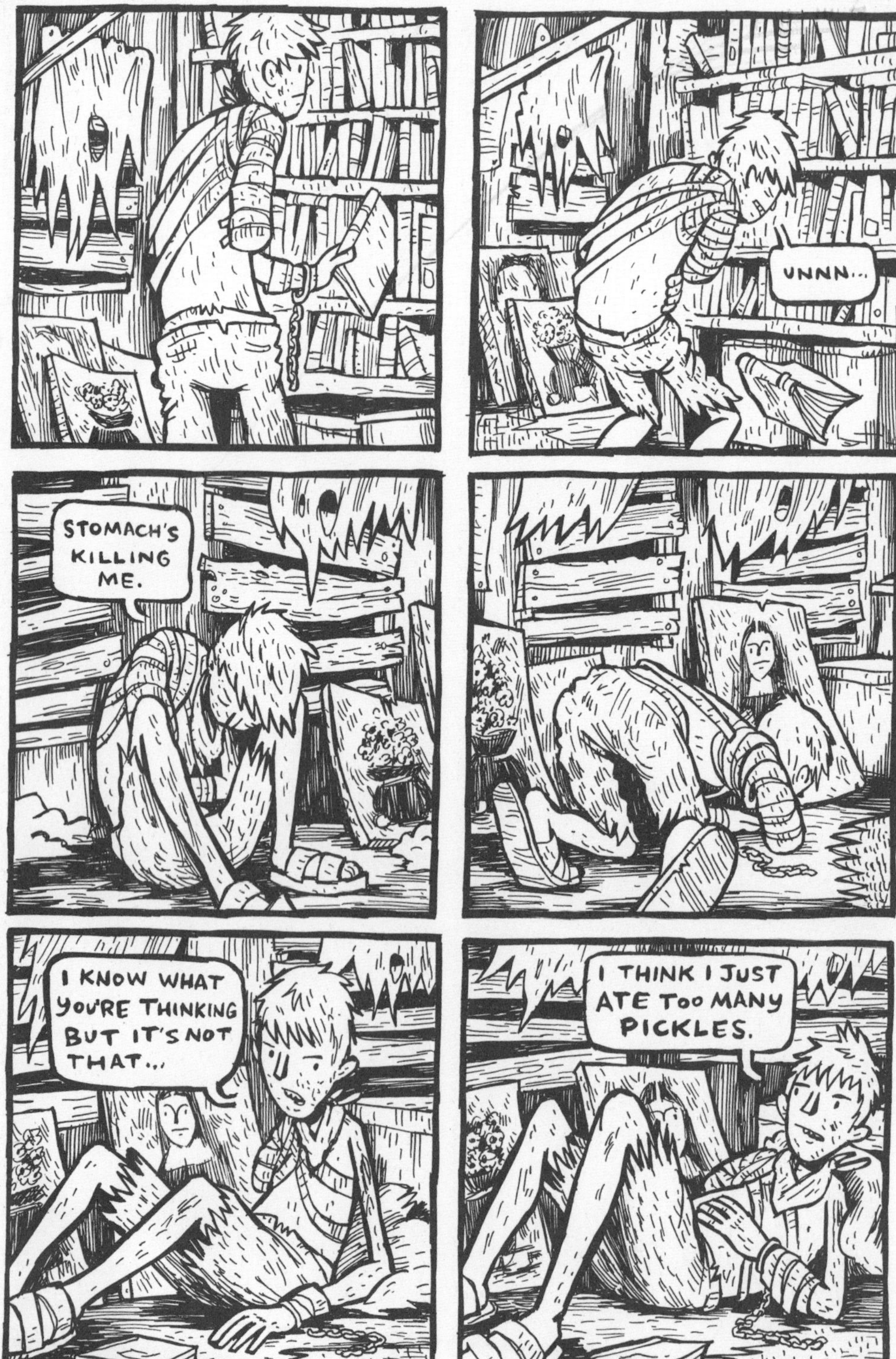
UNNN...
STOMACH'S KILLING ME.
I KNOW WHAT YOU'RE THINKING BUT IT'S NOT THAT...
I THINK I JUST ATE TOO MANY PICKLES.

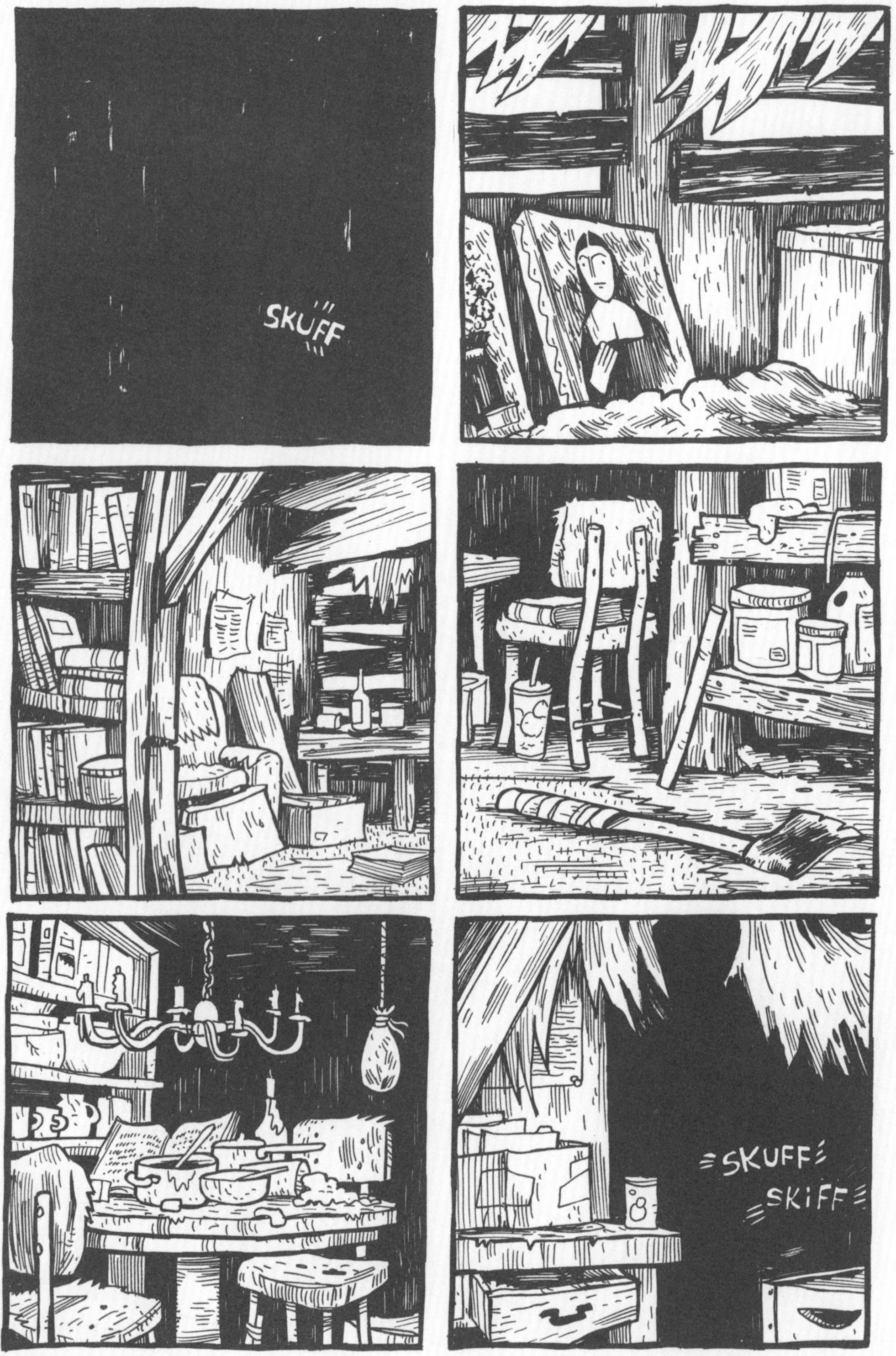
SKUFF
SKUFF
SKiFF

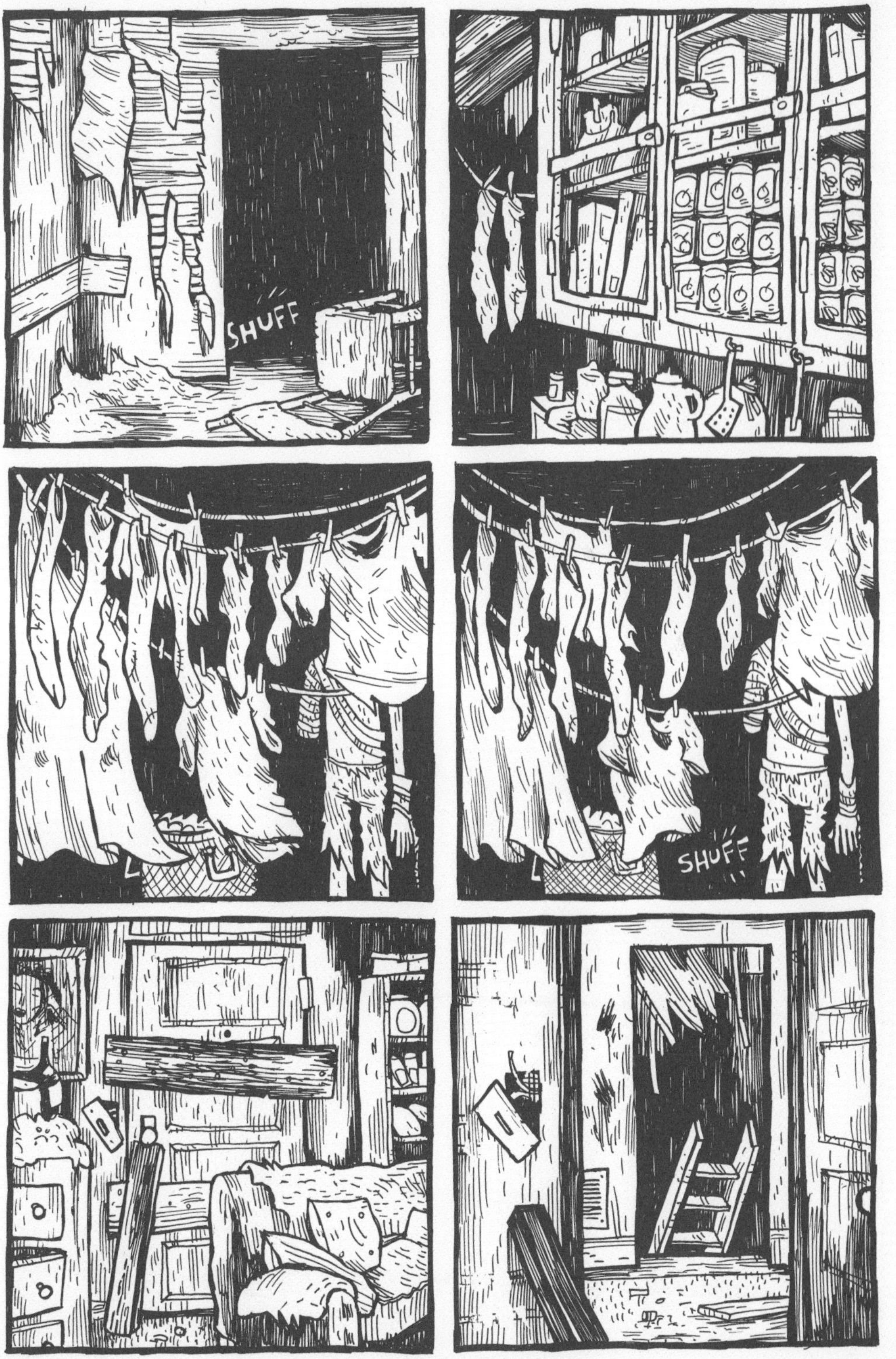
SHUFF
SHUFF

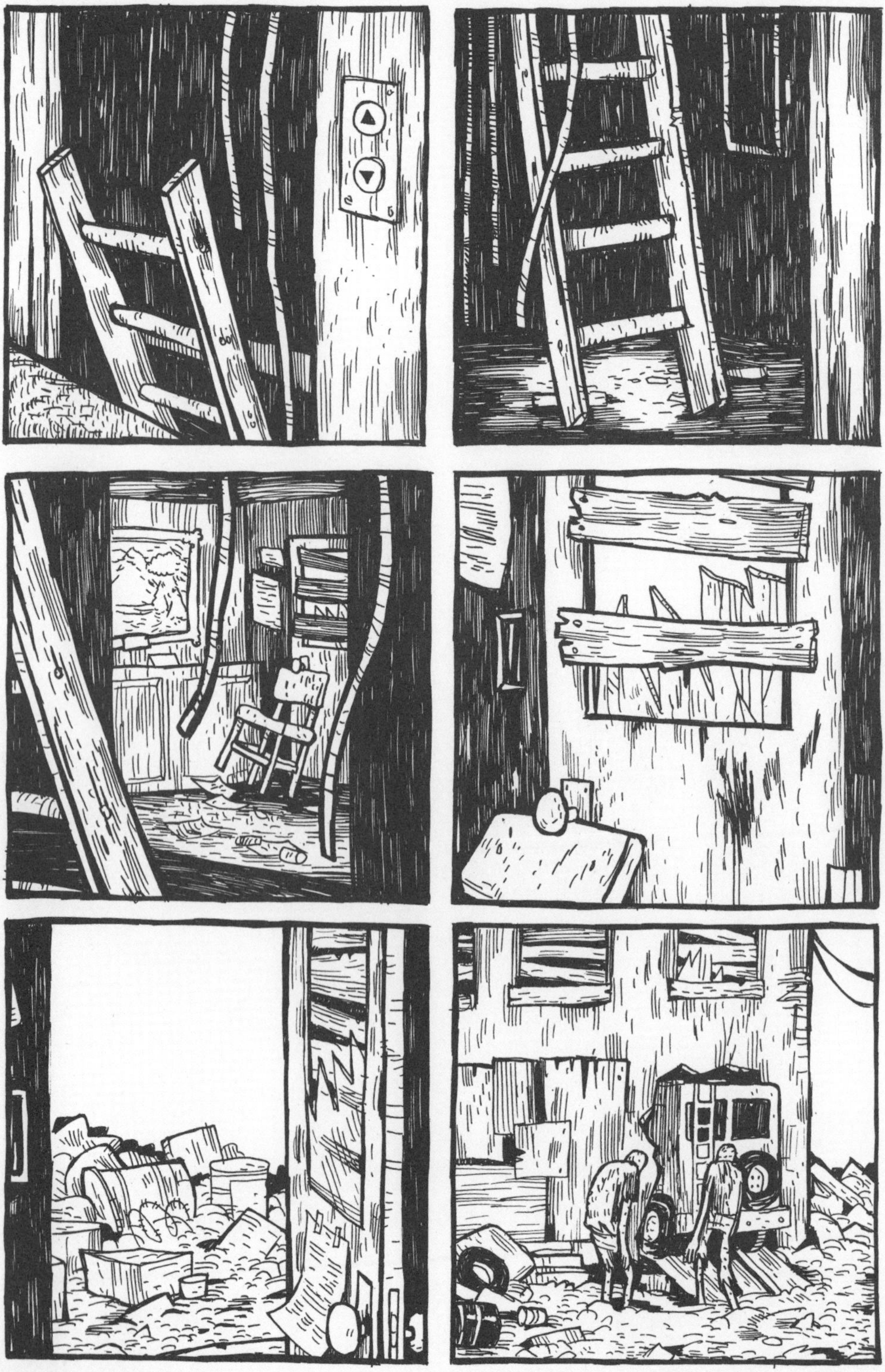

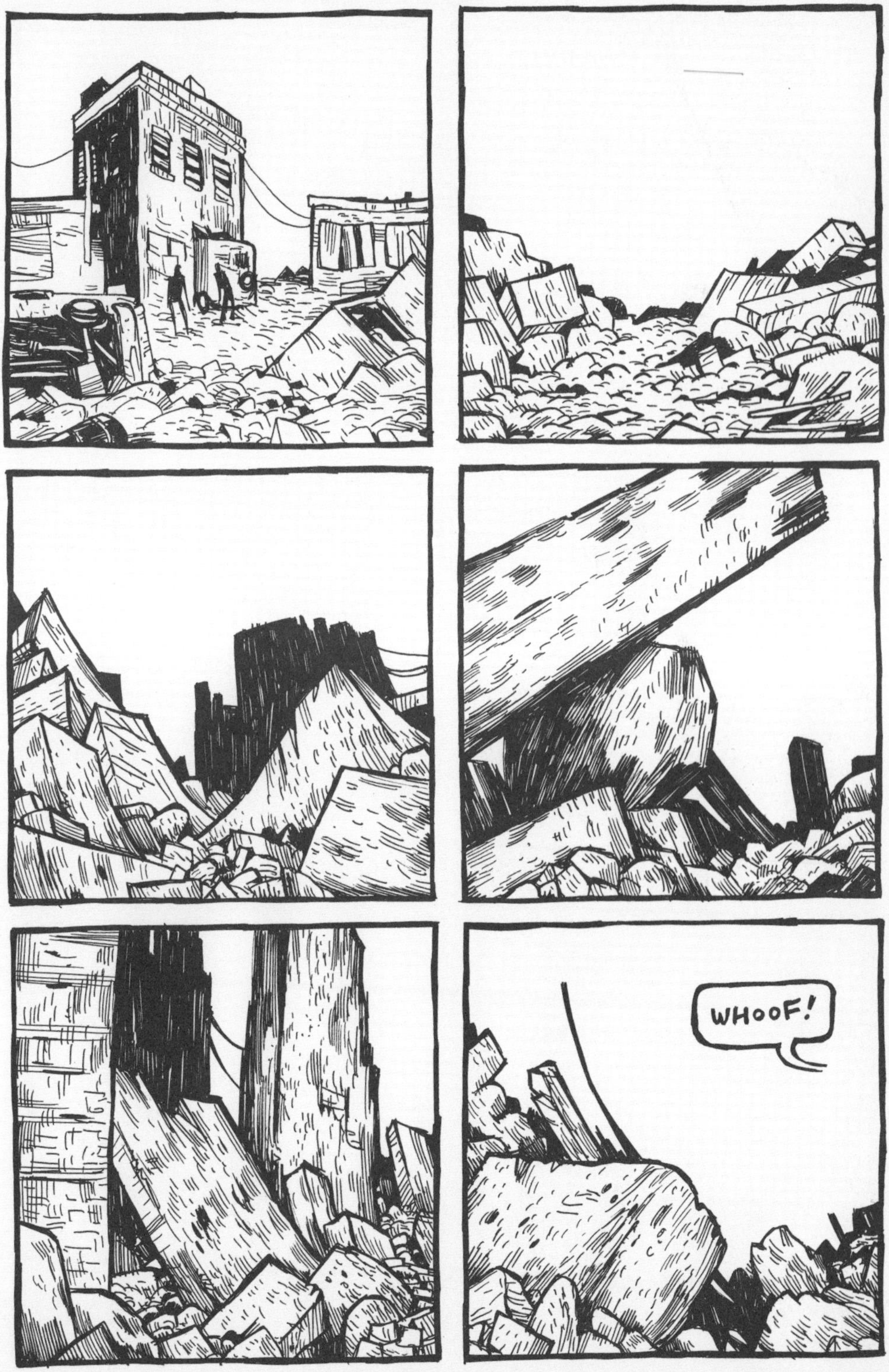
WHOOF!

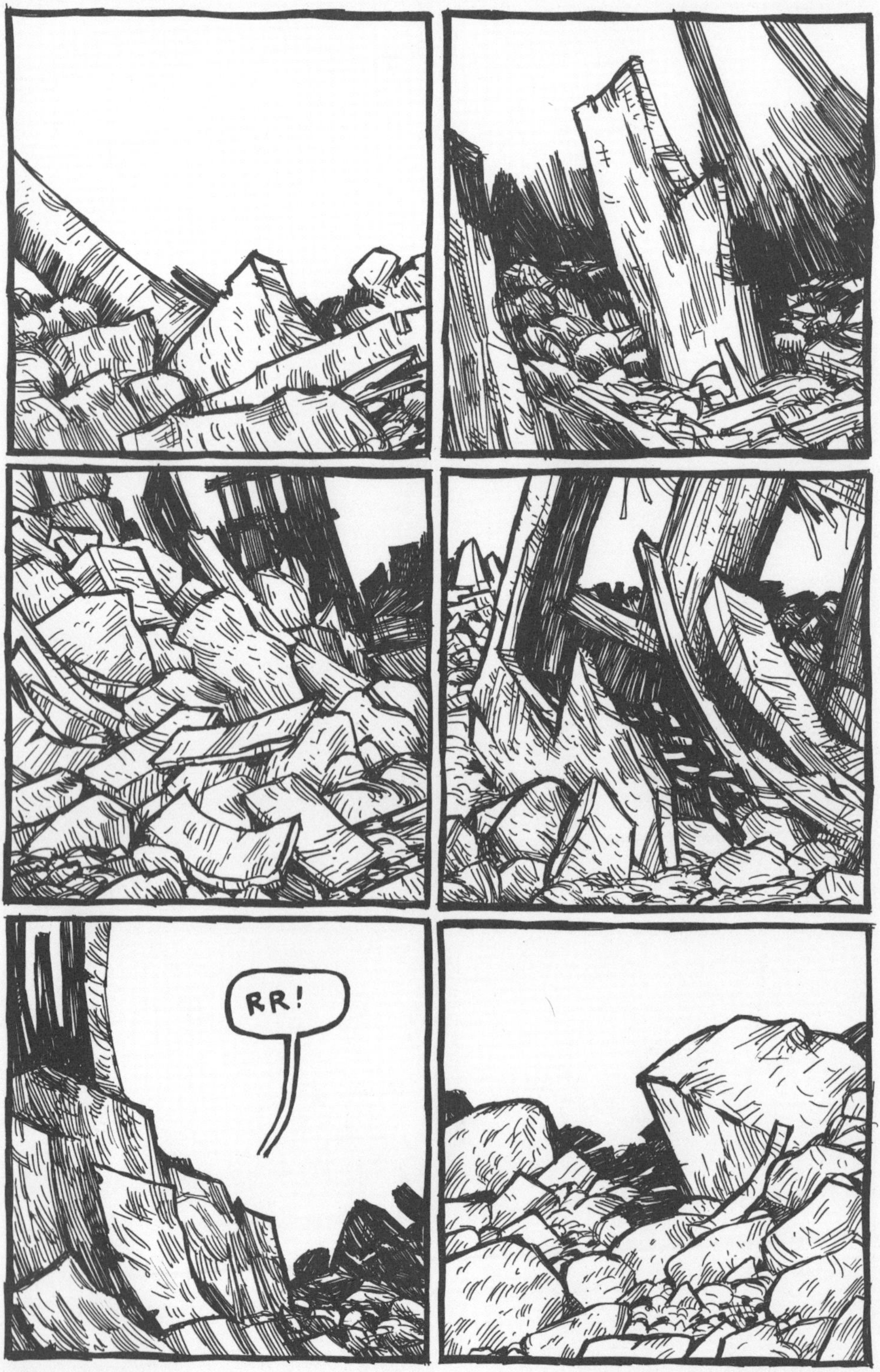
RR!

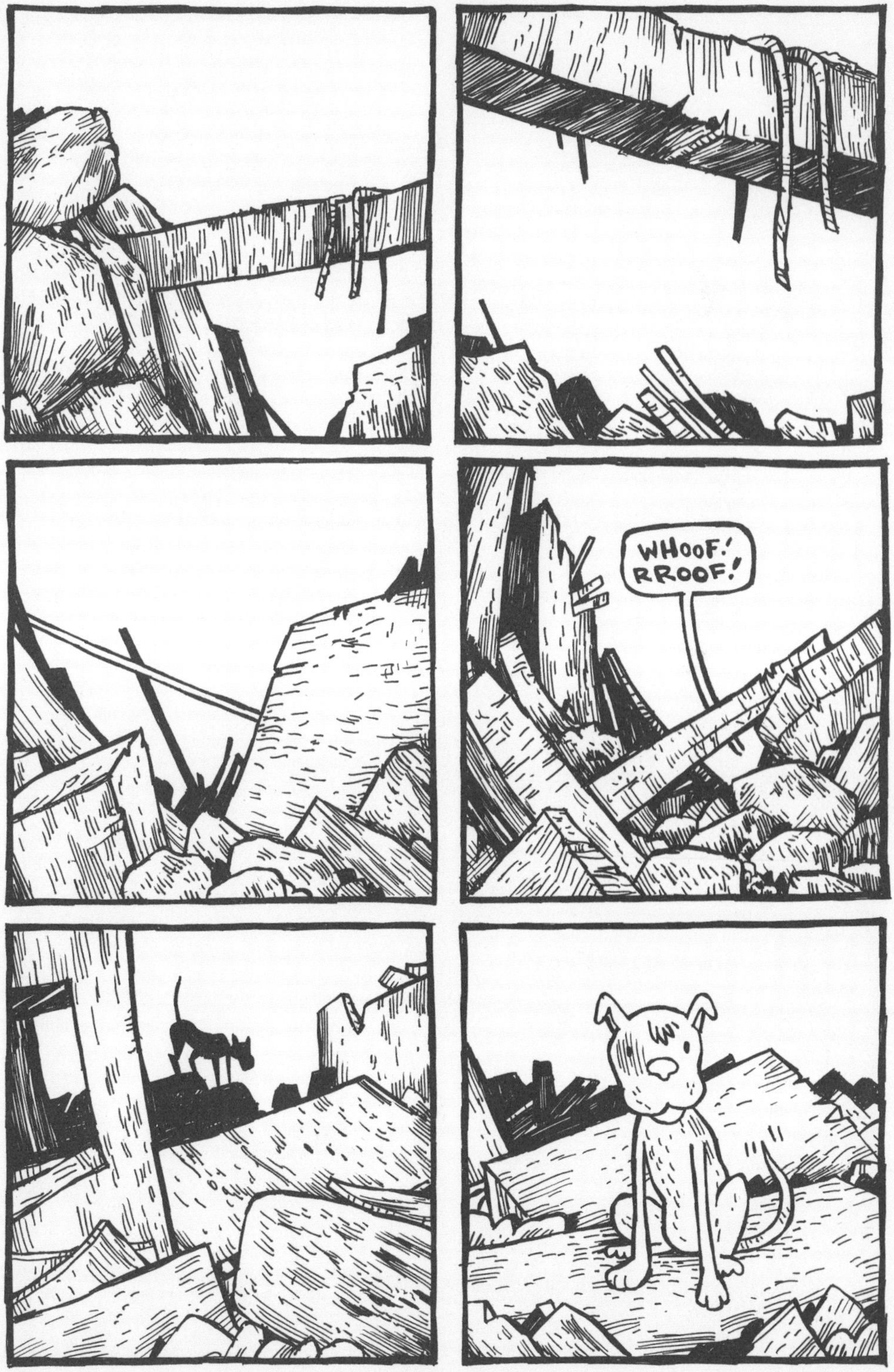
WHOOF! RROOF!

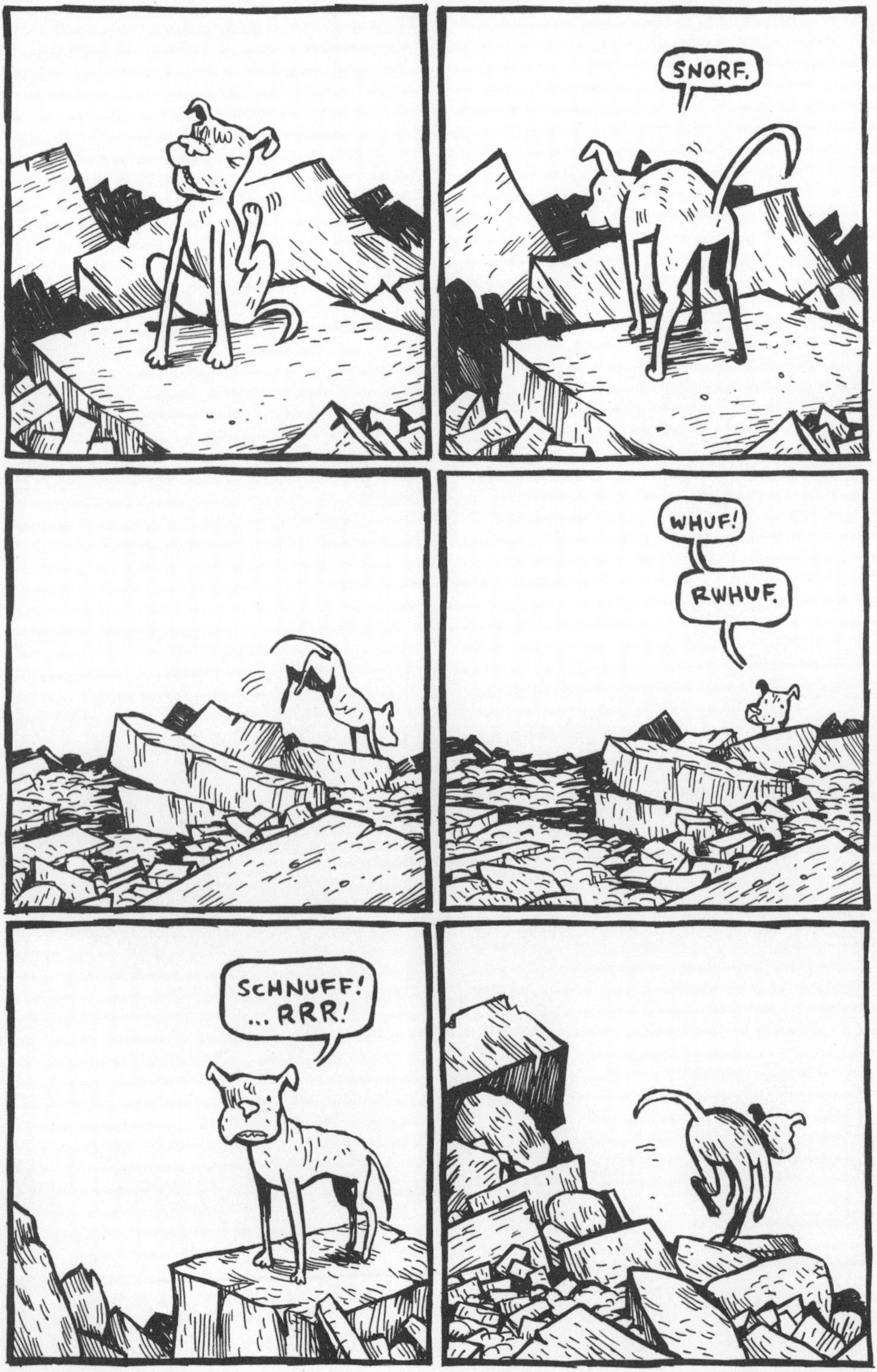
SNORF.
WHUF!
RWHUF.
SCHNUFF! ...RRR!

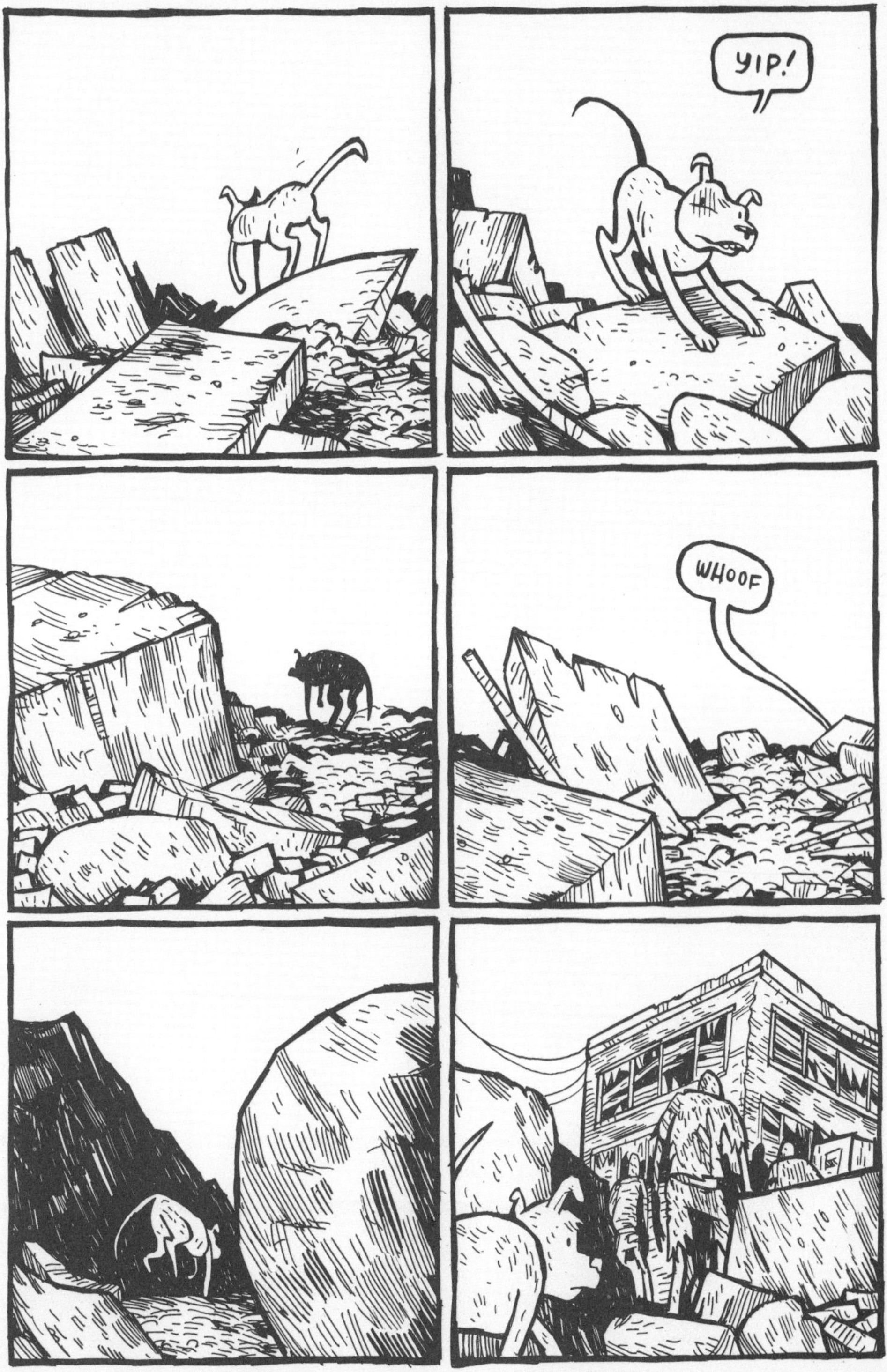
YIP!
WHOOF

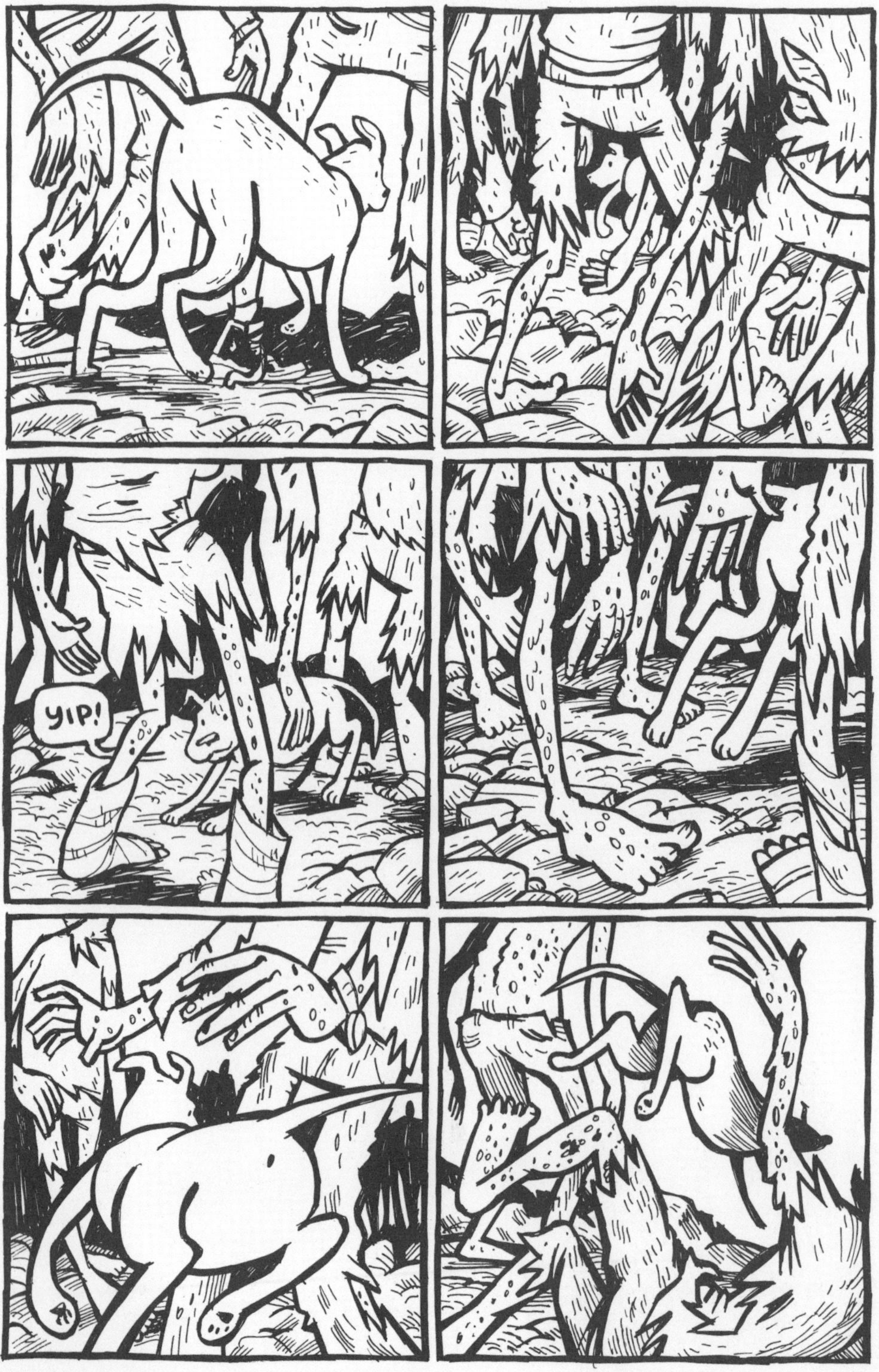
YIP!

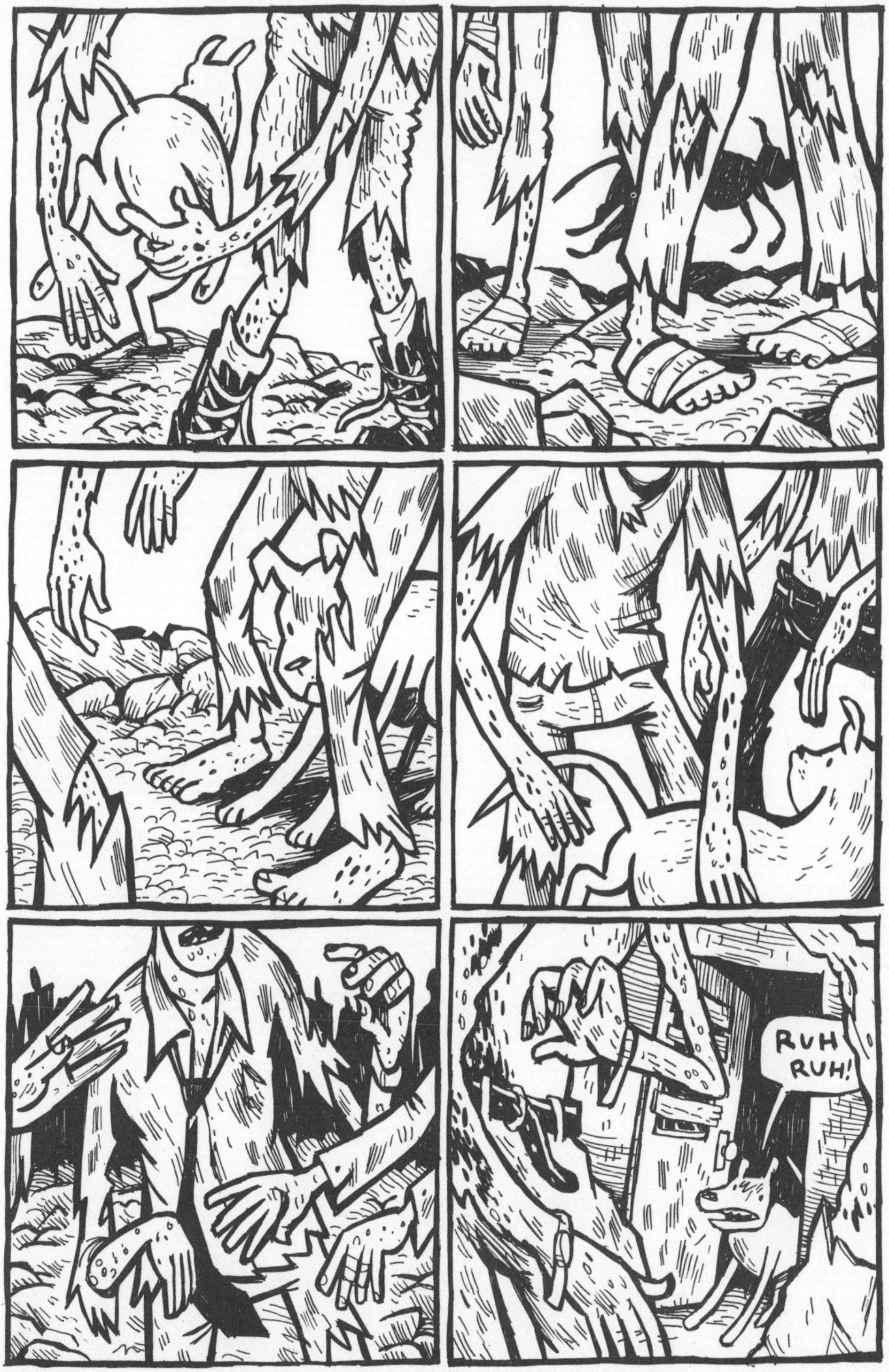
RUH RUH!

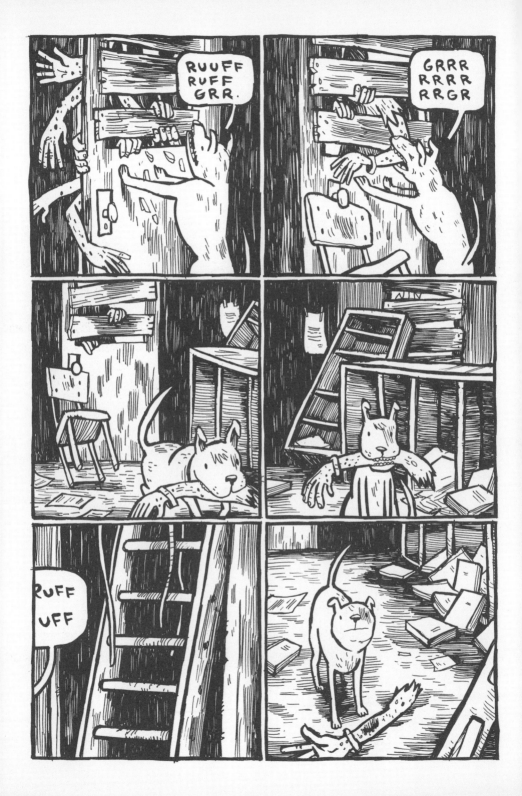

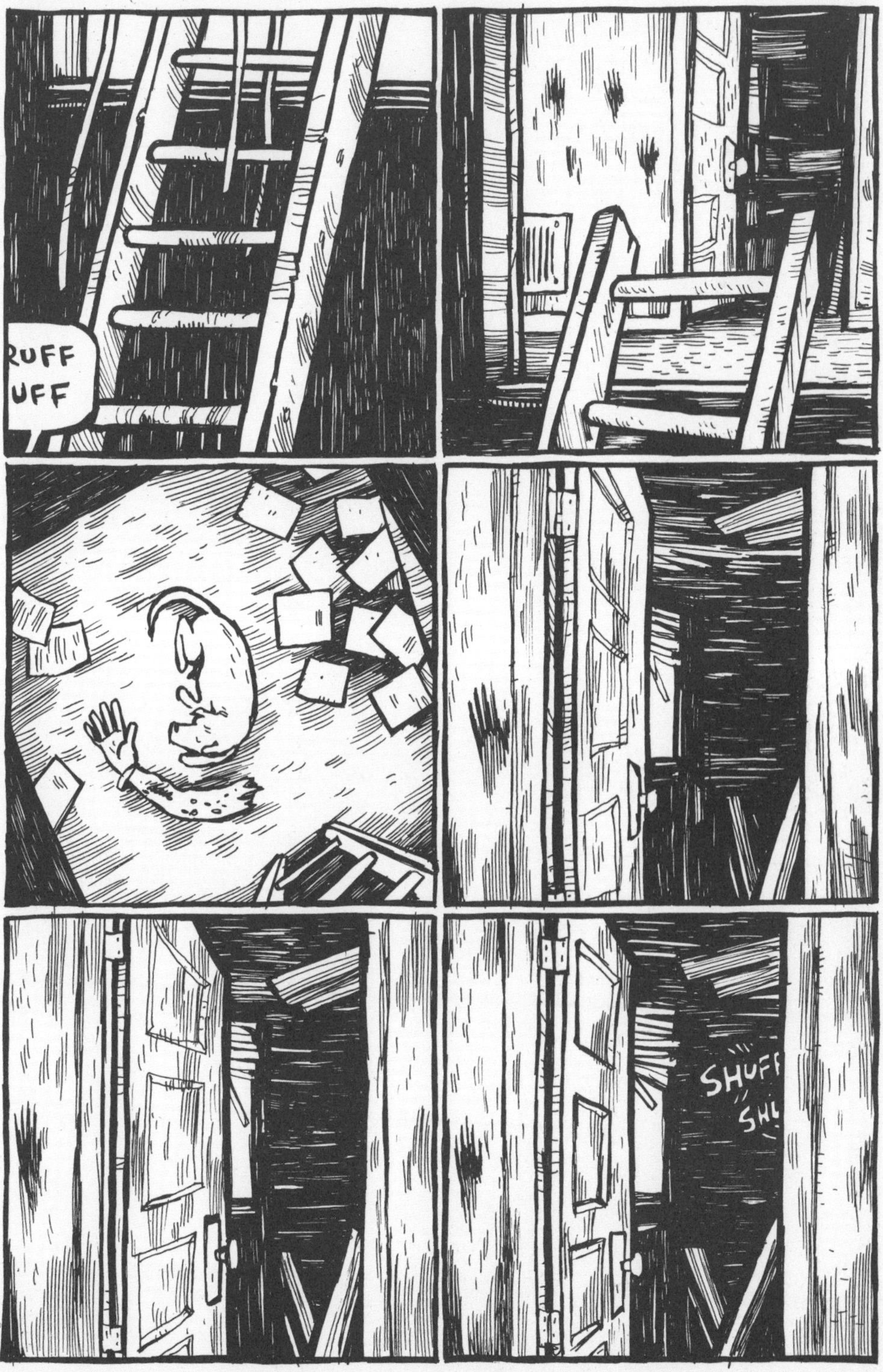
RUFF
UFF
SHUFF
SHU

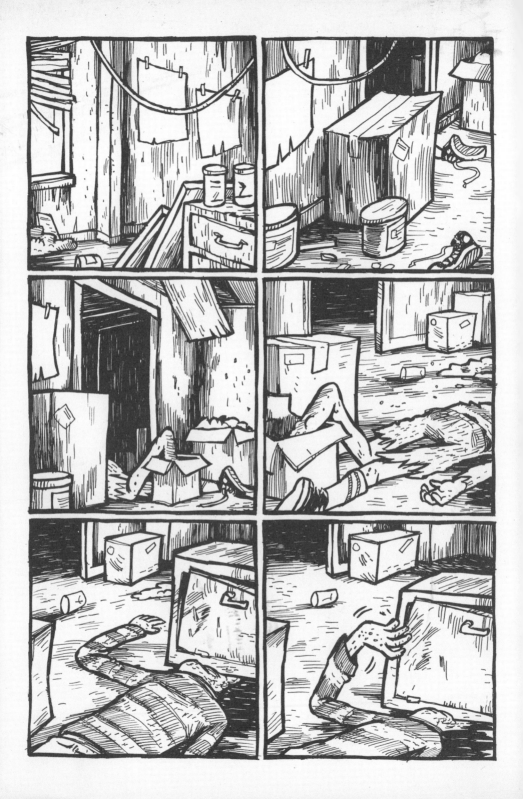

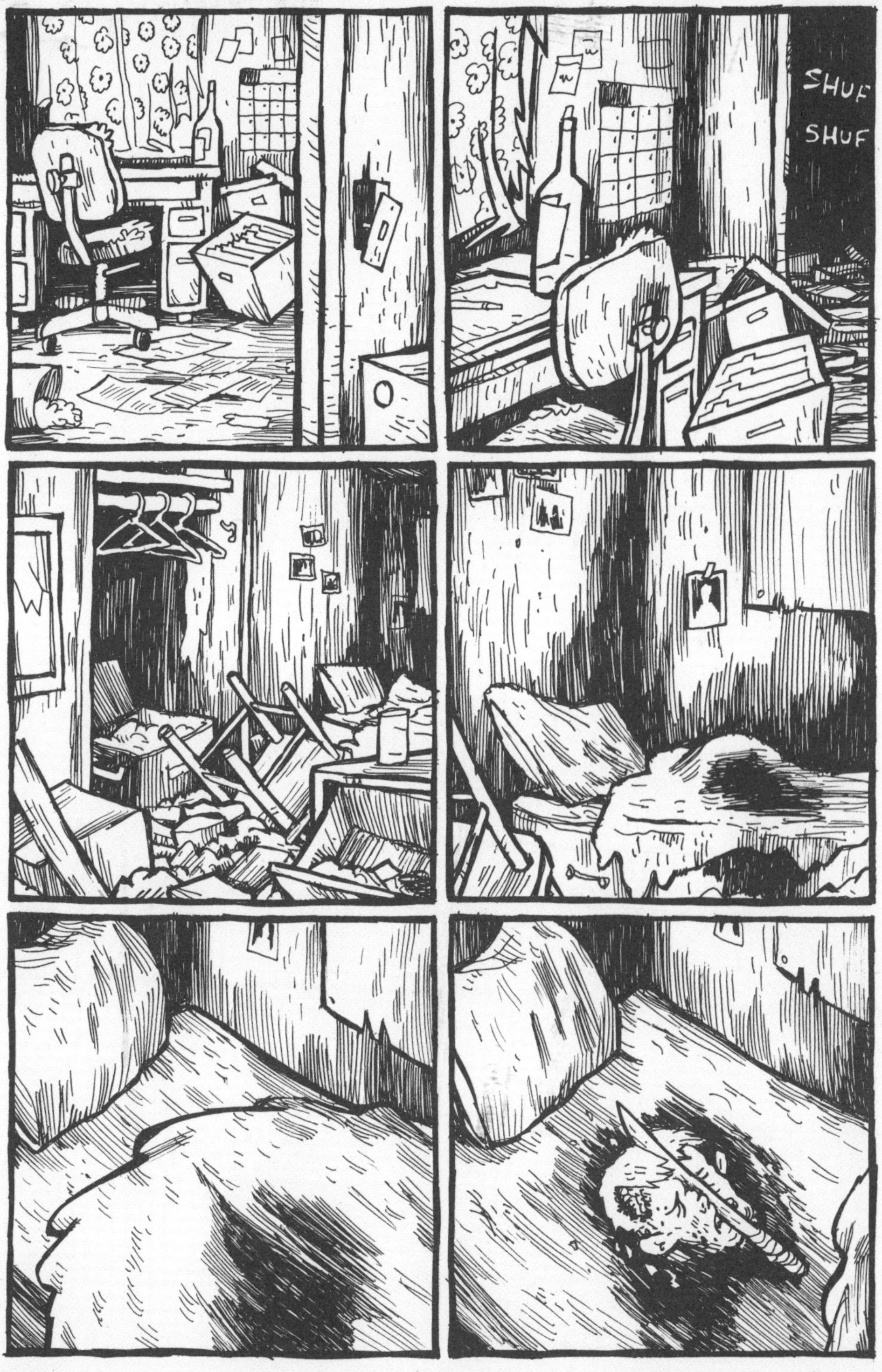
SHUF
SHUF

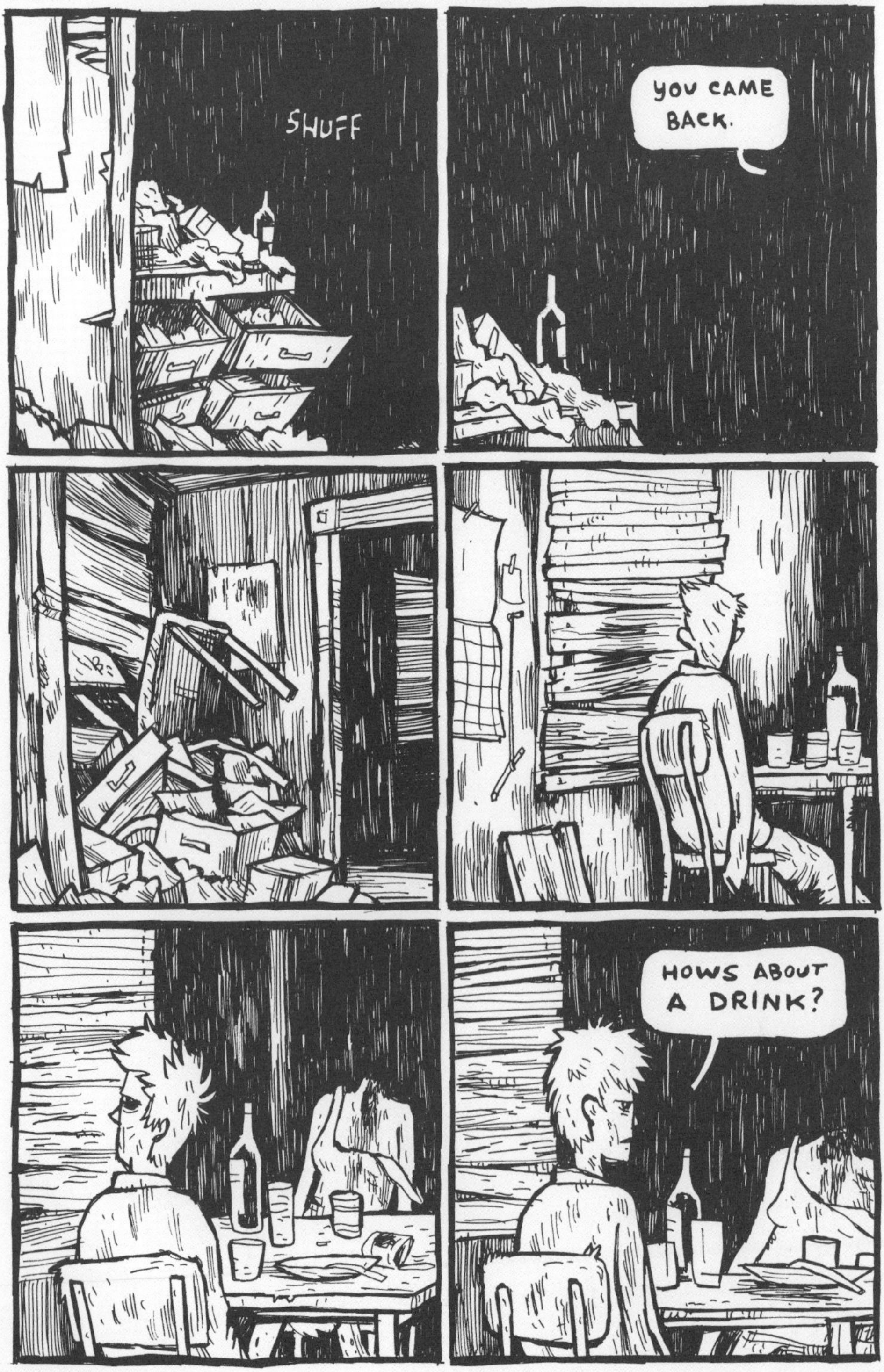
SHUFF
YOU CAME BACK.
HOWS ABOUT A DRINK?

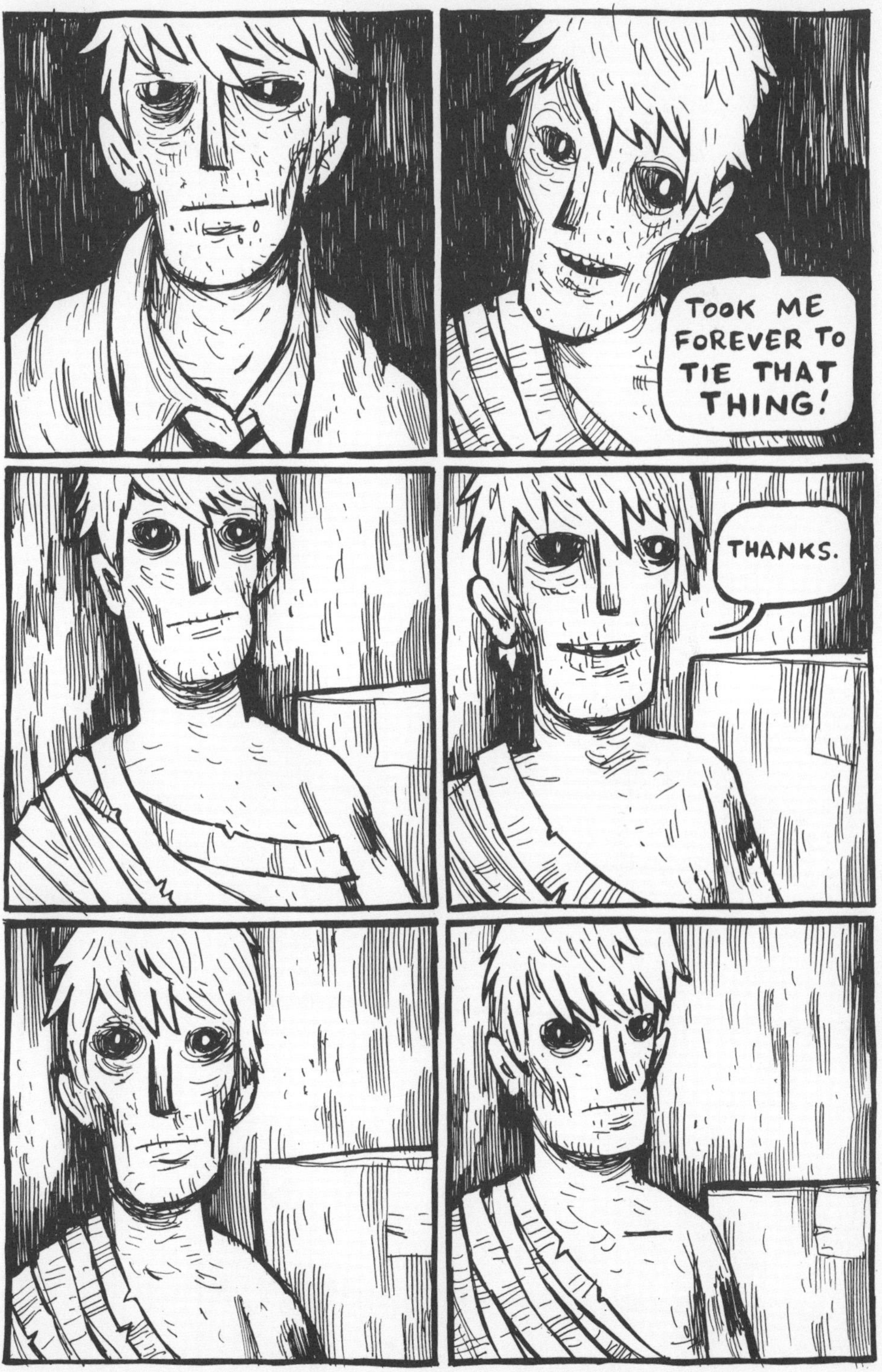
TOOK ME FOREVER TO TIE THAT THING!
THANKS.

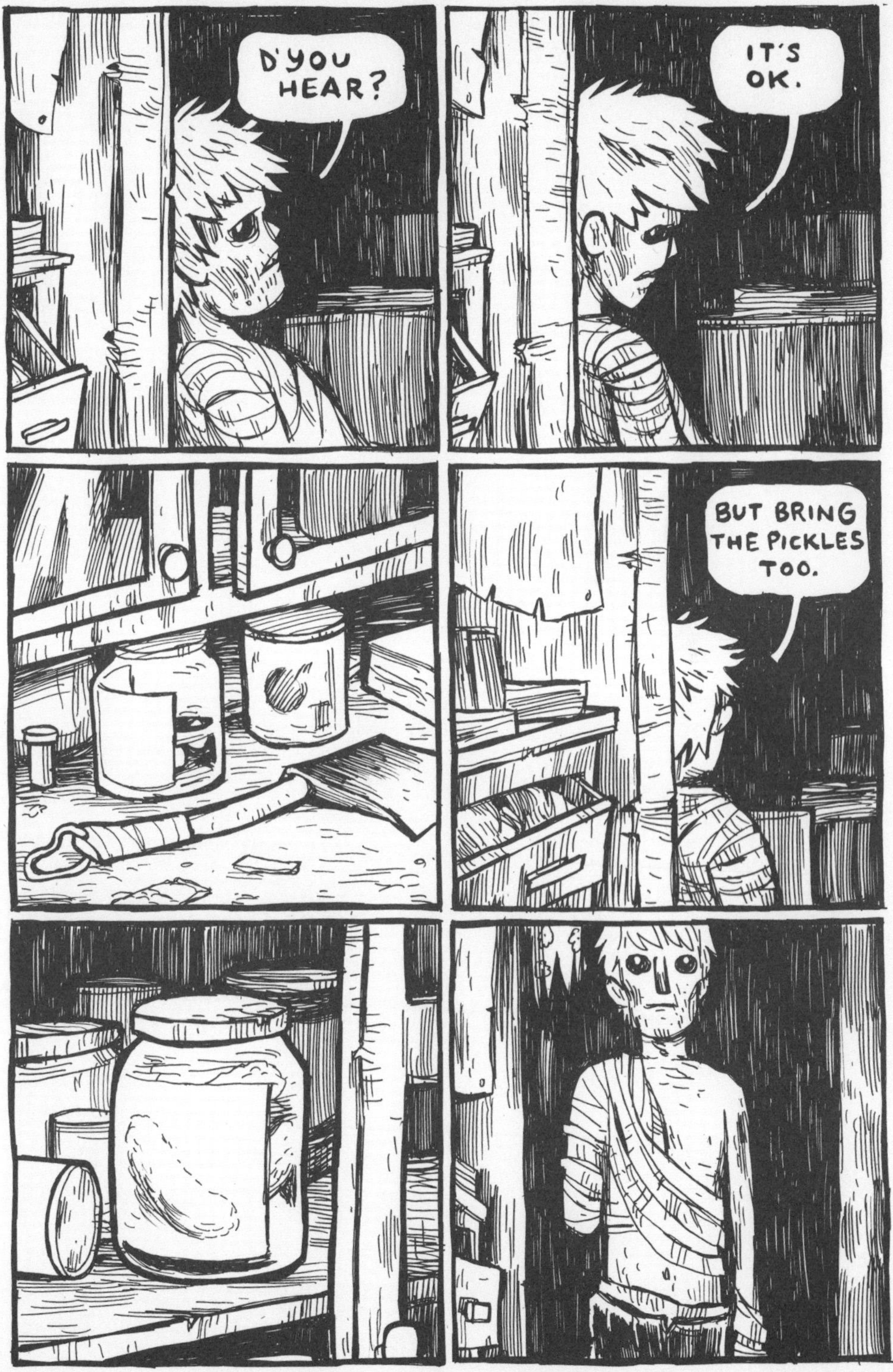
D'YOU HEAR?
IT'S OK.
BUT BRING THE PICKLES TOO.

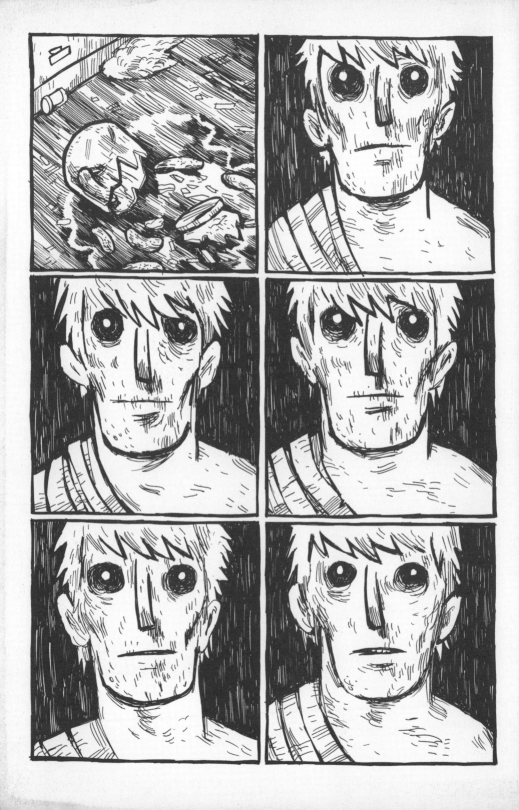

BRIAN RALPH is the cartoonist of the *New York Times* bestselling graphic novel *Daybreak*, as well as the wordless graphic novel *Cave-In* and the *Astro-Boy* tribute *Reggie-12*. He is a founding member of the influential Providence underground art collective Fort Thunder.

He is a RISD graduate and currently teaches at the Savannah College of Art and Design.

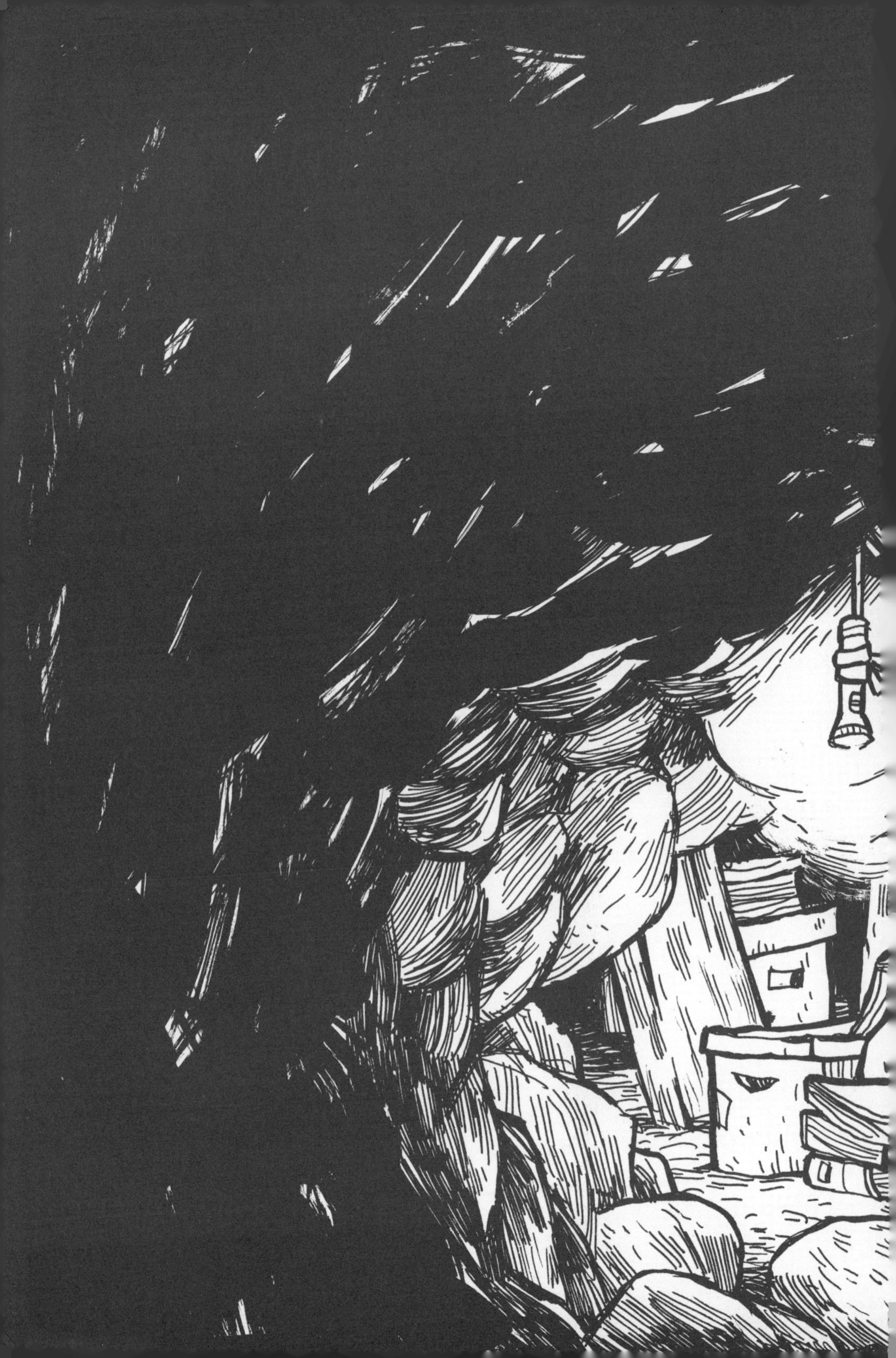

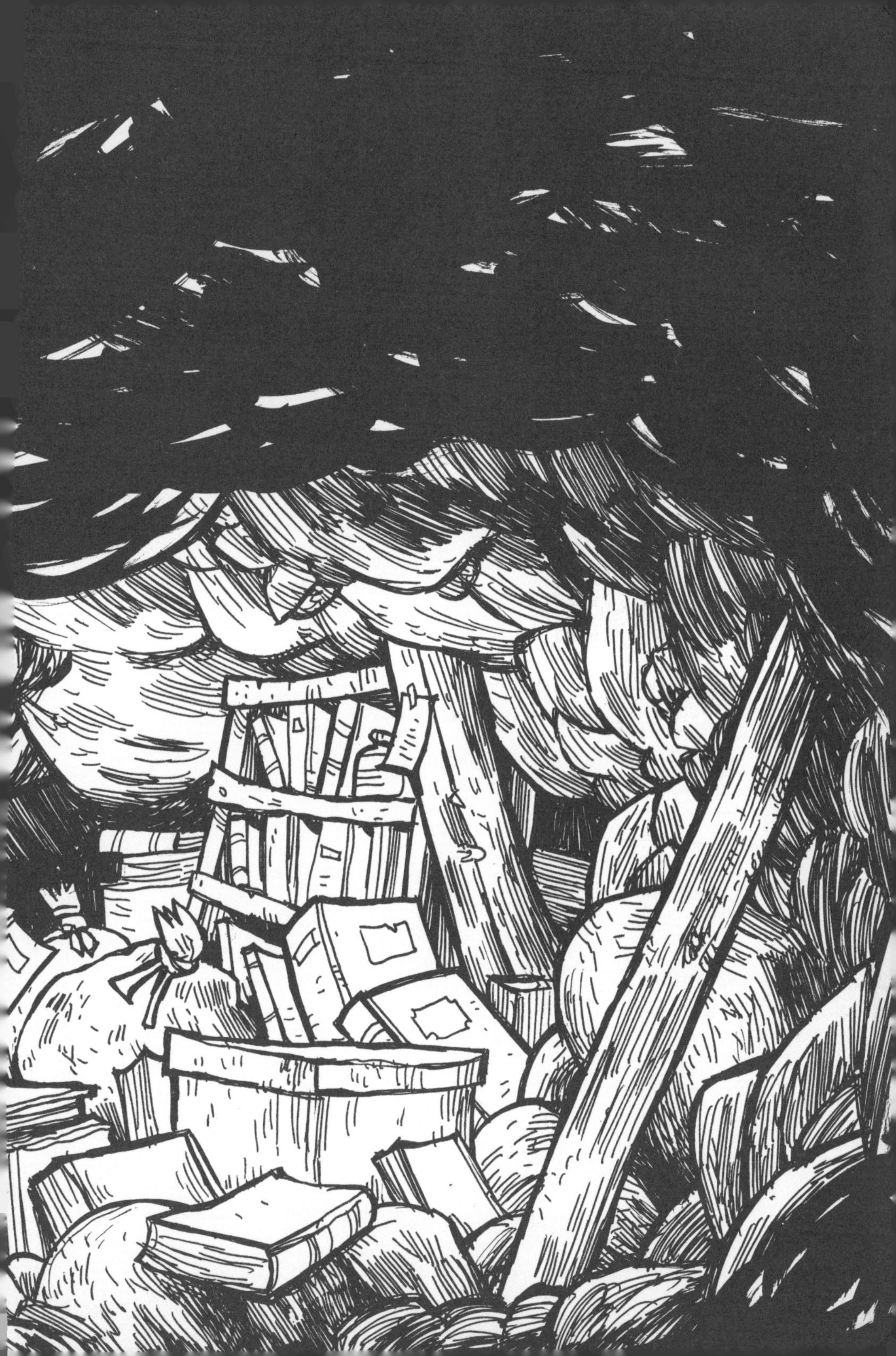

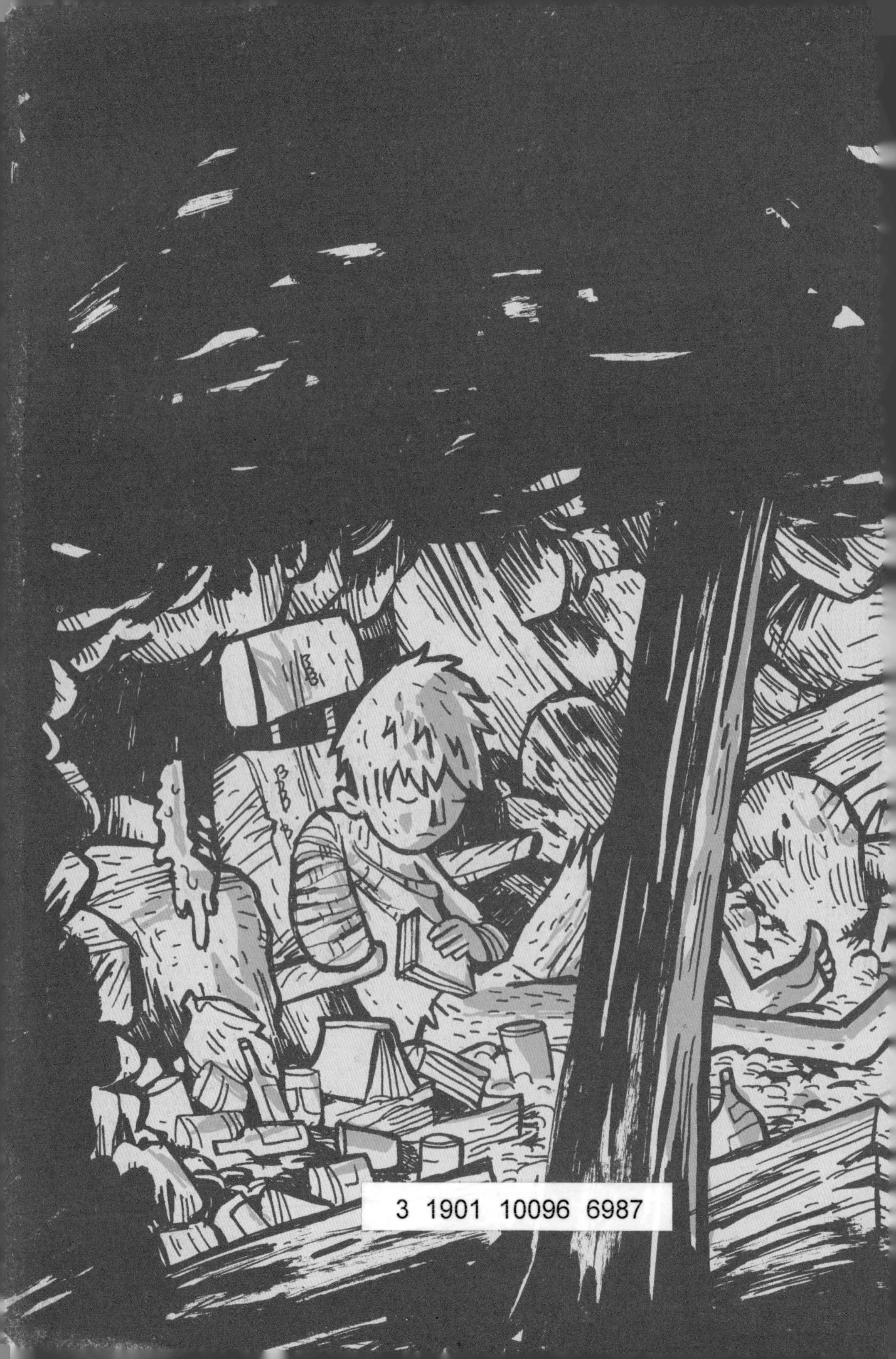